RELIGION AND FILM

'The developing field of religion and film is very new and encourages a wide range of different interests and approaches, as Melanie Wright rightly acknowledges in this substantial contribution to film and religion studies. The whole area has not yet developed very far, is something of a hodge-podge, and to a certain degree we do not yet know what we are doing. By selecting a particular systematic approach to religion and film – which incorporates an analysis of narrative, style, content and reception – Wright makes a great step forward for the whole field. Her cultural studies approach to the topic proposes a clearly defined solution to the subject's fragmentariness: a challenge that is long overdue. Moreover, the account she gives of each film that she considers is thorough, fascinating and enlightening.'

William L Blizek
Professor of Philosophy and Religion, University of Nebraska at Omaha, and Founding Editor of *The Journal of Religion and Film*.

'Many in religion and film studies do little more than use filmed stories to illustrate religious pieties. Melanie Wright is different. In this admirably informed and wonderfully fluent book, she argues for a cultural studies approach to religion and film which attends as much to the production, visual grammar and reception of a film as to its story. For it is only when we understand a film in its structure and cultural contexts that we can begin to understand its many meanings, including the religious. This book is both an excellent introduction to religion and film – to religion in film and as film – and a much needed challenge to a facile use of film by theologians unversed in film studies and cinematic cultures.'

Gerard Loughlin
Professor of Theology, Durham University, and author of *Alien Sex: The Body and Desire in Cinema and Theology*.

'Melanie Wright's scholarship, ease of language, and depth of knowledge make this an insightful, useful, and thought provoking read that examines both religion and film without privileging one for the other. It is an award winner for people who are tired of the low-budget B-movies that litter the field.'

Eric Michael Mazur
Book Review Editor, *Journal of Religion & Popular Culture* and Associate Professor of Religion, Bucknell University.

'Melanie Wright not only provides fascinating discussion of a range of important movies, but also moves the fledgling field of 'religion and film' to the next stage by drawing attention to concepts, questions and themes that undergird this exciting interdisciplinary endeavour. Religion and Film: An Introduction is a must-read for anyone interested in the integral relationship between religion and film in Hollywood and beyond. It will also prove an indispensable text for undergraduates and their teachers.'

Adele Reinhartz
Associate Vice-President of Research, and Professor of Religion and Classics, University of Ottawa

RELIGION AND FILM

AN INTRODUCTION

Melanie J. Wright

I.B. TAURIS
LONDON · NEW YORK

Reprinted in 2008 by I.B.Tauris & Co Ltd
6 Salem Road, London W2 4BU
175 Fifth Avenue, New York NY 10010
www.ibtauris.com

In the United States of America and Canada
distributed by Palgrave Macmillan, a division of St. Martin's Press
175 Fifth Avenue, New York NY 10010

First published in 2007 by I.B.Tauris & Co Ltd
Copyright © Melanie J. Wright, 2007

ISBN: 978 1 85043 759 8 (Hb)
ISBN: 978 1 85043 886 1 (Pb)

A full CIP record for this book is available from the British Library
A full CIP record is available from the Library of Congress

Library of Congress Catalog Card Number: available

Typeset in Warnock Pro by Sara Millington, Editorial and Design Services
Printed and bound in India by Thomson Press (I) Ltd

Contents

I

Preface

The cinema – meaning not just films, but also the institutions that produce and distribute them, and the audiences who are their consumers – has been in existence for just over a century. From early beginnings as a travelling fairground attraction it quickly developed, as both art form and industry. Within a couple of decades, the making and exhibiting of moving images was a worldwide business. In the mid-twentieth century, going to 'the pictures' was *the* social pastime in the West, a status it would soon enjoy globally until challenged, but not eclipsed, by other forms of mass entertainment and communication like television and the Internet. Whilst cinema attendance in the West has declined since the 1950s, India (the world's largest manufacturer of feature films) still has a weekly film-going population of 65 million people. In the UK, there has been an upward trend in cinema admissions in recent years: 2002 saw a high point of 176 million admissions (2.6 per person, compared with 5.4 per person in the USA).[1] The rise of home video, and latterly DVD, has bolstered the status of film viewing as one of the most ubiquitous of leisure activities. In short, film is an enormously popular medium. It shapes and reflects a range of cultural, economic, religious and social practices and positions in modern society.

As old as the cinema itself is its relationship – or more accurately, relationship*s* – with religion. Book titles like *The Seductive Image: A Christian Critique of the World of Film*,[2] or even *Religion and*

Film: An Introduction, perhaps imply that 'religion' and 'film' occupy realms that are distinct from, or even at odds with, one another. Just as Jürgen Habermas associates the growth of print culture in early-modern Europe with a rise in discursiveness and reason and a shift in the Church's status from that of feudal power to 'one corporate body among others under public law', so for some the expansion of film as a medium is linked to a crisis or decline in religious authority and commitment.[3] This view has weighty antecedents. For Theodor Adorno and Max Horkheimer, writing during the Second World War, film typified the 'culture industry'. Its reliance on rationalistic, technocratic forms of organisation meant that it embodied the modern drive to system and unity – responsible for the death of 'local mythologies', and implicated in the advancement of totalitarian ideologies.[4] Accounts of cinema as an agent of secularisation are, however, misplaced. Religion has not been displaced by a new medium: it has colonised it, and has found itself challenged and altered in the course of the encounter.

Religious ideas, rituals and communities are represented or alluded to in a dizzying number of films. In early twentieth-century North America and Europe significant resources were channelled into films that re-presented biblical or moral stories and drew on existing practices of religious dramatisation, including passion plays and (in the case of Yiddish cinema) Purimspiels. *Raja Harishchandra* (Dhundiraj Govind Phalke, 1913), based on a Hindu epic (the *Mahabharata*), is widely credited as the first feature film made in India, where entertainment had for centuries been associated with the temple and religious activity. (Interestingly, plans for the new Swaminarayan Mandir to be built near Delhi – intended to be the largest temple complex in the world – include an Imax cinema.)

Worldwide, a significant number of films continue to rely explicitly on religion for the development of narrative and character. A glance at the list of features released in any given year yields many examples. Thus, *The Chronicles of Narnia: The Lion, the Witch and the Wardrobe* (Andrew Adamson, 2005), released during the final stages of this book's preparation, was based on the similarly named novel by Christian apologist C.S. Lewis and was marketed heavily amongst faith-based audiences in the USA;[5] and the top-grossing film of 2006 is widely expected to be *The DaVinci Code* (Ron Howard, 2006) in which two academics pit themselves against clandestine Catholic groups and unravel clues to discover the 'holy grail'. Countless other productions, whilst not explicitly concerned with religion, have explored themes commonly associated with religion, such as forgiveness, hospitality, redemption, sacrifice or tradition.

Providing a counterpoint to the on-screen treatment of religious themes and subjects are a host of public and private off-screen encounters. In the mid-twentieth century, American Christians figured amongst the harshest critics of the cinema. The morality code that regulated Hollywood film content from the 1930s to the 1960s was drafted by a Catholic priest, and first implemented by a Presbyterian Church elder. In present-day Iran, a country governed by *sharia* (Islamic religious law), film-making is a highly regarded profession. Yet in the late 1970s it was one of the revolutionaries' favourite targets, and arsonists, stirred up by religious rhetoric, destroyed over 180 cinemas.[6]

However, the relationship between religion and the film industry is not always an oppositional one, and has more often been characterised by ambiguity or positive symbiosis: when Anglican authorities at Westminster Abbey refused to allow their building to be used for the filming of *The DaVinci Code*, those at Lincoln Cathedral granted permission, seizing an opportunity to boost church finances (directly through the film-makers' £100,000 donation and indirectly through increased tourism) and raise their profile, whilst also issuing a statement emphasising the story's fictional nature.

There is also a long history of communities and individuals thinking religiously about and around film – of film being perceived and used as a means to reflection and spiritual experience. Those occupying positions of leadership or authority sometimes encourage such activity, identifying and promoting films that are considered to accommodate particular religious sensibilities. In Britain, the Bible Society's 'Reel Issues' project and its sponsorship of *The Miracle Maker* (Derek Hayes and Stanislav Sokolov, 2000), an animated feature of the life of Jesus, evidence a conviction that film can provide a launch pad for discussion and can function as a tool for mission. Many religious newspapers and websites carry film reviews. In Turkey, Islamist parties have promoted *beyaz sinema* ('white cinema'), a genre that champions the cause of devout Muslims within the secular state. Conversely, audiences themselves may seize upon a film as being expressive of religious sentiments and needs. The example of *Jai Santoshi Maa* (Vijay Sharma, 1975), discussed further in Chapter VIII, illustrates the capacity for religious adherents to experience images as embodiments of the divine, and even for film to 'create' or 'manifest' a deity. Some Indian audiences responded to this film with acts of devotion, entering cinemas barefoot and showering the screen with flower petals, rice and money. At times, then, film can assume a sacramental quality.

Several disciplines attempt to grapple intellectually with the diversity of religion–film relationships. A small number of film-makers and academic film critics have asked how film might move from trying to depict religion to 'doing' it. Underlying this quest is an assumption that religion, like film, is in part an aesthetic discourse – a view akin to Rudolf Otto's ideas about the human need to articulate thoughts and feelings in metaphorical and symbolic forms.[7] In other words, religion is (amongst other things) a narrative-producing mechanism, and in this respect can be likened to both literature and the cinema. Reading the discourses of religion and film against each other can, therefore, be fruitful, given that both seek in differing ways to make manifest the unrepresentable. For Paul Schrader, who straddles these two worlds uniquely – as writer of one of the most influential studies in the field, and screenwriter of *The Last Temptation of Christ* (Martin Scorsese, 1988) – religion and film both attempt to bring people 'as close to the ineffable, invisible and unknowable as words, images and ideas' can take us.[8]

Similar convictions have prompted some practitioners of Christian theology to move into the field of 'theology and film', although a pragmatic, instrumental approach – akin to that associated with mission and ministry – is frequently a central motivation. Many writers in theology and film locate their work in a wider context of responses to the challenges posed to traditional faith by the concerns of a modern, apparently secularised culture (see Chapter II). However, the trend is gradually towards a more self-reflective stance, which holds the writer's faith position in dialogical tension with the content of particular films.

Approaches to religion and film that emerge from the context of religious studies are not identical to any of those outlined above. (There is some truth in Brian Bocking's wry observation in relation to theology and religious studies: 'if you don't know the difference, you're a theologian'.[9]) However, they may include a critical examination of any or all of them within their remit. Classically, religious studies does not assume a particular faith stance, and is instead interested in religion as a significant phenomenon of human consciousness and society. In the best sense of the word, it problematises religion, which, in simple terms, individual scholars may define substantively (focusing on the substance or 'content' of religion, particularly vis-à-vis conceptions of the divine) or functionally (focusing on the contribution religions make to meeting the essential prerequisites of society by fostering value consensus and group solidarity), or they may identify it with reference to a number of forms or dimensions (such as community; ritual; ethics; social and political involvement; myth; concept; aesthetics and spirituality). Studying 'religion and film' provides a route into the examination of various topics of interest to religious studies, including the interpenetration of religious and cultural ideas and forms, and the processes at work in mythopoesis and meaning-making.

Despite the many connections between the worlds of religion and film, relatively few extended studies try to tackle the topic systematically. Some works tackle only one aspect of the religion–film nexus, looking at, say, biblical epics or films dealing with other explicitly 'religious' content, such as sainthood. Other studies (typically, edited collections of essays) are broader, but rarely do much to present and defend clearly the approach being taken to a sometimes bewilderingly diverse range of films. It is also accurate to say that, for the most part, existing literature on religion–film relationships shows little or no awareness of critical approaches in film and cinema studies, although it routinely professes interest in these fields. *Religion and Film* aims to fill this gap. It attempts to offer an informed understanding not just of specific films but also of key concepts, questions and themes that can be applied more generally. As the book's title implies, the discussion does not assume or argue for a particular faith position but seeks to move towards an interdisciplinary approach, drawing from the practices both of religious studies and of film and cinema studies.

The first section of the book gives an account of the approach used later on to interpret the films. Chapter II highlights some trends in the analysis of 'religious films' (variously defined by different writers), touching on the theories and methods in the work of those approaching film from the contexts of theology, religious studies and film studies. Readers who are not particularly interested in theory may prefer to skip this chapter; others will no doubt find it the most important one. I have tried to present a range of positions fairly and to resist canonising certain films or interpretations although, inevitably, the discussion is not neutral. I find some theories more amenable than others and I will suggest that, particularly as far as academic writing on religion and film is concerned, many basic issues remain to be addressed adequately. The chapter therefore functions as an argument for my own perspective, and, for those who want to follow up other ideas, as a kind of 'user's guide' to selected approaches in religion (theology) and film.

The main section of the book is concerned with the detailed analysis of particular films. The choice of films has been shaped by a number of criteria. First, all the films selected are available on DVD. Although most films are made for cinema and acquire their reputation through theatrical release, the small screen is now intrinsic to our relationship with film. It is not in the multiplex or art cinema, but in the living room, that viewers typically have the chance to enjoy both an introduction to the breadth of what cinema has to offer and repeat screenings of old favourites. The availability of the films means that they have figured or continue to figure in public and/or popular discourse. Accordingly, the accounts given in this book may be read against those offered elsewhere – online, in print, or in conversation. This matters because, as discussed in Chapter II, the complexity of the film medium itself requires that we view it through multiple lenses. Above all, I hope that readers will be interested to view some or all of the films for themselves. This study tries to bring a number of critical ideas to the fore, but it is for others to make up their own minds about the credibility of my arguments.

Second, all the films discussed are ones in which religion is a dominant or significant feature. The definition of 'dominant or significant' is clearly open to debate. This book adopts a deliberately cautious position. The Bible was foundational for the Western literary canon, and so persists, post-Christendom, as the text that is most widely alluded to in Western literature. Likewise, it is virtually impossible to conceive of a narrative film devoid of *any* trace of the religious impulses that underpin the cultural construction of feelings, institutions, relationships, and so on. However, in a more direct fashion the films in this book deal extensively with religious characters, conflicts, or texts; are dependent upon religious narratives or traditions for plot or narrative; and/or make use of religion for character definition; or are set in the context of a religious community or communities.

Finally, the films have also been chosen to represent something of the range of works that constitute cinema worldwide. Approaching more than one tradition is, as Ninian Smart describes, a feature that distinguishes religious studies from theology.[10] More specifically, it serves the purpose of this book, since the chapters are intended to function cumulatively as an argument for the use-value of the approach outlined in Chapter II. Comprehensiveness is impossible,[11] but I have included features produced by big Hollywood studios, and art films (sometimes called 'Second Cinema') and I also discuss 'Third Cinema' – usually defined as films that are independently made and political in content and practice. Because the films vary, they demand different emphases of analysis, thereby demonstrating something of the approach's flexibility in dealing with the cinema and religion. The films included are as follows:

La Passion de Jeanne d'Arc ([The Passion of Joan of Arc] Carl Theodor Dreyer, 1928) is a French–Danish production about the ecclesiastical trial and execution for heresy of a young girl, who was later rehabilitated by the Catholic church, and declared a saint in 1920. The film, made by a director whose work is often characterised as 'spiritual' or 'transcendent', is sometimes described as representing the heights that silent film was capable of achieving. Following a troubled early circulation history, the film is now accessible on DVD. Indeed, in 2003 the British Film Institute used a still from the film to advertise its Dreyer season, attesting to *Jeanne*'s currency amongst art cinema-goers.

The Ten Commandments (Cecil B. DeMille, 1956) is a well-known biblical epic, made by the director most closely associated with the genre, but whose values are often regarded as far removed from those of Dreyer. Now 50 years old, the film continues to enjoy repeat screenings on television on both sides of the Atlantic. The story it retells is that of the biblical Hebrews and their exodus to freedom from slavery; as such it provides an opportunity to consider how classical Hollywood cinema handles a narrative common to Jews and Christians.

The Wicker Man (Robin Hardy, 1973) is one of the most unusual films to have been made in postwar Britain. It features a Christian policeman, whose efforts to investigate the disappearance of a young girl lead him into fatal conflict with the pagan religion practiced by the inhabitants of Summerisle, a remote Scottish island. *The Wicker Man* is widely regarded as a cult classic, and its study provides an opportunity to explore the 'religious' dimensions of fandom as well as the presentation of religious themes in the film itself.

My Son the Fanatic (Udayan Prasad, 1997) explores intergenerational conflicts within a British Asian community. It centres on the ageing Parvez, and his relationships with Bettina, a prostitute, and his son, Farid, who becomes a Muslim fundamentalist. In broad terms, *My Son* is also about cultural and religious pluralism, identity and belonging.

Keeping the Faith (Edward Norton, 2000) is a popular Hollywood feature, filmed in New York by a director interested in questions of inter-religious and inter-ethnic relations. It is a romantic comedy about a rabbi and priest who both fall in love with the same woman. *Keeping the Faith* has been praised for its sympathetic attention to issues of identity in the modern world and of friendships across religious boundaries, but arguably, it fails to confront them directly.

The final film to be discussed is *Lagaan* (Ashutosh Gowariker, 2001). Indian cinema is the fastest-growing foreign language cinema in Britain, and the Oscar-nominated *Lagaan* exemplifies the recent successes of Hindi film outside of South Asia. Hindu, Muslim, and Sikh characters and Hindu mythology and ritual are significant in its story of a cricket match between Indian villagers and British colonialists. Its study offers an accessible route into Indian film, which has its own unique conventions and history, inextricably entwined with religious tradition and the act of *darśan* ('seeing' the divine).

Many debts of gratitude have been incurred during this book's preparation, particularly since illness unexpectedly disrupted its progress. I am, therefore, especially thankful for the support of colleagues and students at the Centre for the Study of Jewish–Christian Relations, and the Divinity Faculty at Cambridge University. The British Film Institute's library staff were unfailingly helpful. I am grateful to the Centre for Literature and Theology at Glasgow University for an invitation to speak on Dreyer, and to the Divinity Faculty Film Club at Cambridge University for an opportunity to think aloud on *The Wicker Man*. Peter Francis kindly introduced me to the film weekends at St. Deiniol's, Hawarden.

My uncle Robert Isle began this book many years ago, when he dared to take a toddler for her first Saturday afternoon visits to 'the pictures'. For this, and for much else, I am indebted to him and his sister Nancy. Martin Forward (Aurora University) kindly commented on Chapter VI, and Srijana Das and Julius Lipner (both of Cambridge University) on Chapter VIII. It has been a pleasure to work with the unfailingly patient and encouraging Alex Wright and the team at I.B.Tauris. Justin Meggitt has by turns endured and supported my cinephilia and my efforts to say what I think. It was always for you.

II

Some Trends in Religious Film Analysis

Opening Shots

Conversation relating to religion, theology and film is far from new, but the past ten years or so have witnessed a remarkable growth in scholarship predicated on the religion–film interface. In Britain and North America, many of the outward markers of disciplinarity – college courses, conferences, publications, and so on – are now in place. Yet close reading of the literature suggests a more diffident attitude on the part of many practitioners of 'religion and film' (and of practitioners in the related field of 'theology and film') than this flurry of activity might at first be thought to imply. Book introductions regularly contain an apologia, justifying a writer's decision to stray from the territory of more 'respectable' study; they reference the fact that his or her scholarly credentials were earned by prior successful engagement with more conventional subject matter. By implication, the disciplinary model operating (be it that of religious studies or theology) is one that places film work at the periphery, rather than at the centre, of serious enquiry. In other words, religion and film (and theology and film) work, with few notable exceptions, has some way to travel before it is securely established as an independent field of credible, critical investigation.

This chapter explores the contemporary *modus vivendi* of academic work in religion, theology and film, its motivations and limitations (and, sometimes, its merits). Although rooted in the tradition of religious studies rather than in a particular faith community, the discussion will also reference examples of work produced by Christian theologians and other religious adherents. This two-fold concern, signalled by the chapter title, has been adopted for various reasons.

First, as outlined in Chapter I, from a religious-studies perspective different religious positions (including those articulated by professional religious adherents, such as academic theologians) are not the starting points of theory but are themselves data that must not be neglected.[1] Thus the use – including academic 'use' – of film by religious adherents is a topic of enquiry within the field of religious studies. Second, perhaps because film work is a minority interest within the wider fields of theology and religious studies, there is considerable contact between differently motivated practitioners. For example, the essay collection edited by Martin and Ostwalt takes a religious-studies approach but one of its three sections, 'theological criticism,' contains pieces by authors writing from positions of religious commitment. Conversely, Marsh and Ortiz, and more recently, Christianson, Francis and Telford include a small number of contributions influenced by religious studies within what are largely theologically driven volumes.[2] Such boundary crossing is inevitable, as scholars grapple with new subject matter and questions. Moreover, if done with care it can be appropriate, since both religion and film and theology and film conceive of themselves as interdisciplinary practices.

In addition to reviewing existing studies this chapter will suggest ways in which the area of religion and film might develop, arguing that recent trends in religious studies and film studies possess the potential to move towards an approach that strikes a balance between, on the one hand, sensitivity to the medium of film, and on the other, critical regard for the content and concerns of religious traditions and their adherents. Remaining chapters in this book develop the argument by modelling the approach in their treatment of a range of films.

Motivations to Religious Film Analysis

Before analysing the literature, it is important to contextualise it: what lies behind the contemporary enthusiasm for film? Arguably, for academic practitioners, two sets of factors bolster the current surge in interest.

The first grouping is what might be called pragmatic motivations. Academic practitioners of religious studies and theology are conscious of the fact they find themselves in a marketplace. Many teach in institutions hit by funding cuts. Moreover, they typically work in small departments within larger schools or faculties; they most likely compete for promotion or sabbatical leave with colleagues in other, larger (more financially 'successful') subjects. Some institutions lack a single-honours programme in religion – courses are offered as part of a wider arts or humanities menu, and need to be attractive and intelligible to students with increasingly diverse educational and cultural backgrounds (this holds true despite the recent, striking increase in the numbers opting for A and AS level Religious Studies in English and Welsh schools). On both sides of the Atlantic, theology and religious-studies teachers are parties to an unending struggle to secure what one writer gloomily describes as 'a little piece of the diminishing pie'.[3]

In a context of competition and insecurity, introducing film into the curriculum is partly a strategic move in the attempt to appear legitimate in the eyes of university administrators and external agencies. Film is – or is perceived as – both 'popular' and 'relevant'; it appears less esoteric and more 'fun' to study than, for example, textual criticism of the *Assumption of Moses*, or advanced Sanskrit. And it *can* provide a route into the study of religion for students who cannot be assumed to be religiously literate, or to share a common cultural background. Whilst these external pressures are rarely cited as a motivation for research, several authors do position their work vis-à-vis the contemporary higher education system. For Martin and Ostwalt, 'popular films' are 'the films college students are likely to view and know'. Scott speaks of being motivated to develop a hermeneutic of film by the realisation that 'some of my students thought differently than I did'. The interests of 'the humanities faculty' and the 'undergraduate student body' are also associated closely in a review essay by Williams, and a recent piece by Weisenfeld.[4]

Market forces are not, however, the sole or major determinants of academic inquiry. Interest often stems from recognition that the cinema offers a 'rich harvest of films which are of interest from a religious [studies], biblical or theological point of view'.[5] As will already be apparent, the nature of this interest varies considerably. Drawing on Durkheimian or functionalist definitions of religion, some critics see film as a site of religion in modern and postmodern societies. That is, they explore the ways films manage dissent, celebrate the collective and ultimately promote social cohesion through the articulation of commonly agreed values, roles and obligations. (This kind of approach underlies Deacy's study of *film noir* as a site of redemptive activity, and Lyden's book on film as religion.[6]) Alternatively, as touched on later in this book, they may focus more broadly, looking not just at film texts but also noting the structural parallels between cinema-going and religious rituals. Both activities may be understood as distinctively patterned behaviours that take place within spaces specially constructed for their performance (see Chapter IV).

Other commentators who prefer substantive definitions of religion (those giving more weight to the 'content' or 'object' of religious activity), and who may write out of more avowedly confessional positions, wish to subject the voice of film to that of particular theological or doctrinal positions. The task then is to explore film as an example of God's presence in everything, including the products of human culture – to look at how films raise and handle questions of meaning, and in doing so prompt particular religious adherents to think about 'the spirit of the age', and hence the relevancy (or otherwise) of their articulations of the truth as they perceive it.

Forays into film may, then, be variously motivated (the positions described above are just some of the many possible), but are they academically defensible? One Christian theologian writing on film suggests that:

> like the rabbits in the coal mines in nineteenth-century England that were used to sniff out poisonous gases, movies can smell the currents in our society, exploring dimensions of reality that are there for us as well, but which we [i.e. Christian theologians] have not fully perceived.[7]

The implication of this simile is that (like the expendable lagomorphs to which it refers) films exist to provide the theologian with yet more grist to his or her mill. Such a statement would strike most film scholars as cavalier (on account of its sheer instrumentalism and seeming disregard for film per se) and naive (in its confidence about film's ability to 'sniff out' the issues of the day).

Much of what follows will suggest that these responses are, generally speaking, well-founded. But a reasonable case *may* be made for work in this field; the kinds of boundary-crossing activity described in this chapter are not without precedent. As Thompson Klein's work on interdisciplinarity highlights, some disciplines have traditions of being more open than others; more eclectic than purist in their conceptions of themselves. In particular, the addition of the term 'studies' (as in 'religious studies') in a discipline's title often signals a shift away from the notion of the discipline as a discrete set of activities and towards a pluralist approach that is problem- or phenomenon-oriented.[8] (Thus classical studies applies a range of tools to the study of the ancient world; Holocaust studies seeks to describe and explain in historical, philosophical, sociological and other terms the attempted genocide of Jews during the Second World War.) In this vein, religious studies has always practised methodological and theoretical pluralism. It uses insights from a range of fields, including anthropology, art history, economics, history, philosophy, psychology and sociology, to further its goal of producing both an informed account of religious experiences and expressions and, sometimes, a degree of reflection on what gives rise to them in the first place. It follows, then, that a religious-studies approach to film will quite reasonably want to take account of film and cinema studies. This takes the discussion beyond the question of motivations to film analysis, to an examination of the *nature* of contemporary engagement with film. What is being done on the religion–film interfaces, and is it being done well?

On Dialogue

The notion that doing religion and film or theology and film should be an act of dialogue and interdisciplinarity is widely trumpeted by those working in the fields. Arguably, however, there are few writings that live up to this goal or consider seriously what might be entailed in trying to do so. A journey that begins with a personal enthusiasm for film may find its destination in classroom usages, or in print and online discussions, that foster disregard for the practices of film studies and the medium of film itself.

Much work in the fields of religion or theology and film lacks firm foundations. There is, for example, often little critical discussion of the principles that have informed either the selection or the analysis of the films under consideration in a given study. This contention is not made for negative–destructive reasons. The following discussion is as much an exercise in self-assessment as it is an interrogation of others, and it is written out of a desire to see an increased sense of critical depth develop within religion (and theology) and film.[9] New publications in these fields are still regularly hailed as pioneering works, despite the fact that serious writing on the religion–film interfaces began in the 1920s, with critics like Jean Epstein.[10] This constant heralding of the new happens partly because writers rarely engage one another to a sufficient degree. Yet without the more secure infrastructure that forms as a result of critical debate, activity in the field of religion and film is vulnerable to retrenchment. Practitioners need to come together – in agreement, and in friendly, robust dispute – to move the conversation forward.

Film Selection

In numerous religion (or theology) and film books, the choice of subject matter appears to be fairly random. In simple terms, this diffuse approach seems to be underpinned by the assumptions that: (a) films are about 'life' and its meaning; (b) religion is about 'life' and its meaning; ergo (c) all films are 'religious', or are amenable to some kind of religious reading. This position has its weaknesses. As a hypothesis, it is effectively meaningless – so broad that it can be neither proved nor disproved. By declaring any secularism to be merely apparent, virtually nothing of substance is added to an understanding of either religion or film. Moreover, some kind of selection process clearly *is* operative, and in the absence of a serious account of the decisions made, it can seem (perhaps inaccurately) self-indulgent and trivial. Films are chosen because, 'they are the ones we like the most'.[11] One solution to this problem would be to concentrate only on films with overtly religious themes or agendas. (Coates's *Cinema, Religion and the Romantic Legacy* does this well.[12]) However, even assuming that such works are readily identifiable, such a response would be very restrictive in its definition of suitable subject matter. The task instead is for practitioners of religion (or theology) and film to develop broader, yet discerning, approaches.

In much academic discourse on film, discernment is associated with 'taste', and the discerning film viewer perceived to be someone with a preference for 'art' or 'alternative' cinema (the Second and Third Cinemas introduced in Chapter I). Writers on religion or theology and film sometimes select films on this kind of basis.[13] For example, Holloway's 1972 study of the religious dimensions of film focuses on 'art' directors or *auteurs* Carl Theodor Dreyer, Ingmar Bergman, and Robert Bresson. 'Popular' films are dismissed, a priori, as incapable of bearing the weight of scholarly criticism. Their very success is seen as indicative of the passivity of the modern cinema audience and the stifling, pernicious influence of American 'movie moguls'.[14] But the notion of culture or 'taste' as a minority preserve no longer rules unchallenged in the humanities, and with few exceptions the 1990s marked a widening in the interests of religion and theology and film professionals. (Bucking this trend, May privileges 'great films' that are 'noble in vision', but his definition of these categories remains elusive; Coates studies 'works in which the intelligence and feelings of the filmmakers, and hence of the audience, are most fully engaged' – seemingly confident both of his ability to identify such films, and of a congruence between the attitudes of director and spectator.[15]) This more inclusive position is, for example, that of Jewett (a Christian theologian) who claims precedent for his approach in that of the apostle Paul:

> Paul's method was to place himself where other people were... If we wish to follow Paul's cue ... it is essential that ministers, teachers and laypersons interested in the impact of the faith should begin to take more seriously the growing cultural force of the movies.[16]

Marsh and Ortiz also concentrate (not exclusively) on popular films, as do Martin and Ostwalt, and studies by Scott, Miles and Stone each suggest that there is a correlation between the viewing figures for a film and its significance as a vehicle of popular mythology.[17]

It is important to question these strategies. Running parallel to the development of religion and film, and theology and film, is film studies' own growing interest in reception. The work of Staiger, Klinger and Kuhn, for example, has demonstrated the extent to which audiences are active and engage critically with films. Box office receipts are not an index of significance; moreover, we cannot assume that the meanings viewers take from what they see in the cinema are encoded in a film's textual organisation.[18] More fundamentally, it is not clear that the distinction between 'mainstream' or 'popular', and 'art' or 'alternative', cinema is tenable or even helpful. It seems inappropriate to dismiss all mainstream films simply by virtue of their corporate roots. Conversely, it would be unwise to celebrate uncritically all 'alternative' cinema. What is really going on when a film is named as 'art' or 'popular' is sometimes less about studio finances, or about the values the film espouses, than it is to do with product placement. Defining a film in one way rather than another may be part of an attempt to generate enough interest to turn a profit at the (carefully identified) box office.

If the accepted wisdom on the art/popular distinction sometimes looks like received foolishness, is there some other basis on which film selection can proceed? As neither religion nor film is characterised by stasis, it is impossible to work with rigid criteria. Moreover, the different goals of those working in theology and film, who (I deliberately polarise here) are approaching the subject from an 'insider's' position of religious commitment, and others (in religion and film) who want to tackle religions analytically from an 'outsider's' or non-adherent's perspective, will point towards different methodologies. However, the unlikelihood of resolution does not legitimate a failure to debate.

In two recent essays Telford deploys a taxonomy of the types of films that he believes offer scope for study. These are films which either:

(1) make use of religious themes, motifs or symbols in their titles;

(2) have plots that draw upon religion (broadly defined to include the supernatural and the occult);

(3) are set in the contexts of religious communities;

(4) use religion for character definition;

(5) deal directly or indirectly with religious characters (e.g. the Buddha, or angels), texts, or locations (such as heaven or hell);

(6) use religious ideas to explore the experiences and transformation or conversion of characters; or

(7) address religious themes and concerns, including ethical issues.[19]

This scheme needs some clarification. When trying to identify films that present indirect treatments of religious characters (a subcategory of (5) above), over-interpretation is a very real danger, as Telford admits (see also the discussion of *La Passion de Jeanne d'Arc* in Chapter III). Similarly, some critics have seen *all* Hindi films as being rooted in the Sanskrit epics. One might make analogous claims regarding *sharia* and Iranian cinema, in which (for example) the wearing of *hejab* is essential for adult female characters. (Neither of these cinemas are well represented in Telford's lists.) Number (7) appears as a kind of catch-all category, which could leave the way open for a re-emergence of the random or arbitrary approach discussed earlier. Finally, the emphasis on story, character and setting imply, arguably, a concentration on film narrative, in contrast with trends in film studies and theoretical conceptions of 'the religious film', which typically emphasise aesthetic practices (see later, and Chapter III).

However, Telford's survey is suggestive of bases upon which future conversations about the shape of religion and film studies might proceed. The next step is for these categories (or other schemes) to be refined, and brought into dialogue with focused research questions. The criteria by which films are selected for analysis must be explicitly relevant to the problems in hand. Hence, the selection criteria for this book were determined by several factors, including a need to fit with the project's overall aims (see Chapter I). In keeping with its wider goals, the definition of films in which religion is 'dominant or significant' is determined with reference to aspects of film narrative, but also the important issue of whether or not religious qualities may be located in a given film's visual style is discussed further in this chapter, together with the audience's role in constructing film as religious.

Methods of Study

If film choice is sometimes accidental, on occasion the interpretative strategy or method deployed by some religion (and theology) and film writers is similarly free, and might be termed 'association', moving towards allegory or typology.[20] The problem with these approaches is that they are limiting – they address films with a set of presuppositions that close off other routes to understanding. Energetic and exhilarating for the practitioner, these methods may allow for a tendency to see resonances between the film and other texts that are simply not there, except in an individual interpreter's mind.

Consciously advocating a postmodern position, Aichele and Walsh are unusual in admitting that the connections their contributors draw between films and biblical passages may exist only for the writers themselves. Such honesty is refreshing, and may indeed shed light on the 'mechanisms of myth and ideology', as they hope.[21] What is less clear is how this hermeneutic can help the authors prevent their discipline from becoming an isolated intellectual exercise, distant from and irrelevant to the ways that those outside the Academy make meaning from and with the cinema. The interiority of such practice seems, strangely, to run counter to the populist impulses that are purportedly behind it.

Whilst some writers are turning to post-(or even pre-)modern forms of interpretation, Jewett's work exemplifies a different strategy; that of bringing the film medium into conversation with a recent trend in biblical studies. Thus his 1999 book takes as its starting point the claim of Bruce Malina and the Context Group that ideas about 'honour and shame' were fundamental to the ancient Mediterranean world, and therefore provide the hermeneutical key to the New Testament, particularly the Pauline corpus.[22] Since the honour–shame model is the key to Paul, it is also, Jewitt says, the lens through which Christian theologians should read film. Leaving aside questions about Malina's theories, it is clear that this method leads to reductionism. It is an entertaining exercise, offering readings of such delights as *Babe* (Chris Noonan, 1995) and *Babette's Feast* (Gabriel Axel, 1987), but whether it ultimately reveals much about film or about Pauline theology seems questionable.

Jewett's study is an example of an approach to film grounded in a theological context, rather than a religious studies one. However, it illustrates a more general tendency to concentrate on certain aspects of film at the expense of others. Typically, the narrative dimension of the films being studied is emphasised, with little attention to *mise-en-scène* ('what is put into the scene'), cinematography, editing or sound: 'The nature of film *is* story', claims one writer.[23] But as Maisto observes:

> The conflation of story with film, or of techniques of literary interpretation with approaches to film, is typical of many efforts in Religion and Film ... in some cases, treatment of the film and the story combine so seamlessly that it is difficult to tell which is being discussed. This has the effect of denying the particularity of each form, and erroneously equating the two media [i.e. literature and film].[24]

This over-concentration on narrative is understandable. Most practitioners of religion and film and of theology and film trained originally in theology or religious studies. Although religious studies is a less tightly structured field, both disciplines have historically privileged literary texts, or more accurately, certain kinds of literary texts, over other media. Until recently, as Kassam observes, scholars of religion discussed Islam's textual tradition 'without any reference to how Muslims in different parts of the world actually expressed their faith in everyday life and practice'; Strenski speaks of religious studies' traditional neglect of the world of 'things'.[25] The problem is that reading a literary text is a quite different experience from 'reading' a film. A written text draws on verbal sign systems; in film a multiplicity of different signifiers (aural, visual, verbal) are contained within the space of a single frame or series of frames. Engaging with a written text requires us to visualise and subvocalise words printed on the page, whereas film presents images and sounds, making different demands on its audience.[26]

When scholars focus on dimensions that film and text have in common (narrative elements) to the exclusion of aspects that distinguish film *qua* film, limited analysis results. To rephrase the point, film's basic building blocks are the shot (the photographic record made when film is exposed to light, or its digital equivalent) and the editorial cut (the transition between shots, made in the pre-digital age by splicing the end of one shot to the beginning of another) but little religion (or theology) and film work explores these fundamentals. This raises questions about what is really going on in discussions that purport to bring the worlds of film and religion into dialogue. Could it be that – despite the growing bibliography and plethora of courses – *film* is not really being studied at all?

A Proposal

Which way now? Work in religion and film and theology and film has some way to travel before it can be regarded as a credible field of enquiry. Fundamentals need to be reviewed and perhaps overhauled; it is important to think seriously about what is involved in doing interdisciplinary work. Without firmer foundations, particularly an ability to engage film *qua* film, the survival of religion (and theology) and film cannot be assumed. Film work has, for example, failed to secure its place as a topic for routine coverage in many of the longer-established periodicals in theology and religious studies. It is more often the subject of a 'special issue' – positioned as something urgent, but ultimately marginal to mainstream scholarly discourse. Without sounder underpinnings this will not change, and worse still, the work itself will continue to offer sometimes interesting but frequently irrelevant and inadequate readings of arbitrarily selected films.

Addressing the limitations of current work in religion and theology and film requires a willingness to listen to and debate with others engaged in serious writing on the cinema. As the tendency to elide film meaning into narrative illustrates, few writers on religion (or theology) and film address theoretical questions. Some ignore mainstream writing on film; others address it inconsistently. (For example,

Marsh and Ortiz includes an introduction to film language, but the issues raised are not really followed through into actual analysis.[27]) Amongst some scholars there is open resistance to film studies. In confessionally grounded writing this is occasionally born of a desire to see theology re-throned as the 'queen of sciences'. Alternatively, it can stem from the recognition that contemporary film studies, with its roots in Marxism and psychoanalysis, often dismisses or devalues the place of religion in contemporary society: 'It is almost as if the discourse of cutting-edge film criticism is designed to exclude attention to religion', complains Martin.[28] (Film studies' handling of religion will be discussed further in Chapter III.) However, this perception does not provide a warrant for those in religious studies or theology to reciprocate poor practice.

A decent course on film within a theology and/or religious-studies programme should regard familiarising students with key areas of film-studies practice as one of its aims. After all, students who want to progress in other areas are expected to develop a challenging range of competencies. Drury lists as follows the demands placed on Bible students: 'knowledge of at least two ancient and two modern languages, of textual criticism and of testingly obscure episodes in history, of religion in its popular and philosophical manifestations, of a vast and sometimes barely readable secondary literature'.[29] Not teaching the skills needed to address film texts and their audiences implicitly devalues the medium of film, and adds credibility to the position of those who regard the study of mass cultural forms as simply the hors d'oeuvre before the 'real work' of theology and religious studies begins.

There is of course a potential danger hidden in the suggestion that religion (and theology) and film must attend to film studies. Such a move could see one 'tyranny' simply replaced with another (that of film or cinema studies). I am not advocating a wholesale or uncritical adoption of film theory, although achieving the goals of dialogue and interdisciplinarity will impact on the subject, processes and products of research.

Noting that both individual scholars and the institutions with which they engage (including employing universities, and political and funding bodies) are often unsure about how to judge interdisciplinarity, Thompson Klein suggests that the focus should be on two dimensions. The first of these is 'depth', which she defines as competence in pertinent knowledges and approaches to the subject matter; and the second is 'rigor', in the form of an ability to develop processes that integrate theory and knowledge from the disciplines being brought together. According to this model, creating a truly interdisciplinary approach to religion (or theology) and film requires much more than either a simple extension of the subject matter of religious studies, or ad hoc borrowings of tools and concepts from a neighbouring discipline. It mandates a high degree of self-reflexivity, since it is necessary to learn and reflect on how the disciplines involved characteristically look at the world. And it requires the cultivation of a spirit of enquiry, coupled with a willingness to check repeatedly the accuracy and validity of 'borrowed' material and ideas.[30]

I am not advocating that scholars and students of religion and theology start mimicking their peers in film studies. There is already a body of people who do 'straight' film criticism well; it is more sensible to develop approaches to film that will play to the distinctive strengths of religion specialists. Moreover, although ambitious, religion (and theology) and film's oft-stated goals of dialogue and interdisciplinarity are laudable, and cannot be achieved if the insights of religious studies (or theology) are simply cast aside. Film studies, too, is beset with its own debates and difficulties – several of which will surface throughout this book. According to some, it faces a crisis of relevance.

In a piece of 'shameless polemic', Miller castigates contemporary film studies, arguing that for the most part, it 'doesn't matter': it has little influence over discourse on film, public policy, or commercial or not-for-profit film-making practice.[31] Interestingly, similar charges could be levied against religion and film. There are many films handling religious or spiritual themes and topics. The turn of the century saw a number of films dealing with supernatural themes and spiritual questions, like *Dogma* (Kevin Smith, 1999), *End of Days* (Peter Hyams, 1999) and *Stigmata* (Rupert Wainwright, 1999); the past few years have seen the appearance of further popular features, as diverse as *Bruce Almighty* (Tom Shadyac, 2003), *Kingdom of Heaven* (Ridley Scott, 2005), *The Man Who Sued God* (Mark Joffe, 2001) and *Millions* (Danny Boyle, 2005). Moreover, some of the most controversial recent features have handled religious subject matter. Mel Gibson's *The Passion of The Christ* (2004) is one obvious example, and Martin Scorsese's 1988 *The Last Temptation of Christ* another. Describing the former's significance as a marker of (certain kinds of) contemporary Christian identity, *The Economist* went as far as to suggest that, 'The 2004 [US Presidential] election could well turn into a choice between Michael Moore's *Fahrenheit 9/11* and Mel Gibson's *The Passion of The Christ*.'[32]

However, few religion and film (or theology and film) specialists are party to public debates about film. The most prominent participants in the controversies surrounding the production of *The Passion*, for example, were those who wrote or spoke as interfaith activists and New Testament scholars. They judged the film to be in violation of academic consensus about the origins and purpose of the Gospel accounts of Jesus' death and resurrection, and of post-Vatican II guidelines governing Catholic presentation of Jews and Judaism in preaching, teaching and dramatisation. These interventions proved largely ineffectual in persuading Gibson away from elements of the film that some feared might inflame antisemitism – in part because they demonstrated little insight into the specific challenges facing those who try to *film* the life and death of Jesus. In a telling illustration of this gap in understanding, the most vociferous scholars based their initial arguments on their *reading* of the screenplay, whilst Gibson's canny and successful response was to organise screenings that allowed people to *see* a rough version of the film.[33]

Miller's proposal for film criticism is that it achieves relevance through a more extensive integration with cultural studies. He is not alone in making this suggestion: cultural studies has transformed film studies in the past decade. A cultural-studies approach to film does not imply a rejection of previous film theories, but rather a building on older agendas and methods. Traditional film studies emphasises the analysis of individual film texts, their methods of production and associated technologies. Cultural studies looks additionally at film distribution, exhibition and reception. It involves a widening from an interest in the production and interpretation of a film 'text' to an interest in the interrelation of 'texts, spectators, institutions and the ambient culture.'[34] In other words, it is a means of avoiding the twin poles of auteurism and reader response (of regarding either the film-maker or the film viewer as an exclusive, determinative influence). It traces the ways in which films acquire meanings by triangulating between film 'texts', contexts and audiences.

Like traditional film studies, cultural studies approaches are interested in gender, 'race', and queer theory, and in ideas about post-colonialism, post-structuralism and materialism (several of these are discussed in this book). What is particularly relevant for conversations about the future of religion (and theology) and film as a subject area is that proponents of this approach (or family of approaches) to film acknowledge that their practices are multi- or anti-disciplinary, that they are subject to ongoing contest and debate, and that they draw inspiration from anthropology and the study of religion as much as from literary analysis and cinema studies.[35] That is, cultural studies provides a way of examining film that on occasion professes a link to the academic study of religions. (In this respect it may be compared and contrasted with auteurism, discussed in Chapter IV, which dominated 1960s film criticism and is sometimes loosely associated with theology.)

Unsurprisingly, the relation of cultural studies to film studies is itself a subject of debate. As Stam notes, the name 'film studies' implies attention to a single medium, and 'cultural studies' points to wide interests.[36] Culture may be defined in extremely broad terms as referring to all human production, including concepts and social structures as much as objects or artefacts. And as a cultural form that is produced by mass industrial techniques and is ultimately marketed for profit to consumers, film may be likened to a host of other things including television, music CDs, clothing, the microwave or the bicycle. In this way, cultural studies may be perceived as a threat to film studies' founding principle: the distinctiveness of film. But others see cultural studies as an organic, necessary development of film studies, pointing out that much traditional film theory, with its positing of ahistorical, decontextualised film viewers and concern with the production of signifying systems (see Chapter III), was becoming alienated from its object of study.

Further objections are raised by those sceptical of the willingness of cultural-studies proponents to look at not only high art but also popular films, and the surrounding culture of fandom (discussed in Chapter V). For Willemen, known for his work on Third Cinema, this risks the de-skilling of the profession: film studies may slide into popularism, losing its critical edge and traditional concern for aesthetic value.[37] In response to this, the limits of the art/popular distinction have already been discussed, whilst Chapter VIII questions the Western Academy's ability to determine aesthetic value. It is also a mistake to hold that cultural studies does not analyse film 'texts', or that a study of the popular necessarily implies popularism.[38] Nevertheless, these cautions about cultural-studies approaches to film are pertinent.

I suggest, then, that the territory of cultural studies, into which much of film studies has been shifting, offers a discursive space in which the oft-touted dialogue between religious (or theological) studies and film studies is perhaps newly possible. For religion specialists, there is an opportunity to engage with film criticism in a way that does not imply a subordinate relationship, in which the exchange of insight is not a one-way process *from* film studies *to* religion (and theology). Crucially, cultural studies too rejects the kinds of totalising (and atheistic) explanations that earlier ways of theorising film, such as Marxism, structuralism and psychoanalysis tended to espouse.[39] It is inherently dialogical and does not automatically assume secularism as a given, nor does it exclude the possibility that those with an expertise in religious studies (or theology) may bring to film competencies and insights that are both distinctive and worthwhile.

The movement towards establishing some kind of common ground is not confined to developments within film and cinema studies. Ever-omnivorous, religious studies shows increasing interest in cultural studies. One of the leading British advocates of this approach, Nye, has argued that the study of religions should in fact be reconceptualised and renamed as 'religion and culture', observing that 'what we think of as "religious studies" is, in many ways, a form of cultural studies, or at least there is much in cultural studies that those in the study of religions need to be aware of'.[40] Why is this? On the other side of the Atlantic, Ochs notes that 'more scholars of religions are now acknowledging what religious or spiritual people worldwide ... have long known, from observation, lived experience and intuition: that material objects – things made by people – are vessels that create, express, embody and reflect sacredness'.[41]

This approach argues that religion is embedded and enacted in material culture and artefacts. It contends that the material (including books, films, or art) has no intrinsic meaning of its own, and that it cannot be 'read' without attention to historical context:

> Meaning ... is not given in some independently available set of code, which we can consult at our own convenience. A text does not carry its own meaning or politics already inside of itself; no text is able to guarantee what its effects will be. People are constantly struggling, not merely to figure out what a text means, but to make it mean something that connects to their own lives, experiences, needs and desires.[42]

FILM OR RELIGION

In short, it brings to the study of religion(s) a heightened focus on the material dimension and on occasionality – the details of the conditions in which religious meanings are re-created and expressed. In the growth of cultural studies' approaches to film, and concern on the part of proponents of religious studies for the enacting of religious ideas and beliefs in the material world, we can begin to see how a way of doing religion and film might develop that strikes a balance between respect for film and film studies, *and* a regard for religious traditions and their adherents. There is potential here for the fields to grow towards each other, creating an interface of theories and subject matter – the kind of genuinely interdisciplinary work that has rarely happened to date.

What might religion and film studies look like if conducted in this way? What would it tell us? In her 1998 study, Miles models one way of using cultural studies to explore the presentation of religion and values in popular film. She is interested in the social and political matrices within which films are produced and distributed;

her starting point is to see each film as demonstrating one or more social problems and proposing a resolution. Miles also takes an interest in reception, although this is principally in the form of press reviews, and she does little to flesh out her suggestion that 'most filmgoers ... will see and discuss the film they watch in relation to the common quandaries of the moment.'[43] Although this book evolved independently, it might be viewed as developing Miles's in several respects. In particular, it seeks a more consistent engagement with scholarship in and around cultural studies, and it recognises that cultural studies is more deeply implicated in the current practice of film studies than Miles allows (notwithstanding her brief observation that cultural studies does not reject other approaches to film). Acknowledgement of this strengthens the account of films as cultural products with specific histories of distribution and exhibition, and facilitates a more extensive dialogue with film theory, particularly in the areas of aesthetics and reception.

The discussion of each film addresses four areas: narrative; style; cultural and religious context; and reception. Film narrative has been discussed earlier in this chapter, and includes in this instance the characters populating films, as well as story and plotting. Style embraces aesthetic and audio-visual dimensions, including *mise-en-scène* (the staging of shots), cinematography, editing and sound. As already noted, it is often in style that the few film critics who have shown an interest in such matters have located a given film's spiritual or transcendental qualities. Cultural and religious context has been touched on briefly in the general discussion of cultural-studies approaches to film. Finally, reception (sometimes termed 'secondary production', because of the active role that cultural studies attributes to film audiences) tries to chart the ways in which a film has been interpreted. It is difficult (particularly when dealing with older films) to map all the variations of interpretation: 'the film *we* saw is never the film *I* remember.'[44] Nonetheless, it is possible to explore the forms (reviews/fan activities/industry, government or other agency documents) that articulate a range of possible responses to a film.

In order to demonstrate this approach more clearly, Chapter III is quite densely written and discusses *La Passion de Jeanne d'Arc* under these four broad headings.[45] The subsequent chapters divide along less pedestrian lines: replication of a method does not guarantee its value. In several instances I try to model in more detail particular strategies that can be deployed, and questions that can be asked, when adopting a cultural-studies approach to religion and film. For example, the chapter on *The Ten Commandments* looks at analysing trailers, and at genre, and that on *The Wicker Man* considers fandom.

The overall goal of this multi-dimensional approach is to offer a richer account of the films concerned, which develops an appreciation of their nature and functions as film 'texts' operating within – and constructing – particular contexts. Looking at film in this way makes it possible to gain a sense of what 'film' is, both as a series of images projected onto a screen (large or small) and as a social artefact. Just as today in film studies, 'the aesthetic and the cultural cannot stand in opposition', so in order to deploy film effectively in the study of religions, it is possible and necessary both to 'see more, and reflect more upon that seeing'.[46]

Conclusion

This chapter has suggested ways in which religion and film analysis could be enhanced by focusing on the verbal, visual, distributional, promotional and other dimensions of the film experience, in addition to the narrative or textual ones. Specifically, it has argued that cultural-studies approaches to film have much to offer. A willingness to take on board findings and perceptions from those working in a variety of fields means that cultural studies is integrative of a range of strategies used by specialist film critics. That same openness allows for conversation with the particular specialist knowledges and methodologies that practitioners of religious studies (and theology) can bring to film.

Doing religion (or theology) and film well does not entail a rejection of previously held assumptions, competencies and passions. Nor does it mean that one should seek to do everything in an account of a film or films. What is instead called for is a focusing in on one or more of the religion–film interfaces, coupled with an awareness of what is being undertaken elsewhere. If we can do this then we will not just have created a dialogue, we may also find ourselves working in that rarest of fields, a discipline that (to evoke Miller's phrase) *really matters.*

III

La Passion de Jeanne d'Arc
(Carl Theodor Dreyer, 1928)

Jeanne d'Arc n'a pas quitté l'histoire sur le bûcher de Rouen[1]

Has anyone ever been more exposed on film than Jeanne?[2]

The Remarkable Story of *La Passion de Jeanne d'Arc*

As described in Chapter II, there is no consensus amongst religion and film practitioners about which films to study, but most would surely consider *La Passion de Jeanne d'Arc* acceptable. Its subject matter is the ecclesiastical trial and death of a young woman (1412–31) who, believing that she had been divinely commissioned to save France, led an army to victory over the English and their Burgundian allies, and was burnt as a heretic-witch; but was subsequently rehabilitated, and ultimately declared a saint by Pope Benedict XV in 1920. Moreover, Dreyer is a director who used terms like 'spirit' and 'soul' when talking about the cinema, and whose work deals repeatedly with themes such as individual faith versus communal intolerance, miracles, martyrdom and witchcraft.[3] He has been characterised as 'one of the few really great cineastes ... able to deal in a serious way with the claims and pretensions of religion' and his style described as 'transcendental' or 'purified' – descriptions with strong religious overtones.[4]

Despite these factors, there are few detailed treatments of *Jeanne d'Arc*. Dreyer is a 'director whose work everyone reveres and no one bothers to see'.[5] This may be because he is perceived to be challenging or difficult. However, setting aside Dreyer's reputation as an auteur, there are other reasons for *Jeanne d'Arc's* neglect.

Notoriously, its fate has been almost as remarkable as that of Jeanne herself. The film opened in Copenhagen in April 1928, but complaints from French nationalists led to censorship, and the Paris premiere was delayed until October. In December the negative (the film used to make positive prints for projection in film theatres) was destroyed by fire; a second, made by Dreyer using out-takes and rushes, was also lost. (Early nitrate-base film burns easily at low temperatures.[6]) For many years the most widely circulated *Jeanne* was a mutilated version that incorporated a later soundtrack, and was based on a poor-quality print of the second negative. There were other more 'reputable' prints in the *Cinémathèque Française* (Paris) and the Museum of Modern Art (New York). The National Film Archive (London) also had a copy, which was shorter than these, but included shots they did not have. In the 1980s yet another version was constructed by the Danish Film Museum. In simple terms, then, studying *Jeanne* has historically been difficult, because of the instability of the film 'text' itself. Which of the Paris, New York, London or Copenhagen prints was closest to the film Dreyer had intended viewers to see?[7]

For many years, it seemed that the 'ur'-*Jeanne* was irretrievable, until in 1981 a cleaner discovered some film canisters in a psychiatric hospital near Oslo. In a move paralleling Jeanne's own resurrection as a national heroine, the Norwegian Film Institute opened them some three years later, revealing a print of Dreyer's first negative, in its original wrapping, and bearing the 1928 Danish censor's seal.[8] How the print found its way to the asylum is the subject of much speculation; critics also disagree as to how significantly it differs from the versions that have been circulating for years. But what *is* clear is that after years of obscurity, *La Passion de Jeanne d'Arc* is newly accessible.

Whilst the problems associated with the copies of *Jeanne* circulating pre-1985 no doubt impeded study, it is important to note that much (but not all) of the growth of the discipline of religion and film (and of its relation, theology and film) has happened since 1990, by which time practical obstacles to research on this particular work had been largely overcome. Are there then other factors leading religion and film practitioners to shy away from *Jeanne*? Chapter II suggested that much of the film analysis in departments of religion or theology over-concentrates on the narrative dimension, and fails to adequately engage film *qua* film. Arguably, a film like *Jeanne* is a stumbling block to such approaches. The detail of its style will be discussed later, but it is enough at this point to observe that *Jeanne d'Arc* is a silent film.

Indeed, it is one of the last silents, made at the moment that sound-on-film became possible. (Newspaper advertisements for *Jeanne* appear alongside ones urging readers to 'Hear Douglas Fairbanks Speak in "The Iron Mask"' and 'Listen in Today. She Speaks! Wait until you HEAR Clara Bow in "The Wild Party".'[9]) Silent films are a distinct art form with their own qualities and styles of production, exhibition, and viewing. Without some appreciation of film practice, *Jeanne*'s distance from the dominant conventions of contemporary Hollywood makes it difficult to approach. In this respect, the challenge of working with *Jeanne* may serve as a test for methodologies in religion and film. The otherness of its conventions lends new urgency to the call for something more than narrative exposition. If we cannot grapple with 'the affective film *par excellence*', we may as well pack up and go home.[10]

Film Narrative

Academic and popular discourse on *Jeanne* is complicated by the fact that those involved in making and viewing the film possess(ed) a (more or less) substantial pre-knowledge of the underlying narrative of Jeanne d'Arc's life and death. This at once empowers and circumscribes the activities of Dreyer and his interpreters. In the decade in which *Jeanne* appeared, her story was a national preoccupation in France. Two accounts of Jeanne's life from this period are particularly significant. The first is a critical text of the trial account, published by independent scholar Pierre Champion in 1921, just after Jeanne's canonization. It portrayed her as the pious product of an idealised rural France, and cast the Sorbonne theologian–priests who condemned her as sordid careerists. The other is a 1925 biography by Joseph Delteil, a literary critic with an interest in Catholic tradition and chivalry. He asserted the reality of Jeanne's voices (the saints whom she believed had commissioned her), her virginity and her sainthood. In addition to these accounts, there was a centuries-old tradition of re-presenting Jeanne in popular culture and elite art. The early cinema shared this passion for Jeanne: Margolis counts seven films made before 1928.[11]

One of the dangers in approaching a film like *Jeanne*, which handles a historical figure about whom much has been written, is the seductiveness of what McFarlane, in discussing films based on novels, calls 'fidelity criticism'.[12] That is, there is a temptation to measure the film against what we feel we already know of the 'facts' of Jeanne's life, and inevitably to find it wanting. This strategy is dangerous. It fails to recognise the nature of film, and arguably, of history itself.[13] Yet in *Jeanne d'Arc*, Dreyer invites viewers to relate the world of the screen to that which lies beyond, especially the trial account, the best known narrative of the later stages of Jeanne's life. So, it is appropriate to compare the film to these written texts, provided that this method is not taken to imply that either presentation of Jeanne is the proverbial yardstick against which others are to be measured.

The *Société Générale des Films*, which commissioned Dreyer, bought the rights to Delteil's biography, but Dreyer largely rejected it, preferring Champion's edition of the trial records, and employing him as a consultant. (However, as described later, *Jeanne* is sporadically dependent on Delteil, particularly for the presentation of Jeanne's *passion*.) *Jeanne* begins with a shot of the trial transcript, inviting viewers to draw connections between off- and on-screen realities. Various shots in the film show the scribe writing or carrying this record of events: he is in Jeanne's cell when she is interrogated there, and in the cemetery, whither she is led to sign an abjuration document rejecting her claims to divine inspiration. This repeated reference to the book is sometimes seen as staking a claim for the film's historicity: Dreyer is claiming to show his audience the events as they were recorded at the time. But equally, the motif may signal the constructed, artificial nature of film – as Dreyer's acknowledgement of what Bordwell calls the film's 'pre-text':

The [opening] shot is emblematic: we come to a familiar tale, equipped with familiar knowledge. Jeanne's peasant ancestry, her religious impulses, her military fervor, and her heroic death: Dreyer assumes that we know all this, takes it as the pre-text of his film, and frees the narrative of an expository apparatus.[14]

As discussed later, Dreyer *was* striving for a kind of realism in *Jeanne* – but it is a realism that locates authenticity in the evocation of the animating spirit of characters and moments, rather than in the replication of factual detail. For Dreyer, 'cinema must work itself away from being a purely imitative art.... *It is not the things in reality that the director should be interested in, but, rather, the spirit in and behind things.*'[15]

The sense that, for Dreyer, an authentic narrative is not necessarily a factually reliable one and indeed, that 'realism, in itself, is not art',[16] is borne out by a closer analysis of *Jeanne*. Most obviously, it attends only to the trial, omitting the military campaigns and Jeanne's childhood in rural France. This differs from the strategy of other silent film-makers. (Compare, for example, *Joan the Woman* (Cecil B. DeMille, 1916) in which Jeanne is a sturdy countrywoman, first seen working at a spinning wheel.) It also cuts across the dominant trends in nineteenth-century and early twentieth-century iconography, which typically showed Jeanne either as a country girl or in warlike terms, as an equestrian soldier.

Significantly, Dreyer also compresses the lengthy trial process (which ran from January to May 1431) into a single day. In this respect, he is influenced by classical conceptions of drama, especially those originating with Aristotle's *Poetics*, which emphasised the importance of the three unities of time, action and place. The time allowed for the action of a neo-classical tragedy was usually deemed to be 24 hours, and the place the stage represented was restricted to a number of points within a single larger area, such as a castle, city or palace. *Jeanne* meets these criteria: the focus on the trial lends coherence to the action. It is possible that Dreyer's approach to tragedy was influenced by Scandinavian dramatists (for example Ibsen, Strindberg) who had sought to revive formal approaches to the genre: he would have encountered their work during his early career as a newspaper entertainment critic. More significantly, this use of classical form reinforces the notion that Dreyer sought a kind of non-imitative realism. The 'three unities' were intended to assist a writer seeking to render truthfully the realities of human nature and experience. To echo Pope and Hurd, they were, 'nature methodized'.[17]

Dreyer's narrative retains several features prominent in the medieval trial transcripts. For example, the film depicts Jeanne being questioned on a number of issues, (notably the reasons for her adoption of male dress) and the judges' attempt to manoeuvre her into declaring herself to be in a state of grace (heresy in the eyes of the Catholic church) together with her disarming, confounding, response: 'If I am, may God keep me there. If I am not, may God grant it to me.' For some critics, the depiction of Jeanne's faith in these exchanges is a factor that lends the film spiritual weight.[18]

Dreyer also depicts the bleeding of Jeanne to lower a fever, although not the cause of the historical Jeanne's sickness, a meal of carp.[19] Instead, Jeanne's collapse follows a scene in which she is threatened with the torture chamber. This presentation would have resonated with Dreyer's audiences in the 1920s, when the human sciences were offering new, psychological accounts of illness, and sometimes (as with Freudian psychoanalysis) pathologised the religious adherent.

Similarly, Dreyer 'recreates' Jeanne's recantation, giving shape to the narrative in a way that some viewers found indefensible, but which resolves inconsistencies and gaps in the accounts from the trial and vindication hearings of 1455. The medieval texts are unclear about whether Jeanne realised that the retraction she signed in the Rouen cemetery stated that she had lied about her voices, and was guilty of deceiving herself and others. It is also uncertain whether Bishop Cauchon, a prime mover in the proceedings, wished to offer Jeanne a way to avert death, or sought to manipulate her, knowing that she would regret her retraction and in doing so become a relapsed heretic, whom he could legally hand over to be burned.[20] The film sweeps such ambiguities aside. Jeanne agrees to sign the recantation *in extremis*: recently bled and weakened, emotionally and physically, she gives way after a priest taunts her with the sacrament. With few exceptions the clerics in the film are presented as firmly allying themselves with the worldly power of the occupying English (represented by Warwick) against the naive, God-intoxicated Jeanne.

Whereas the narrative in *Jeanne* is structured to transform a chaotic, confused series of events into a unified drama, and the bleeding and recantation are recast in simplified terms, two key aspects of the conflict between the historical Jeanne and her judges are absent from Dreyer's film: namely, the witchcraft accusations laid against her, and her self-proclaimed status as 'la Pucelle' – the virgin–maid.

As Warner notes, the word *sorcière* does not appear in the official trial accounts, but Jeanne's 'crimes' included activities and attitudes commonly ascribed to witches. In 1433, the Duke of Bedford attributed English losses in France to Jeanne's sorcery.[21] It is interesting to consider why Dreyer omitted these charges against his heroine. It may be that he felt the medieval preoccupation with magic would alienate twentieth-century audiences, who might appreciate the potential seriousness of theological and political disputes but have little empathy for characters who took for granted the reality of such powers. But elsewhere, Dreyer directly challenges the viewer to accept miracles. In *Ordet* ([*The Word*], 1955) Johannes – a former seminarian who, his family believes, lost his sanity after studying Kierkegaard – raises his sister-in-law, Inger, from the dead. Alternatively, it is possible that Dreyer saw the witchcraft charges laid against Jeanne as functions of a larger fear of heterodoxy, simply one manifestation of the underlying ideological conflicts separating accuser and accused. Seen this way, they could be omitted, with little violence done to the core dynamics of the narrative.

Similarly, *Jeanne* glosses over its heroine's virginity and there is no reference to the sexual violence she experienced in captivity.[22] Jeanne herself emphasised her virginity (adopting the title 'pucelle') and was subjected to several physical examinations. This attention to her body is attributable to popular medieval belief that the devil could not deceive a chaste woman; for Jeanne and her supporters, intactness could function as a proof that her voices were not evil spirits. Jeanne's body became even more prominent following her rehabilitation, when her story was subsumed to the familiar patterns of Christian sainthood: virginity was essential to her role as saviour of

France. Why, then, does Dreyer not touch on this? There are probably several reasons. Propriety may have been a factor, but is unlikely to have been the primary motivation. Earlier films had depicted threats of rape; neither Delteil nor Champion's writings avoided it. Arguably, the threats against Jeanne's person *are* present in Dreyer's film, but the typological construction of its heroine (discussed later) lead to their being transposed into the tauntings of the prison guards, which she endures with Christ-like sorrow and patience. It is not insignificant that the film places the mocking of Jeanne after her recantation and before its withdrawal – that is, at the same point in the narrative at which the rehabilitation witnesses claimed the historical Jeanne's guards had attacked her.

Film Style

Studying *Jeanne d'Arc* demonstrates the need to attend to style and form as well as narrative; it is the aesthetics of the film (the photography, sets, editing and so on), which are commonly thought to define it as avant-garde, as opposed to mass entertainment. More significantly, there are specific reasons for its being important for religion and film practitioners to consider style. Subject matter alone does not make a 'religious film' (whether one interprets that as meaning 'a film which resonates meaningfully with the experiences of religious adherents', or 'a film which may be examined by practitioners of religious studies in order to gain insight into the religious ideas and commitments of others' – or both). It is necessary to probe more deeply. What are the qualities of Dreyer's *Jeanne* that have led many to speak of the film in near-religious terms?

One way of analysing film art is the thematic approach, which reads stylistic effects as symbolic or metaphoric expressions of narrative themes. Directors sometimes use visual figures in this way. For example, as its heroine burns, *Jeanne* cuts to shots of birds rising in the sky. Dreyer probably intended their flight to function metaphorically, evoking the ascension of Jeanne's soul to the heavens. This method of 'reading' style is at some levels satisfying, because it leads to the construction of meanings, which can be readily remembered and discussed. In religion and film studies in particular it is popular because interpreting film in such terms allows particular works to be identified as expressive of specific religious concepts or dilemmas, or as typological re-presentations of the lives of significant religious figures.[23]

The problem is that the search for elements in a film that can first be read as metaphors, and second, cohere to form a narrative, tends to push towards over-interpretation. Individual moments and entire films can be inappropriately forced to illustrate preconceived themes existing only in the mind of the critic. Intrinsic to thematic criticism is the danger – of which students of religion have long been aware – of confusing the act of 'translating' a symbol with understanding or explaining it. There is a sense in which the critic's decoding of visual events produces a 'discourse in symbolism' (projecting his or her own preoccupations) rather than a useful conversation about it. Why might a director use metaphor? How have different people responded to symbolic cues in a film? These are questions that the thematic approach cannot tackle.

In part as a reaction against thematically driven tendencies to privilege aspects of films that are linked with narrative continuity and coherence, formalists emphasise the aesthetic (unities and) disunities in a given film. According to this approach, the most discussion-worthy aspects of *Jeanne* are those that disrupt viewer expectations – the unusual structuring of the shot and the cut. The fundamental emphases of the film are perceptual contradiction and discontinuity. According to Bordwell, one of the most well-known exponents of formalism, Dreyer's goal in *Jeanne* was to 'withhold the smoothly flowing pleasure of viewing', to make it hard for his art to be consumed.[24]

Again, there is some appeal in this position. The emphasis on disruption highlights aspects of *Jeanne* that are noticed by all viewers of the film, namely the extensive use of close-ups and unusual camera angles and framings. However, this attention to visual perception and disorder creates an account of film that affords little room to the emotional and cognitive dimensions of viewer experience. Audiences do not relate to films as the formalists classically view them, that is, as series of microscopic units, capable of expression in diagrammatic or tabular form. In *Jeanne d'Arc*, Dreyer defamiliarises and disorients viewers, but the film is about more than a desire to challenge the style of his artistic contemporaries.

This section will discuss the style of *Jeanne* in a way that negotiates a moderating path between the extremes of thematic and formalist criticism. This kind of approach (not an identical one) is advocated by Carney in a study of some of Dreyer's other films.[25] First, the film's use of figures suggestive of the Christ narrative will be considered. This will be followed by a discussion of its deployment of disruptive style. Whilst Dreyer's style is often strange, and is not only a function of the film's themes, at the same time, style and narrative are not wholly unconnected in *Jeanne*.

The title of the film, *La Passion de Jeanne d'Arc*, itself suggests that Dreyer intends to draw comparisons between the trial and execution of Jeanne and the suffering and death of Jesus of Nazareth. Numerous images and sequences evoke the Christian gospel stories. There are repeated visual references to the Crucifixion. Cross shapes are formed by the bars on the windows of Jeanne's prison cell, and their shadow projected by sunlight onto its floor. They appear in the gravestones in the Rouen cemetery, and on top of distant church towers; and at the end, the crucifix itself is held first by and then before the burning Jeanne.

It is significant that in one early scene Loyseleur, the judge who later decides to use the torture chamber and guides Jeanne's hand as she struggles to sign the abjuration, is shown treading on the shadow cross as he steps into Jeanne's cell. The implication is that in contrast to the faithful Jeanne, his piety is a sham: he has no real regard for the Christian message. Additionally (as noted earlier) Jeanne is tormented by her jailors, who, evoking Mark 15:17–19 and parallels, dress her in mock regal garb (a straw crown; a sceptre made from an arrow). In an echo of Matthew 27:37, the charge against Jeanne ('relapsed heretic, apostate, idolater') is nailed to the stake above her head. Finally, as she makes her journey to the stake, a bystander offers Jeanne a drink (compare Mark 15:21–23), and another later declares, 'you have burned a saint' (see Mark 15:39).

In what sense are viewers being encouraged to read Jeanne's suffering as a re-enactment of the Christ event? It could be that the images are intended to suggest to the audience that this is how Jeanne herself made sense of her experiences. For example, changing facial expressions seemingly imply that she feels strengthened by the appearance of the shadow cross on the cell floor. It is at the moment when the prison guard is sweeping away the straw crown that Jeanne makes her fateful decision to withdraw the recantation and reassert the reality of her voices, a move the trial clerk notes as '*responsio mortifera*'. (For the historical Jeanne, resumption of male dress was the fatal relapse.) The crown becomes for Jeanne the symbol of her torment, and provides the sense of her purpose as one of martyrdom. 'His ways are not our ways', she tells Houppeville; her deliverance will be death.

This is perhaps the crucial point at which the film best captures the dynamics of religious experience: Jeanne perceives her message and mission as suprahistorical. Ordinary discourse is turned inside out; she will save France not by intervening in earthly affairs, but by dying at the stake. Her stance is visionary. Of course, it remains unclear whether Dreyer intends the audience to comprehend Jeanne's self-understanding at an intellectual level, or to empathise with her, or, as Baugh suggests, to *share* the meanings she finds in her experience, also seeing her as a figure of Christ.[26] The ambiguity is perhaps intended.

Exegesis determined by Jesus typology does not exhaust *Jeanne*. There are many dimensions of the gospel story not present in the film, and there are other aspects of the film that are not helpfully described as 'Christ-like'. If the Jesus typology allows some viewers to feel 'at home' with dimensions of *Jeanne*, as touched on earlier, Dreyer's style is often perceived to make the film an exhausting, disorienting one for audiences.

Almost all critics who discuss *Jeanne* comment on its unrelenting, exhausting use of the close-up. 'Jeanne suffers, but the spectator suffers no less', quipped one reviewer.[27] There are no true establishing shots in *Jeanne* (long shots that orient the viewer, making subsequent action and space understandable). The face of Jeanne (played by Marie Falconetti – her appearance in the film has become an important aspect of the film's mythology) is ever-present, filmed without make-up, and so tightly that small movements, blemishes, and pores are all visible. Jeanne is also characterised by stasis, a lack of movement giving her character an almost statuesque quality. According to Dreyer, this technique was suggested by the trial transcript, which evokes a series of 'talking heads' engaged in mortal combat.[28] Certainly, the spoken word is hugely prominent in the film, perhaps because Dreyer had at one point hoped to make *Jeanne* as a sound film, only to discover that European studios lacked the necessary finance and facilities. Unusually for a silent feature, the actors seem to enunciate the words reported in all but one of the 174 intertitles.

The close-up does not only focus attention on the verbal combat between Jeanne and the judges. For the late Gilles Deleuze, a French philosopher who wrote extensively on the cinema, the close-up is the 'affection-image'.[29] Seen at such close quarters, all faces look alike; Dreyer's strategy means that Jeanne's experience absorbs viewers in a way that transcends cognitive processes. In psychological terms, our individuation is suspended. We are drawn into the image – hence the feelings of disorientation and exhaustion. In using these stylistic techniques, Deleuze says, Dreyer is able to show both the trial (the historical 'realities' – the characters, the connections between them) and the *passion* – the internal and the suprahistorical dimension of Jeanne's experience.[30] Sarris similarly suggests that in its use of close-up, Dreyer's 'film had found its way to *human* representation'.[31]

Almost as remarkable as *Jeanne*'s use of close-ups are the framing and the cuts between shots. Conventional editing privileges continuity, typically achieved either by the shot–reverse shot or the eyeline match – cutting from a shot of a person talking or looking, to a shot of the person being addressed, or the object being looked at. *La Passion de Jeanne d'Arc* rejects these norms. It also films characters from unusual angles and rarely places the principle action in the centre of the frame. At times, Jeanne's face is cut horizontally, vertically, or obliquely by the frame-edge.

From a thematic perspective, this style might be illustrative of Jeanne's and her interlocutors' isolation from one another. For formalists, they are about perceptual contradiction and a desire to encourage the viewer to reflect on the way the film is being constructed cinematically. But it is equally possible that the unorthodox techniques are intended to serve more 'conventional' functions. For example, a priest's head may suddenly appear in the side of a frame, as he questions Jeanne. This is visually striking, but also a stock move: Dreyer shows in the frame what Jeanne sees, offering a type of point-of-view

shot. It is as if the priest suddenly intrudes on her as well as our attention. Similarly, when the camera pans rapidly back and forth across the
faces of the judges, this evokes the chaos sweeping them, disturbed by
Jeanne's responses to their questions. Also when, in a down shot of
an alley English soldiers appear as helmets, swinging arms and shoul-
dered spears, the absence of the soldiers' faces from the frame suggests that they are less people than tools of an occupying authority.

At this point, it is worth briefly relating *Jeanne* to other examples
of Dreyer's work. Many commentators have noted that the sets were
designed by expressionist Hermann Warm (renowned for his work
on *The Cabinet of Dr. Caligari*, Robert Wiene, 1919) and have a
starkness that negates viewer perception of depth and perspective,
complementing the use of close-ups.[32] Partly on the basis of Warm's
reputation some writers have categorised the film as avant-garde,
but since it was intended for a popular audience (see later) there are
perhaps more plausible explanations.

Jeanne's style represents a deliberate move away from the 'mistakes'
of Dreyer's earlier film, *Der var engang* (*Once Upon a Time*, 1922), a
dull presentation of a fairy tale about a Danish prince who disguises
himself as a tinker and wins the hand of a beautiful but haughty princess.
Just as the *Société Générale des Films* hoped to use cinema to bolster
French national pride, so those who encouraged the production of
Der var engang were keen to develop a Danish national cinema (films
made in Denmark and bearing the distinctive imprint of its character).
But Dreyer found the characters offered by folklore too flimsy and
two-dimensional, later writing that he had learned 'that one cannot
build a film from atmosphere alone', as 'people are above all interested
in people'.[33] *Jeanne*'s rejection of make-up and the use of minimalist
sets, built in three-dimensional form so that the actors became used
to negotiating them, is a reflection of Dreyer the craftsman, feeling his
way towards a style that does justice to history without succumbing to
the temptation to picturesqueness that dogs the period drama:

> Handling the theme on the level of a costume film would probably have
> permitted a portrayal of the epoch of the fifteenth century, but ... what
> counted was getting the spectator absorbed in the past.... The year of the
> event seemed as inessential to me as its distance from the present.[34]

In this sense his approach is not so much avant-garde as experimental.[35] The film's aesthetics reflect his assessment of the best tools for the job of connecting audiences with Jeanne's inner experience.

In conclusion, the use of close-ups, the repeated and challenging cuts, the negation of depth and so on, may function partly to emphasise that meaning is enacted. But in combination they divert attention *away* from externals in a way that encourages viewers to experience the encounter between Jeanne and her judges as a timeless and present conflict, rather than a significant but distant historical event. From a religion and film perspective, this emphasis on interiority is particularly interesting, since it resonates with the ideological subtext of the film, and suggests that religiosity, or spirituality, stands in opposition to institutions and outward forms.

Cultural and Religious Context

As the epigraph to this chapter suggests, Jeanne d'Arc is one of France's most enduring symbols. However, as students of religion have long been aware, common myths do not have to be read the same way: Jeanne's persistence is testimony to the malleability of her story. As Winock remarks, 'Jeanne the Christian, having had the consideration to be sentenced by a man of the Church [a priest] can appeal to the clerical and the anticlerical equally; each recognises himself in the scene.'[36] Those who would claim her as their own are able to select those elements of the Jeanne 'myth' that resonate with their cause. Dreyer's film, then, inescapably and only exists in relation to other images of Jeanne.

In the late nineteenth and early twentieth centuries, right-wing nationalists in France appealed extensively to the story of Jeanne. While the figure of Marianne served as the symbol of liberty and the Republic, Jeanne became the icon of integral nationalism, and her birthday celebrations an alternative to those commemorating the storming of the Bastille. Her identity as a patriotic Catholic, royalist and virgin made her the ideal symbol for the notorious *Action Française*, who rejected the values of the Republic in favour of a mystical Catholicism, xenophobia, and a glorification of violence and war. According to one 1920 *Action* text:

Jeanne of Arc is rebirth ... the fertile peace after a cruel war. She is the motherland once again taking charge of its destiny.... She is the eternal youth of our people, who after heroism produce work and, after death, bring forth life.[37]

The right wing did not only seek to claim Jeanne as its own; it was acutely sensitive to the *processes* of image-making, attacking rival interpretations of the French heroine, such as that offered in the biography written by the secularist Anatole France.[38] (As a young man, Dreyer's collaborator Champion worked as an assistant to France.) This history of the use of Jeanne by reactionary forces, and the flurry of popular interest and pagentry accompanying her declaration as venerable (1903), her beatification (1909) and eventual canonization as a saint (1920), and the quincentenary of her victories (1929), provide important context for the reception of Dreyer's film (see later).

The film does not depict Jeanne in battle. It downplays her virginity. It also pays little attention to her relationship with Charles VII, for whom she fought, and whose coronation she attended in 1429. However, Dreyer's depiction of Jeanne is nevertheless political. By ignoring her military genius and leaving the question of the authenticity of her voices 'open', Dreyer challenged the version of the Jeanne myth that the right wing was working hard to establish. More significantly, *Jeanne* depicts its heroine's abjuration, a historical detail largely overlooked or downplayed by the nationalists. As Warner notes, it is fundamental to the concept of Jeanne's heroism that she died to testify to her truthfulness, and her seeming willingness to recant for fear of the stake challenges this image of the staunch, guileless peasant.[39] In depicting the recantation, therefore, Dreyer's film drew attention to precisely that element of Jeanne's biography that her champions desired to forget.

Dreyer was not ignorant of the significance of Jeanne in 1920s France. Arguably, his focus on Jeanne's *passion* is a critique of those who located her significance in militarism. However, this is not to say that *Jeanne* is completely at odds with the wider religious and cultural context. DeMille's *Joan the Woman* drew links between fifteenth- and twentieth-century Europe when it depicted the ghost of Jeanne appearing to an English soldier in a First World War trench, to suggest that 'the time has come for thee to expiate thy sin against me'. In Dreyer's film, similar notions of the transference or persistence of English guilt are found, albeit in more muted form (see later section on reception). Moreover, Jeanne's death prompts the onlooking crowds to riot. This scene, with its anachronistic shot of traversing cannon, is Dreyer's salute to Sergei Eisenstein's *Battleship Potemkin* (1925). Reinforced by the final intertitle, which speaks of 'Jeanne, whose heart has become the heart of France; Jeanne, whose memory will always be cherished by the people of France', it also evokes the popular conflation of Jeanne and French national destiny.

Director and screenwriter Paul Schrader, adopting a modified form of the thematic approach, describes this as the point at which the religiously non-committed Dreyer retreats from the transcendent (defined by Schrader as the sense that humanity and 'the All' are in a deeply felt unity): the film's attention to context and action at this climactic moment gives unhelpful licence for the viewer to evaluate Jeanne's martyrdom in social or historical terms, and detracts from its value as religious art.[40] However, this interpretation ignores the camera's return to the stake and the cross in the final shot.

Moreover, Schrader's assumption that social concerns are necessarily opposed to religious ones is not as obvious or as universally applicable as he suggests. In his view, 'sparse' artistic means are better able to depict and foster a sense of the transcendent than 'abundant' ones, because they alone point viewers beyond the emptiness of the everyday, to higher, divine, realities. (This interest in what Schrader himself has subsequently termed, 'the cinema of denial' may be rooted in his own Calvinist background – he once studied for the ministry, and was not permitted to watch a film until he was 17 years old.[41])

Conversely, within many religious traditions (such as Hinduism, as is explored in Chapter VIII) superabundance is believed to point the adherent towards, and not away from, the divine. Since the 1970s, Christian theological speculation (the religious tradition against which Schrader is measuring film) has generally moved towards an admission or celebration of context. Dreyer's depiction of the riot does not preclude the possibility of viewers interpreting or experiencing the film religiously, but fits with the perspective of those in early twentieth-century France for whom the meanings of Jeanne transcended her death, and were resonant moments in the divinely ordained life of the nation.

Reception

As described in Chapter II, a focus on viewers as active agents who see films in specific contexts is one of the distinctive emphases of cultural studies. In their classical forms, psychoanalytical and structuralist approaches to film effectively imply that the ordinary viewer is 'duped' by what he or she sees – specialist skills are needed to describe what is really happening on screen. Cultural studies takes a more empirical, evidence-based approach, arguing that films are not containers of immanent meanings, but are interpreted by viewers in ways that vary (but are not random), and are capable of investigation and relation to historical, social and political factors.[42]

In a brief study such as this, it is impossible to do justice to this area of inquiry, and the problems are compounded when trying to study an older film's period audience. Whilst reviews are relatively accessible, evidence of non-professional and non-elite interpretations is hard to find. But as Smoodin suggests, it is possible to study the 'rhetoric of reception' – that is, to look at all or some of the forms that articulate responses (including, where available, academic writings; exhibitor reports; fanzines; promotional materials; reviews) and gain a sense of the ways in which audiences have interacted with a given film in particular locations.[43]

La Passion de Jeanne d'Arc is widely hailed as a masterpiece. Its landmark status in the history of silent cinema was recognised early on: in a 1929 review one critic asserted that it took precedence over anything previously produced, and made worthy pictures of the past 'look like tinsel shams'.[44] But Dreyer did not make the film with cineastes and scholars in mind; he wanted *Jeanne* to be his commercial breakthrough, to attract a mainstream, popular audience.[45] Likewise, the *Société Générale des Films*, in its desire to counter the increasing dominance of Hollywood cinema in post-First World War Europe, hoped for a film with mass appeal. At its instigation, *Jeanne* was even shown to an early focus group, composed mainly of intellectuals, journalists and clergy, in Paris in April 1928. According to Dreyer, the feedback was such that if all objections to the film were acted upon, nothing would be left to screen, which suggested that it should in fact appear without *any* revision. However, the staging of this unusual preview itself perhaps indicates that prior to its release, there was some feeling of unease amongst Dreyer's backers.

In Copenhagen, where *Jeanne* was premiered, unemployed Danish workers were invited to a free screening at the instigation of a Social Democrat politician. The audience was encouraged to fill in response cards, which were generally positive, and illustrated the tendency for some viewers to draw links between their own day and that of Jeanne. 'There are women today who are as tortured morally by society as was Joan of Arc', commented one.[46] However, in France, where viewers had firmly established ideas about the narrative and meanings of Jeanne's life and death, the film was less liked. Critics like the *Candide* reviewer quoted in 'film style', characterised *Jeanne* as painful to watch. They catalogued well-known incidents from Jeanne's life that were absent from the film, and also noted the lack of visual reference to famous paintings of the saint, describing the film in terms of 'an absence of what they had expected'.[47] For nationalists, the fact that a Danish director had been chosen to make a film about Jeanne was a scandal: the involvement of a foreigner in such a project could only be detrimental to French national culture.

The Catholic church had additional difficulties with the film: before the preview, the Archbishop of Paris threatened a boycott. Much dissent turned on the handling of the role of the church authorities in Jeanne's death. The canonization document described her as a loyal Catholic who was attended regularly by her confessor; it depicted her judges as schismatics. It also characterised her as a virgin, not a martyr. Although *Jeanne* does show Houppeville declaring her 'a saint', the film presents Jeanne's conviction about the truth of her *in-ward* experience as being in fundamental and inevitable conflict with the *institutional* church. Specifically, Cauchon appears attempting to pressurise Jeanne into signing the retraction. He threatens that, 'The Church opens its arms to you ... but if you reject it the Church will abandon you ... and you will be alone ... alone!' But Jeanne's response – 'Yes, alone ... alone, with God!' – reveals that she is guided by a different set of values. Cauchon then taunts her by offering, but at the last minute withholding, the Eucharist. This scene (cut for the Paris screening; missing from the London print) proved highly offensive to Catholic sensibilities. It suggested that leading Church figures were devious and demeaned the Host, implying that it could be used as a political weapon. From this troubling incident emerge the limits of the ability of the Catholic church and Dreyer to comprehend one another (Dreyer's protestant (or Protestant) desire – his adoptive parents were Lutherans – was to subordinate externals to 'the spirit in and behind things').

While the *New York Times* praised Falconetti for revealing the 'faith that guided the girl knight of France', and found the cinematography 'effective', other objections to the film came from the English authorities, where *Jeanne* was banned for a year because of alleged anti-English bias.[48] The story of Jeanne was not in itself the problem. A performance of George Bernard Shaw's (admittedly satirical) play, *St. Joan*, was broadcast on radio in spring 1929, and the British press reported the celebrations of Jeanne's quincentenary in detail and with some sympathy, in features illustrated by stills from Dreyer's film.[49] However, in the film's opening scene, the stage is set for Jeanne's trial by an English soldier who sets her stool down upon the floor – suggesting that the English military will control what follows. The widely perceived similarity of the helmets worn by Dreyer's soldiers and those donned by English troops in the First World War, and the depiction of Warwick, pressing for Jeanne's conviction and determined to deny her 'a natural death', were also sources of contention.

Eventually, however, the film was screened in London in November 1930, when reviewers and advertisers carefully avoided politics and stressed style, describing Falconetti as 'poignant', but finding the film's style strange, as opined by *The Times*:

The film is a brave attempt to render on the screen the spiritual suffering of Jeanne of Arc ... the predominant use of the 'close up' tends to monotony, and a feeling of almost hysterical relief is experienced when the camera is allowed to show a more distant view. [50]

There were reservations, too, about 'inaccuracies' of detail. Critics ridiculed the bespectacled priest, pointing out that glasses had not been invented in Jeanne's day. However, a focus on such issues seems reductionist and misplaced. As described earlier, Dreyer's approach did not associate realism with recreation of 'the look'.

Whilst in the 1920s most negative responses to *Jeanne* stemmed from the film's lack of fit with prevailing versions of the Jeanne myth, and so can be attributed to wider cultural and religious factors, its subsequent reception has been shaped by other forces. As described earlier, studies have been circumscribed by the lack of availability of a stable and reputable print. But as the decades have passed, *Jeanne* has been subjected to many different forms of criticism.

In the theoretical seventies, Nash's study, influenced by Marxism and psychoanalysis, pronounced *Jeanne* to be a performance of 'politico-religious doctrinal struggles within the context of a patriarchal order marked by Judeo-Christian monotheism'.[51] Scholars of religion and film might wish to question the assumptions underpinning Nash's work, including those reflected in the misnomer, 'Judeo-Christian' and the implied (unchallenged) causal link between monotheism and patriarchy. Just a few years later, Malpezzi and Clements assessed *Jeanne* quite differently, declaring the film to be a masterpiece precisely because it *transcended* politics.[52] The approach adopted in this chapter, informed by cultural studies, suggests that such an interpretation of the film is simply not plausible. However, as these brief notes indicate, one of the advantages of studying such an old film as *Jeanne* is that by comparing how different scholars have evaluated it, it is possible to chart both changing trends in cinema studies and the general contours in a particular film's reception over time: all the works referred to in this chapter form part of *Jeanne's* reception history.

Whilst for multiple reasons *La Passion de Jeanne d'Arc* has been a difficult film to watch, it continues to attract the interest of art film-goers and students, including those of religion and film (and theology and film). A measure of its iconic status as a piece of 'spiritual art' is the frequent citation of the film in a host of media. Baugh's study of Jesus and Christ films devotes less than two pages to Dreyer's film, but an image from one of its final scenes appears on the book's cover. Shots of Jeanne's upturned face also appear on the cover of Carney's earlier study of Dreyer's style (although its primary focus is on *Day of Wrath* (1943), *Ordet* (1955) and *Gertrud* (1964)) and on the summer 2003 publicity leaflet for the British Film Institute's Dreyer retrospective at the National Film Theatre (London) and the Edinburgh Filmhouse.[53] At the cinema, Jean-Luc Godard's 1962 *Vivre Sa Vie* and Philip Kaufman's *Henry and June* (1990) used images from Dreyer's film to counterpoint the banality of modern culture, whilst the video for Sinead O'Connor's 1989 hit song, 'Nothing Compares 2 U', famous for its desaturated colour and unflinchingly long close-ups of the shaven-headed singer's tear-stained face, evoked *Jeanne* to great effect.[54]

Why is this? Without doubt, 'myth' and mystery play a significant role. As outlined earlier, there are well-known, arresting resonances between the fate of the historical Jeanne and the film bearing her name. Both were railed against and ravaged by fire, but restored to better fortunes years later. Dreyer's choice of actress Marie Falconetti for the film's starring role also proved fortunate. The historical Jeanne's early death ensured her status as icon: she remains forever young, and an unfailing hero in whom much meaning may be invested. Likewise, Jeanne is the only screen role of Falconetti, which makes her brilliant performance even more compelling. Like the historical character she plays, her brief appearance before us attains a special status partly because it leaves the viewer pondering what might have been, but also because there are no disappointing follow-up roles to tarnish her reputation.

La Passion de Jeanne d'Arc is, then, a film that depicts a moment in religious history, and assumes a 'religious' quality in its efforts to capture both the ideological conflict between Jeanne and her opponents, and Jeanne's interior life – her struggle to discern and realise her spiritual vision. Dreyer does not offer a view as to the ultimate source of Jeanne's conviction, but he nonetheless succeeds in disclosing something of the character of religious experience. (For this reason, Luis Buñuel called the film, 'one of her little tears, which wandered our way, in a little celluloid box. An odourless, tasteless transparent tear, a droplet from the purest fountain.'[55])Yet for all its merits and its cultural capital the film did not initiate a trend in the handling of religious themes in the cinema. Whereas (for director and commentators alike) *Jeanne*'s spiritual quality lies in its visual style – Dreyer once claimed that *Jeanne* was his greatest film, because he had been able to make it without the use of make-up – few directors have shared either Dreyer's personal interest in the intersection of the everyday and the supernatural, or his intensely precise approach to film-making. The advent and rapid development of sound technology presented new possibilities and challenges to those involved in making, exhibiting and viewing films. The medium and the industry moved on.

By the mid-1930s Hollywood's dominance was near complete, and most films, including those dealing with religious subject matter, used a set of stylistic conventions (rules concerning framing, editing, and *mise-en-scène*) to present a clearly structured, linear narrative, in which individuated characters acted in a coherent space and time, in keeping with carefully established personality traits and motivations. This classical Hollywood style, still highly influential today, is clearly embodied in the biblical epics of the 1950s, and strongly associated in academic and popular discourse with iconic figures like director–producer Cecil B. DeMille. It is to *The Ten Commandments* (1956), his final film – and one that earned Paramount studios an at-the-time record-breaking $34.2 million dollars – that the next chapter will attend.

IV

The Ten Commandments
(Cecil B. DeMille, 1956)

Roughly comparable to an eight foot chorus girl – pretty well put together but much too big and much too flashy[1]

Moses ... for generations of people all over the world, looks like Charlton Heston[2]

Moses at the 'Movies'

For quite different reasons *The Ten Commandments*, like *La Passion de Jeanne d'Arc*, is oft referenced and rarely discussed. *Jeanne*'s reputation as a spiritual masterpiece seems almost to place it beyond routine criticism: *The Ten Commandments* is ubiquitous, regularly and dismissively cited as the biblical epic *par excellence*.[3] One recent study of theology and the arts describes religious films as ranging 'from Cecil B. de Mille's [*sic*] Biblical spectaculars like *The Ten Commandments* to Martin Scorsese's *The Last Temptation of Christ*'; a contributor to a digest of contemporary thinking on film considers *Commandments* to be, 'DeMille and 1950s Hollywood at either their best or their worst, depending on one's ... penchant for sentiment and spectacle.'[4] The gist of these remarks is that films like *Commandments* occupy a position at one end of a spectrum; that they constitute an approach to religious subjects concerned with visual excess and lacking in depth. 'Spectacle' suggests showy, perhaps ridiculous, display. However, given the significance of epic films as circulators of biblical narrative and interpretation (a reality underscoring the second quote at this chapter's head) it is important to consider seriously how and why they picture the biblical past in the ways they do.

As suggested in Chapter III, *The Ten Commandments'* depiction of the biblical universe – its presentation of an empirically credible world (which is *not* necessarily the same as an historically accurate one), its psychologising treatment of the protagonists and its concretisation of the miraculous – exemplifies classical Hollywood style, a mode of cinematic representation that dominated narrative film-making at the height of the studio era (1930–60) and remains influential to this day.[5] In typical fashion, *The Ten Commandments'* story takes place in an 'external' world, witnessed largely from outside the action (the camera becomes something akin to, but not identical to, literature's 'omniscient narrator'). The narrative proceeds in linear fashion, with beginning, middle and end, and focuses on a central character (Moses (Charlton Heston), acting as God's prophet) with clearly established personality traits and motivations, who has to overcome various antagonists (principally Pharaoh Rameses (Yul Brynner), Nefretiri (Anne Baxter) and Dathan (Edward G. Robinson)) before realising his goal, which is to lead the Hebrew slaves out of Egypt, to freedom under God's law.

The exodus story's place in Jewish and Christian scripture implies for adherents of Judaism and Christianity that it is literally or figuratively true. Setting this substantial but distinctive factor aside, two stock devices encourage the suspension of disbelief in the film's neatly constructed tale. First, (although the film naturalises the supernatural) human agency is strongly inscribed into the narrative: the chain of events is governed by the characters' actions and motivations. Nefretiri's fury at her rejection by Moses prompts her to 'harden Rameses' heart' against the slaves, for example. Second, locations, sets, costumes and props are used to construct a credible fictional world, and are filmed in ways that enable the spectator to watch with little conscious effort: like most films of the era (and in contrast to *Jeanne*) *Commandments* uses a range of shot types (for example, close shots are interspersed by long ones that establish perspective and spatial relations) and continuity editing.

As this quick sketch illustrates, *The Ten Commandments* is able to bear the weight of critical analysis. Before turning in more detail to its handling of the Bible, other preliminary questions remain to be addressed. Why were biblical epics made? And, given the tendency to regard this genre as inseparable from the DeMille persona, how helpful is the concept of auteurism for an understanding of *Commandments*?

In a rare critical analysis of the biblical epic, Babington and Evans describe it as 'the last of the great Hollywood genres to find its proper level of attention'.[6] Epic film-making (following Babington and Evans, I take 'epic film' to denote a large-scale cinematic treatment of a significant moment from a culture's history or mythology) peaked during 1915–30 and in the 1950s. In the earlier period, biblical features were, together with film treatments of literary classics and famous historical subjects, known as 'quality films' and the industry expended disproportionate amounts of money, time and technological expertise in their production.

During a time of growing calls for censorship and regulation (in which the voices of some Christian clergy were prominent) pictures with biblical subjects reflected the need to realign a medium often regarded as morally suspect with the symbols of respectability, decency and high culture. 'When ... stories from the Bible are used as a basis for moving pictures', asserted Frank Dyer, of the Motion Picture Patents Company, 'no fair-minded man [*sic*] can deny that the art is being developed along the right lines'.[7] Later, in the early Cold War era, biblical themes were attractive to an industry seeking to defend itself against charges of Communist infiltration.[8] The officially atheist stance of the Soviet Bloc meant that the foregrounding of religious subjects could serve as an assertion of loyalty to the American way of life. 'In God We Trust', adopted as the country's official motto in 1956, the year of *Commandments*' release, could easily have been the film's tagline.

Additional factors encouraged epic production. Hollywood in the 1950s faced the challenge of television, a mass medium compatible with the privatised lifestyles of the increasingly suburban population.

(The association between the success of the television as a consumer product and the conservative emphasis on the merits of the domestic life in the 1950s is effectively evoked in Todd Haynes' 2002 film, *Far From Heaven*.) The film industry responded with a number of technical developments, for which the epic was an effective showcase: *Commandments* was filmed in VistaVision, Paramount's new widescreen format, and won an Academy Award for special effects the like of which no television company could afford. More specifically, the cultural currency of biblical stories, whilst sometimes circumscribing creativity, provided a framework of shared knowledge and meanings that could be exploited to great effect.

Notoriously, the sex and violence in the Bible narrative afforded opportunities to circumvent censorship regulations. *The Ten Commandments* suggests a sadomasochistic relationship between Rameses and Nefretiri, when he says to her:

> You are going to be all mine – like my dog or my house or my falcon, only I will love you more and trust you less.
>
> … You will be my wife. You will come to me when I call you and I will enjoy it very much. Whether you enjoy it will be your affair, but I think you will.

Lilia (Debra Paget) becomes a sex slave to save the life of her sweetheart Joshua (John Derek). The film also rewards the heterosexual female (and male homosexual) gaze with displays of hyper-masculinity, particularly in the revealed bodies of Rameses and the young Moses. (In a controversial 1960 essay, Michel Mourlet wrote of the 'beauty' that Heston's 'pent-up violence' instilled in a film.[9])

Finally, epic films were enormously popular, which ensured the perpetuation of the genre. Although critical opinion has tended to regard their abundant style as evidencing questionable artistic and spiritual values, large audiences were willing to view and re-view lavish screen presentations of religious texts.[10] This may have been partly because they offered socially legitimated forms of access to otherwise transgressive pleasures. However, the reception history of *The Ten Commandments* indicates that many viewers also found religious meanings in epic style.

How far is it meaningful to interpret a film like *The Ten Commandments* as the product of a single personality, Cecil B. DeMille? Auteurism, the attempt to understand film as the work of an authoring director, dominated film criticism in the late 1950s and 1960s, and is of relevance to religion and film (and theology and film) scholars for several reasons. Its presentation of the director as author of 'visual text' was partly a reaction against literary critics who, like some scholars working in religion today, castigated the 'cheap and easy pleasures offered by the cinema', downplayed the medium's distinctiveness, and thought that the most important part of a film was the dialogue, to which the director simply added pictures.[11] Moreover, auteurism's attention to the image was often linked to mystical notions of the cinema as revelatory. For critic and film-maker Jean Epstein (who first described directors as auteurs in 1921) the effect of the moving image was to transport and transform; it offered spectators an 'essentially supernatural' experience, which reverberated 'through the entire physique'.[12]

DeMille actively presents himself as *The Ten Commandments'* auteur or organising principle. In a pre-credit sequence he appears on screen, to address and instruct the audience as to the film's significance and meaning. The opening credits begin with the Paramount logo, and announce *Commandments* as 'a Cecil B. DeMille Production' – suggesting his status as auteur and/or commodity (given the film's subject matter, the Paramount peak also plays a thematic role here; much later it reappears in a dissolve blending a final shot of the dejected Rameses with one of Mount Sinai).

However, as the film's reception history reveals (see later section) DeMille was unable to control its interpretation; therein lies one of auteurism's difficulties. As Stam notes, auteurism anthropomorphised the critic's love of the cinema.[13] The idea that the genius of an individual personality provides the hermeneutical key to a film is a distortion of the real puzzle, namely, the difficulties associated with explaining the source of film's ability to move and affect viewers. The conventions that govern academic writing testify to the place of auteurism in establishing and legitimating film studies in its early years. In a book like this one, the first reference to a film is followed immediately by the director's name, as if this conveys something of significance for the following discussion. However, contemporary emphases in cinema studies (whilst not abandoning the director tag) query auteurism, foregrounding the collaborative, industrial nature of film-making and challenging the notion that any film has a single, intrinsic meaning. They question the extent to which particular motifs are the result of choices that could only have been made by a particular director, rather than decisions that might have been made by others handling similar material in the same context. Rather as biblical scholars may use the names 'Mark', 'Matthew', 'Luke' and 'John' as shorthand labels for the various contributors and processes they believe to stand behind the gospel texts, so those working with film today rarely regard a given feature, even a 'DeMille film' like *The Ten Commandments*, as being completely the product and possession of its director.

Screening the Scriptures

DeMille's speech in the opening sequence of *The Ten Commandments* stresses the film's origins in the Bible, and DeMille has been characterised as 'a devout believer', who wanted to make scripture 'attractive and fascinating to the masses in an age of increasing materialism.'[14] *Commandments'* approach to the Bible is, however, more complex than such comments suggest.

In places, *Commandments'* position appears strikingly literal and pietistic. By the 1950s, the historical–critical method of biblical study, which had taken as one of its starting points the interrogation of Jewish and Christian traditions identifying Moses as the author of the Pentateuch (the books of Genesis through to Deuteronomy), was firmly established within the Academy and exerted an influence far beyond its walls. Its identification of different sources behind the final form of the text weakened the Law's association with Moses and the exodus. Moreover, many dismissed the biblical miracles as fanciful creations of 'primitive' minds, or rationalised them as freak combinations of natural phenomena.[15] *The Ten Commandments* resists these trends and refuses to deconstruct the exodus.

In an establishing scene, the narrator (DeMille) speaks in terms redolent of Genesis:

> And God said, 'Let there be light', and there was light.... And man was given dominion over all things upon this earth, and the power to choose between good and evil.

> ...But each sought to do his own will because he knew not the light of God's Law. Man took dominion over man ... the weak was made to serve the strong. Freedom was gone from the world.

Juxtaposed with long shots of men dragging blocks of stone, the speech presents Hebrew slavery in Egypt as a violent intrusion upon the divinely established order. Miracles such as the burning bush, the plagues, the parting of the Red Sea, and the giving of the Ten Commandments are portrayed as actual events. In the film's final scene, Moses hands Eleazar the scrolls of the Pentateuch and reminds him that they were written at divine behest.

However, this literalism slots into a narrative within which extra-biblical material predominates. The film's most obvious innovation is its portrayal of a romantic *ménage à trois* involving Moses, Rameses and Nefretiri. Pharaoh's wife is mentioned nowhere in the Bible, but Nefretiri's vengeful attitude to Moses, fuelled by his rejection of her sexual advances, is crucial to *Commandments'* plot. Elsewhere, the biblical account is not merely supplemented but altered. Modifying Exodus 2:15, Moses does not flee Egypt, but is exiled; worshippers of the golden calf are killed by thunderbolts and earthquakes, not the Levite swords of Exodus 32.

Many of these innovations are in fact loosely derived from the Bible and implicitly reinforce its primacy. When Moses, having discovered his Hebrew ancestry, decides to experience slavery for himself, the narrator quotes Exodus 2:11; Nefretiri's manipulation of Rameses is explicitly cast as an attempt to 'harden Pharaoh's heart' (compare Exodus 4:21; 7:3).[16]

It is not just the Hebrew Bible that influences the film's construction of events. In the film Moses describes his commission at the burning bush thus: 'He revealed His Word to my mind and the Word was God. He is not flesh but spirit, the light of eternal Mind and I know that His light is in every man.' The reference to spirit seeks to clarify the implications of the previous scene's visual pyrotechnics, often regarded as an inappropriate attempt to imprison God within the confines of Hollywood style, but intended by DeMille to invoke awe and wonder (in the medium and/or the message). At the same time, the concept of God as divine and in-dwelling Word draws on Johannine vocabulary (compare John 1:1-15; 14), and illustrates *Commandments'* wider tendency to Christianise the exodus. Like other works of exegesis, *The Ten Commandments* recreates the Bible narrative as it retells it.

Although the exodus is foundational for Judaism, and the biblical account speaks of 'my people... Israel' (Exodus 3:10), *The Ten Commandments'* exodus participants are largely departicularised. The slaves' ethnic identity is modified or weakened by the inclusion in their ranks of Nubians and sympathetic Egyptians. As Smith notes, the film is, perhaps, ultimately concerned less with divine power than with interior change.[17] In keeping with this and with classical Hollywood's emphasis on psychological causation, the film visions societies ordered by choice, not birth or fate. Despite the significance of bloodlines implied by the plague of the firstborn, membership of the Chosen People is presented as a voluntary, self-selected identity – a post-Enlightenment, and in this instance, modern Christian position, best illustrated by the career of Moses' adoptive mother, Bithiah. Her rejection of Egypt and desire to learn about God brings her to the table for the celebration of the first Passover; she joins the exodus, and her 'conversion' is evidenced by good works when she gives up her chariot for the infirm and defends Moses against his critics in the wilderness.

Whilst Bithiah models Christian discipleship, *Commandments'* tendency to subsume the Hebrew Bible within a Christian framework is clearest in the scenes charting the period from Moses' discovery of his origins, to his exile. Moses' decision not to conceal his birth but to throw his lot in with the slaves in Goshen prompts a 'Lukan' declaration from his birth mother, Yochebel. Combining themes from the Magnificat and Anna's speech in the Temple (see Luke 1:46–55;

2:36–8) she prophesies that in Moses she beholds her deliverer, and is blessed above all mothers. *Commandments* also has its 'Simeon' (Luke 2:25–35), in the form of an elderly mud-treader working alongside Moses in the brick pits. In contrast to the Lukan visionary, he dies believing his prayers for a deliverer to be unanswered. The irony is that although neither he nor Moses realises it, the old man's request *has* been granted. A gap opens up between the characters' perspective, and that of the audience. The film's transformation of Luke thus heightens the narrative tension (how will Moses' status be made known?) whilst asserting that despite appearances, prayer *is* answered.

The Ten Commandments also conceives of Moses' downfall (his capture and exile) in Christianising terms. Whereas the Bible has Moses flee after impulsively killing an Egyptian taskmaster, in the film he is banished from Egypt because of suspicions that he may be the slaves' long awaited deliverer.[18] Like Judas in Mark 14:10–11 (and parallels) Dathan (Edward G. Robinson) receives financial reward for betraying Moses to the then Prince Rameses, and when Moses is charged in the Pharaonic court, his response, 'I am the son of Amram and Yochebel, Hebrew slaves', evokes Jesus' enigmatic replies at Luke 22:66 ff. and parallels. Pharaoh Seti, like Pilate, realises that in the face of Moses' intransigence he must order his death, but cannot bring himself to pronounce sentence and hands him over to another agency, his son Rameses, for punishment (Matthew 27:24–6).

New Testament imagery and language also abound in Moses' banishment to the wilderness. The narrator's description of the desert as a place 'where holy men and prophets are cleansed and purged for God's great purpose', emphasises Moses' interior 'preparation' for his mission, recalling Luke 4 and parallels. Just as Jesus is mocked as 'King of the Jews', and dressed to parody regal wear (Mark 15:16-20 and parallels; John 19:2,5), so Rameses taunts Moses as 'the slave who would be King', and 'Prince of Israel.' He is dressed in a 'Levite cloth', 'his robe of state', and handing him a binding pole (Moses has previously carried the pole in such a way as to evoke Christian iconography of the cross; later in the film the pole becomes his miraculous 'weapon' against unbelieving Egypt) Rameses tells him that, 'here is your king's scepter, and here is your kingdom. You have the scorpion, the cobra, and the lizard for subjects. Free them if you will, leave the Hebrews to me.' As in the scene with the mud-treader, DeMille plays with the audience's foreknowledge of the exodus. Rameses' comments are closer to the truth than he imagines. Moses will prove to be the Hebrews' leader, just as for the evangelists Jesus *was* King of the Jews.

The Ten Commandments' handling of the Bible is, then, a complex blend of the conservative and the hubristic. For critics dismissive of the epic, this inconsistency is indicative of its flippant approach to matters religious. But a good deal of this ambiguity is a necessary part of the film's response to the challenges involved in reworking a familiar text. Attaching creations like the Moses-Nefretiri-Rameses triangle to biblical verses is partly about the clever licensing of audacious innovations. Within a genre much concerned with display, it is also an assertion of the cinema's ability to enflesh the text, and its *need* to do so. *Commandments'* audiences know 'what will happen next': DeMille and other biblical film-makers capture interest by shifting attention to *how* things happen – to questions of narrative theme, character relation and the ability of the medium itself to represent the fantastic. Pardes' claim that in a scene depicting his oversight of the construction of Seti's treasure city, Moses is posed to resemble 'more a film director than an architect' is perceptive. Seen this way, the image illuminates not just *The Ten Commandments*, but the furthest reaches of a too frequently dismissed genre.[19]

Why the Slaves Don't Cross the Red Sea

The Cold War, which imposed specific pressures on Hollywood, was an important political context for the production and early viewing of *The Ten Commandments*. On the one hand, the potential for the cinema to communicate a vision was widely recognised. Eric Johnston, President of the Motion Picture Export Association, characterised American films as 'messages from the free country'.[20] On the other hand, the conviction that film influenced public values, coupled with a lingering distrust among conservatives of Jews and the foreign-born, made the industry a target for anti-Communist investigation. Boycotts, blacklisting, and the picketing of movie the-atres all encouraged studios to adopt more conservative production policies.[21] The classic Hollywood film narrative of the 1950s patrioti-cally upholds the 'American dream', focusing on 'economic success, individual achievement and social mobility, equality of opportunity, competition, and winning'.[22]

Produced at the high point of Cold War hysteria, *Commandments* is an avowedly anti-Communist film. Moses, as guardian of a divinely willed freedom, becomes a cipher for the American nation, and more specifically, its self-understanding as a second Israel (in the sense of both Promised Land and light for the nations).[23] The (unseen) Promised Land is characterised as an ordered but open society, where individuals will be free to pursue their own happiness in the form of acquisition and ownership. Moses tells the slaves, 'tomorrow we go forth a free nation where every man shall reap what he has sown', and the narrator describes exodus participants as yeoman farmers: 'planters of vineyards and sowers of seed, each hoping to sit under his own vine and fig-tree'. As various commentators note, Moses' final words in the film are, 'Proclaim liberty throughout all the lands, unto all the inhabitants thereof' – the text drawn from Leviticus 25:10 and engraved on the Liberty Bell in Pennsylvania. A closing shot, in which Moses is posed to resemble the Statue of Liberty, reinforces the suggestion that the (Christianised) Israelites are the spiritual precursors of America.[24]

Conversely, the autocratic Rameses, who subjects the masses to lives of drudgery enforced by the threat of state-backed terror, stands for the powerful, demonised Soviet enemy. (The casting of Yul Brynner as Rameses is pertinent: his Eastern-European accent hints at parallels between the Egyptian regime and that in the USSR, and his appearance in such films as *The King and I* (Walter Lang, 1956) means that he brings a subtext of powerful Otherness to the role.) At various points in the narrative, *Commandments* stresses that, in contrast to the godly slaves, Egypt, like Communist Russia, is no nation 'under God'. Echoing Marx's and Lenin's characterisations of religion as the 'opium of the people' and 'a kind of spiritual gin' (a social construct that dulls the pain of a harsh world and justifies inequalities of power and wealth[25]) Rameses explains the Egyptian belief system sociologically, claiming that 'you prophets and priests made the gods that you may prey upon the fears of men'. Like the present-day editors of the *Oxford Annotated Bible*, he also attempts to rationalise the first plagues as freak natural phenomena (a work of deconstruction trumped narratively by DeMille's/Moses' immediate invocation of a plague of hail). As if to reinforce the political connections stylistically, the scenes depicting Rameses' palace in the wake of the exodus and the failed attempt to recapture the slaves see the screen flooded with crimson tones. By contrast, the film depicts the biblical Red Sea as deeply blue, and the word 'red', then synonymous with Communism in popular discourse, was deliberately omitted from the dialogue.[26]

Governed as it is by Hollywood conventions, *Commandments* does not simply re-present the Cold War, it also promises resolution of the conflict between America and the USSR, suggesting that one culture will be triumphant, the other overcome. When a dejected Rameses finally proclaims that 'his [Moses'] god is God' the implication is that despite current fears (concentrated around the Korean War and the Suez Crisis) the Soviet threat will be extinguished. Moses (and America) can win through.

It is not only international politics that surface in *The Ten Commandments*. As highlighted earlier, the film identifies slavery as unnatural and contrary to God's purposes. ('God made men [*sic*]. Men made slaves', says Joshua.) In 1950s America, when racial segregation (part of the aftermath of African American slavery) was a live social and political issue, Moses' denunciation of 'the evil that men should turn their brothers into beasts of burden … only because they are of another race, another creed' is not simply a declaration of an abstract principle.[27] Discrimination against individuals on racial grounds is specifically rejected in the Memnet subplot. It is Memnet's (the royal nurse-maid's) misplaced belief in the importance of the racial purity of the Egyptian ruling class (the influence of modern eugenics and Nazi ideology appears reflected in the dialogue articulating her belief in the paramount importance of the 'blood' of Rameses and Moses) that leads her to plot against Moses and reveal the secret of his Hebrew origins. Her actions bring exile and grief into the lives of

Nefretiri, Moses, Seti and Bithiah, and lead to her own death. They contrast sharply with the attitudes and behaviour of Bithiah, whose early willingness to incorporate Moses within the royal household implies a differently based and positively sanctioned construction of social organisation and leadership. Whereas Bithiah's convictions are a route to life (the infant Moses is rescued from the Nile; Bithiah joins the exodus), the film suggests that prejudice such as Memnet's can engender only violence and death, and will eventually destroy even that which it misguidedly seeks to preserve.

Just as its handling of the Bible can at first sight appear capricious, so *The Ten Commandments* may appear to offer unstable political meanings to its viewers. In presenting a binary opposition between on the one hand, Israel–America, and on the other hand, Egypt–USSR, *Commandments* reinforces the basic anti-Communist premise that Communists are inherently disloyal enemies of the nation. Yet a more liberal ideology seemingly underpins the critique of race politics. Each of these 'contradictory' impulses can be understood within the broader context of the film's commitment to the American dream. *Commandments* rejects racism since it, like the command economics of the Soviet Union, is a perversion of the American dream's belief in the power of anyone to pursue the 'good life' and fulfill her or his desires. Ambiguity therefore blends into consistency, a trait emphasised in the reception and promotion of the film, to which the analysis will now turn.

Trailing *The Ten Commandments*

The cinema experience is sometimes described as a communal ritual analogous to churchgoing or other worship activities:

> We gather together, seated in rows, necks craned, silently facing the screen of light and revelation … we share food uniquely blessed for movie time … in specific, movie-house-only vessels and portions; we follow a carefully patterned … familiar liturgical sequence, from meeting the well-dressed usher at the entrance, to the obligatory announcements of forthcoming events, to the opening reminder to be still and keep silence, to the Feature Presentation … to a well marked conclusion with credits and a closing song as we file out in silence, crossing back over into the monotony and homogeneity of the ordinary world.[28]

Cinemas...are 'the temples of modern India'...monumental spaces gleam with light and colour, vestibules are plastered with posters of gods and goddesses, red carpets exude desire and wantonness. Devotees come in huge numbers to worship...at the shrine of the new image, the oneiric image that will create their new gods and even their new beliefs.[29]

If access to the divine is to be had in secular life, perhaps it is in the cinema that people most closely approach communion.[30]

The analogy can be pushed too far. One purchases admittance to a cinema; and for most religious adherents, a non-material but real deity is the object of devotion. However, these accounts highlight a number of typical elements. As the first quote describes, one of the ritualised aspects of the cinema-going experience is the screening of trailers or short films announcing forthcoming features. Contemporary trailers fall into two categories. The brief 'teaser,' usually thirty seconds or so in length, functions to create an air of anticipation several months before a film's release, and to alert audiences to its name and website. Standard trailers are around two or three minutes long. They establish genre, sketch plotlines, and introduce stars.[31] Fast cutting (consecutive brief shots) injects energy or urgency (in *La Passion de Jeanne d'Arc* Dreyer very occasionally uses fast cutting in this way, for example to evoke the oppressiveness of the torture chamber) and presents information economically.

Trailers are so intrinsic to the cinema experience that many DVDs include them as 'special features' (see Chapter V). They can provide an indication of how the film was first positioned by the industry. Consequently, their study sometimes reveals a distance between a studio's expectation of a film, and its actual reception. Analysis of different trailers produced for *The Ten Commandments* additionally charts the changing reputation of the film and the epic genre.

The 1956 trailer is an extraordinary nine-and-a-half minutes long. *Mise-en-scène*, editing and dialogue are used certainly to establish DeMille as auteur but also to promote multiple avenues of access, to make *Commandments* resonate as extensively as possible and attract the largest possible audience.[32] After a title card, the first image is a close-up of a reproduction of Michaelangelo's famous statue of Moses, from the Church of St. Peter in Chains, Rome. The camera then pulls back, to reveal that the statue is standing on a desk in a study. The suggestion is that it is DeMille's room: he appears on the screen to negotiate the viewer around the space, and to introduce the film. His first move is to 'explain' Michaelangelo's work. The famous horns on the statue are, he reveals, the result of a misinterpretation of the Hebrew term *keron*, which early scholars translated as 'horns' but which we now know refers to 'rays of light' surrounding Moses' head as he descended from Sinai. Only then is a photograph of Charlton Heston, posed with the Rome statue, shown to the viewer, who is advised to 'notice the likeness' between the two profiles. In this way, DeMille establishes himself as the personality behind *Commandments*, and aligns the film with high culture, suggesting that it, like Michaelangelo's statue, is informed by the best available scholarship of its day.

These associations are carefully sustained. The objects in the study are a mixture of film props (the tablets of the law; the reed basket) and artefacts, such as a Van Dyck painting of the infant Moses. DeMille comments that the latter has 'never before been exhibited' – simultaneously evoking cinema's revelatory potential, and claiming for it a status akin to that of the art gallery or museum. He also addresses the film's need to supplement the biblical story with incidents from Moses' youth. Citing as his sources Philo and Josephus, DeMille identifies them as 'ancient historians', who had access to traditions in destroyed or long lost documents 'like the Dead Sea Scrolls'. Significantly, these figures are also oriented historically in relation to important events in early Christianity: 'Philo wrote during the lifetime of Jesus of Nazareth ... Josephus wrote some 50 years later.' It matters little that Philo and Josephus are historically irrelevant as far as attempts to construct the historical Moses are concerned, or that *Commandments* makes very little use of the first-century authors.[33] By referencing ancient documents and traditions, which many at the time believed could hold vital information about early Christianity and Judaism (especially in America, where biblical archaeology remains a field of popular Christian interest, and expectations concerning the potential import of the Qumran material ran high in the 1950s) DeMille associates the film with a reverential but scholarly faith.

The next section of the trailer, introduced by a description of Moses' life as a great 'adventure', sells the film more conventionally. Images from *Commandments*, or alternative takes, are used to introduce the characters and stars. Fast cutting and rhetorical questions ('How did God harden Pharaoh's heart?' 'Who organised the exodus?') define the film as a drama, with action and romance. Finally, the Cold War relevance of the story is underlined. 'All this happened 3000 years ago, but we are still fighting the same battle that Moses fought,' says DeMille (in words repeated in the film's prologue). 'Are men to be ruled by God's laws or are they to be ruled by the whims of a dictator, like,' here DeMille pauses – allowing space for a 1950s audience to insert the name of Hitler, the more-recently dead Stalin, or Krushchev – 'Rameses? Are men the property of the state or are they free souls under God?' In suggesting that *The Ten Commandments* champions a vision of a society 'under God,' the trailer firmly establishes its representation of the biblical narrative as one replete with meaning for mid-twentieth-century America.

The context of *The Ten Commandments'* theatrical re-release in 1989 was markedly different from that of the 1950s. In that year the Soviet Bloc collapsed, leaving Communism much diminished as an ideology and as a political movement. At the cinema, attendances had declined throughout the 1980s, and television and home video seemed dominant. Few in the West predicted the rise in cinema attendances that was to happen in the years following 1990. Conventions from art cinema, and postmodern elements (such as 'quotations' of classic scenes and genres) had been grafted into the classic Hollywood style, reflecting a more self-conscious approach to film-making and spectatorship.[34] These factors are reflected in the promotion of *Commandments* for its re-release.

The 1989 trailer is just over 90 seconds long. It promotes *Commandments* on two related bases, both of which assume a 'film literate' audience, reflecting its distribution on the art cinema circuit. First, the trailer's voice-over evokes nostalgia for the golden age of Hollywood: 'There was a time when the cinema was a place of spectacle and wonder, when unforgettable films played on gigantic screens that overwhelmed the imagination. Now that time has come again.'

The staid language recalls the 'historical' vocabulary of the film's opening prologue – but it is the mystery of cinema, rather than any divine secret, that is being invoked.

Second, the trailer visually asserts the superiority of seeing the film on a large screen, rather than on video or television at home. As the voice-over begins, the screen is empty, save for a tiny image (evoking the small screen of the television) of blue-black stormclouds, and a hint of light showing behind them on the distant horizon. This image is gradually enlarged until, at the point at which it fills the whole screen, it cuts to show Moses/Charlton Heston. Whereas the 1950s trailer deliberately withheld images of the parting of the Red Sea, this trailer displays them, as well-known evidence of the film's epic credentials. Fast cutting creates a montage of close-ups of the lead characters, and long shots drawing attention to the film's juxtapositioning of well-known stars and a ubiquitous 'cast of thousands'. The voice-over also announces that *The Ten Commandments* is newly restored 'and presented in 70 millimeter VistaVision, with a six track Dolby stereo sound,' emphasising that image resolution and sound quality far exceed anything available at home.

The 1989 trailer reflects the ways in which, 33 (now 50) years since its initial release, *Commandments* has been incorporated into popular awareness of the history of the cinema, a move that is just beginning to be paralleled within the worlds of cinema studies and religion. In its foregrounding of the medium, it is also a sobering reminder of the distance between the 'overwhelming' formats for which biblical epics were designed and first viewed, and the experience of watching and critiquing them subsequently in diminished version (on television, video or DVD).

Reception

DeMille's name ensured a substantial amount of press coverage in 1956 and 1957, but could not secure automatic praise for *Commandments*. The film's lavish sets, array of Hollywood stars, and three-and-a-half hour duration prompted *The New Republic* reviewer Evett to quip, '*The Ten Commandments* is longer than the 40 years in the desert.'[35] As touched on in Chapter II, the consumption or non-consumption of cultural artefacts is a means by which individuals ally or distance themselves from particular peer groups. In the case of 1950s newspaper and magazine film critics, the kind of 'knowing' tone adopted by Evett marked the writer's membership of an elite subgroup of professional viewers, who routinely contrasted Hollywood productions with motion picture 'art', and castigated the former for its elevation of spectacle over substance.[36]

Nevertheless, reviews in general-interest publications like *The New Republic*, *The New York Times*, *Nation*, *New Yorker*, *Newsweek* and *Time* all engaged to some extent with DeMille's claims for *Commandments*, and attempted to measure the film against them. Film periodicals such as *Sight and Sound* and *Films and Filming* also published reviews.

Newsweek was largely positive, judging that *Commandments* might be 'a trying experience now and then, but a very educational one'.[37] Other writers took issue with the film's scholarly credentials. Writing for *The New York Times*, Crowther hinted that some 'frank apocrypha' had been added to the biblical story, to produce 'a lusty and melodramatic romance'.[38] Evett, noting the screen credits' emphasis on texts and research, suggested that the use of such material was superficial, giving the film 'an odd, almost highbrow patina'.[39]

It was, however, the attempt to combine religious experience with entertainment that most exercised the early commentators:

> Cinemogul DeMille claims that he has tried 'to translate the Bible back to its original form,' the form in which it has lived. Yet what he has really done is to throw sex and sand into the movie-goers' eyes for almost twice as long as anybody else has ever dared to,

declared *Time*.[40] The editor of *Films and Filming* complained that the film moulded religion into a set pattern of Hollywood conventions. This idea was advanced in the present chapter – but Baker goes further, suggesting that the strategy inevitably led to a production lacking in 'true' spiritual content.[41] Reviewers also protested the film's romantic plotlines and the sexual overtones of Moses' relationship with Nefretiri: DeMille had 'exercised heroic bad taste to create an epic of balderdash'.[42]

Time went further in castigating *Commandments'* 'taste'. 'Is this blasphemy?' pondered the reviewer, deciding, 'technically not; but it is sometimes ... impossible to avoid the impression that the movie maker, no doubt without intending to, has taken the name of the Lord in vain'.[43] *Sight and Sound* made a similar point in less restrained terms: 'When Moses first says "Let my people go", *The Ten Commandments* gathers some momentum ... Dilute it with "I belong to you, Moses", or "Worship whatever God you please, so long as I can worship you", and a rooted vulgarity is exposed', claimed Kitchin.[44]

Interestingly, the film's special effects, recognised with an Academy Award, were identified as highly problematic by the professional reviewers. *Time* objected that the burning bush scene made God sound like a television advert voice-over.[45] The pestilential mist used to signify the death of the Egyptian first-born was derided as, 'fit for a stage production of *Dracula*'.[46] Finally, in characteristic fashion, Evett suggested of the miracles that:

> For a film on the Ten Commandments, this is a splendid demonstration of how to violate the first three. In making the Almighty talk as if He were at the bottom of a well, and by showing Him as a sort of suburban show-off and spoilsport, determined to toss off miracles as if they were parlor tricks, DeMille has given us a vision of God so shocking in its naivety that even an atheist must blanche at the idea of disbelieving in anything so inconsequential.[47]

The Ten Commandments' reception in the religious press was widely divergent, as typified by a debate in *The Christian Century*, initiated by Union Theological Seminary's instructor in religion and drama, T.S. Driver. Driver was strongly critical of *Commandments'* presentation of the Moses–Nefretiri–Rameses triangle, and the portrayal of the divine voice, declaring them as not just irrelevant, but idolatrous. The Church 'must object when the primary drive and thrust of a picture, its conception, idiom and style, are in a direction exactly opposite from that of the Bible'.[48] For Driver, whereas religion was essentially an internal matter of personal faith, *The Ten Commandments*, with its star-studded cast and lavish sets, was dedicated to the public and the external. To some extent, he deemed the source of this weakness to lie in the nature of Judaism and Christianity as historical religions. Their ultimate grounding in events linked to concrete times and places might tempt the believer to feel that the meaning and significance of a biblical event could be accessed by 'recreating' those times and places in great detail, but the result was a misrepresentation of God. 'The DeMille God is imprisoned in the DeMille style, which means in the irrelevant minutiae of Egyptian culture and the costume director. He bears no resemblance to the Old Testament Lord of History.'[49] (The proximity of Driver's and Dreyer's views on this issue is striking.)

Confident of his ability to function as an arbiter of aesthetic and religious merit, Driver urged clergy to oppose the film publicly on faith grounds:

This three-hour-and-thirty-nine-minute-god must be rejected quite as absolutely as the god of the Golden Calf was rejected by Moses, for he is, in fact, his latter day descendant ... When the minister is invited to participate in the advertisement of this film ... he will be unwittingly invited to choose whom he will serve.[50]

In effect, he claimed that those who saw some religious or spiritual value in the film were idolaters, no better than those whom the Levites slaughtered (Exodus 32:27f.).

The Christian Century printed correspondence from several people who felt that Driver's anger was misplaced and inappropriate. Kennedy, a Methodist Bishop, was typical in his suggestion that 'it does not seem quite fair to expect Hollywood to create on the screen the atmosphere of a seminar discussing neo-orthodoxy'. There were problems with the film, but it made Moses 'alive and great', and stressed the place of God as the foundation of human freedom. Rochester churchman H.L. Clark expressed similar views, arguing (realistically? condescendingly?) that Driver asked too much of a film produced for a mass audience. Lindsay Young, representing the National Conference of Christians and Jews in Los Angeles, suggested that Driver's comments revealed more about *his* attitudes to religion and representation than about *Commandments* itself, asking,

Was he [Driver] not moved by the unconquerable will to freedom on the part of the people, a will born out of faith in God? Was he unimpressed by the portrayal of a loyalty to God that transcended allegiance to any state?[51]

From this sample of materials several trends emerge (Smoodin's 'rhetorics of reception'). There is considerable disparity between the readings of *The Ten Commandments* promoted in the trailer and opening credits, and actual interpretations of the film. This further undermines methodologies such as auteurism, which locate a film's meanings in directorial activity and intention. Moreover, the diversity of opinions expressed by commentators writing within a few months of *The Ten Commandments*' release is a reminder that a film's meaning is not self-evident, uniform or unchanging. Finally, the reception of *Commandments* touches on more widely relevant questions about the handling of religious themes and subject matter at the cinema. Some viewers, represented by Lindsay Young, were 'too engrossed with the message to be unduly concerned about the wrapping'.[52] For others, such as Driver, 'message' and 'wrapping' (visual display; fictional subplotting) were inseparable, and certain kinds of 'wrapping' were, a priori, anti-religious. By attempting to capture the events of divine history on screen, Hollywood created petty gods or idols, a process antithetical to the fostering of true religious sentiment.

The discussion of *The Ten Commandments* has, then, travelled full circle. Is the epic genre, with its emphasis on large-scale, heavily visual treatment of biblical subject matter, inherently irreligious?

As noted earlier, biblical epics such as *Commandments* have frequently been the object of religion and film scholars' at best benign neglect, and at worst, sneering derision. But cultural studies, taking on board Bourdieu's arguments about the relationship between taste and power, has challenged the wholesale dismissal of popular and mass culture. Empirical research from the 1950s onwards has also indicated that cinema audiences, including viewers of epics and 'blockbusters', choose what to see and hear, and how to interpret it.[53] These factors necessitate a re-visiting of the epic's visual culture. Is it in fact in the visual excess castigated by so many commentators that *Commandments*' religious significance may lie?

The past decade has seen a new willingness to consider the biblical epic in less negatively judgmental terms. The work of Wood and of Babington and Evans forms part of this history and has been discussed. A number of other critics have been prompted to re-evaluate *The Ten Commandments*, particularly in relation to more recent cinematic representations of the exodus, chiefly *The Prince of Egypt* (Brenda Chapman, Steve Hickner and Simon Wells, 1998). In keeping with New Hollywood trends (see Chapter VII) this animation feature cites the 1956 film in plotting (it borrows motifs like the sibling rivalry between Moses and Rameses) and visual design (the realisation of the 'hounds and jackals' gameboard that appears in scenes in Seti's palace; the colours of Moses' garments; and the parting of the Red Sea), strategies that invite critics of the film to reflect on its predecessor.[54]

Juxtaposed with *Prince of Egypt*, some of *Commandments'* distinctive qualities emerge more clearly. *Prince of Egypt's* Moses, having led the slaves to safety, appears broken by Rameses' loss of his son, embodying the film's struggles to come to terms with the partisan character of the biblical text. Likewise, the use of overtly stylised graphics to depict the plague of the firstborn (shown in monochrome) and Pharaoh's slaughter of the Hebrew children (presented by animated Egyptian hieroglyphs) foregrounds the film's status as a *representation* of events as well as the confines imposed by a need to appeal to families with young children. In impulse and outcome, this is far removed from classic Hollywood's efforts towards realism, and potentially encourages spectators away from literal viewings. *Prince of Egypt's* closing message, voiced in the song, 'When You Believe', places emphasis not on the object of devotion, but on the importance of self-reliance and commitment as the means for achieving one's goals:

Who knows what miracles
You can achieve
When you believe
Somehow you will –
Now you will,
You will when you believe.

In contrast, *The Ten Commandments* depicts the massacres and the miracles as literal, visceral events: in the trailer DeMille claims, 'these *very* tablets, are *actually* carved from the stone of the mountain'; 'we rolled our cameras across the *very* ground on which Moses trod'. These phrases propose cinema as a pilgrimage event, an experience that enables viewers to connect, through an audio-visual medium, with salvation history.

Commandments' insistence on the miraculous (underlined narratively by the rejection of Rameses' naturalising rationalisation of the plagues), and its celebration of God's triumph over Pharaoh, may appear unpalatable to some: one early reviewer joked that 'no one ought to be admitted unless accompanied by an Egyptologist, on account of the...anti-Egyptian bias'.[55] Yet in many respects this position resonates with the Bible's own account of 'signs and wonders' (Deuteronomy 34:11). As Pardes notes, much of the *Commandments'* appeal to mass audiences may lie in the potential for its visual abundance to capture something of popular religion's historic connection of seeing with belief – an association voiced in the Bible: 'And Israel *saw* the great work which the Lord did against the Egyptians, and the people feared the Lord; and they *believed* in the Lord and his servant Moses'[56] (see Exodus 14:31).

The ability of visual phenomena to mediate an experience of the divine is further suggested by *Commandments'* focus on Moses' response to God's activity. The film's most obvious attempt to present religious experience lies in its depiction of the changing facial expressions of its lead character, as he variously reacts to the giving of the Ten Commandments, the burning bush, or the miracle of Passover. As Sheen notes, 'one of the most important features of this film...is the way Moses' face *keeps* changing, *keeps* changing, *keeps* recording for us the presence of that absolute other outside the frame'.[57] Moreover, Moses' body, displayed to viewers as a sexual commodity in the first half of the film, is hidden after his commission at the burning bush. From this point onwards, his hair ('Moses, your hair!' exclaims Sephora, in an illustration of the knowingness of DeMille's style[58]) is styled to resemble the Michaelangelo statue used in the film's publicity. In an era in which conservatives worried over the presence of 'secret Commies' in American society, *Commandments* adopts the reassuring strategy of collapsing the distance between inner commitment and outer form; appearance and reality.

In this displaying of the potential of the visual and 'the look', *Commandments* stakes a bold claim for the film medium – one akin to that made by *The Passion of The Christ* (see this book's concluding chapter). Simultaneously, it serves as a reminder that a consideration of a film's religious qualities, like that of its meanings more generally, is not something that an individual critic can determine once and for all, but is instead a 'volatile, essentially cultural phenomenon'.[59] The elusiveness of the answer to the questions about what makes a 'religious film' may be heightened when studying a film like *Commandments*, which presents a narrative foundational for Judaism, and in many ways, for Western culture as a whole. It is more readily apparent in studying a film like *The Wicker Man,* which focuses on a faith position largely alien to that of most of its viewers (paganism) but has become the inspiration of a range of devotional practices and cult-like activity, as explored in Chapter V.

V

The Wicker Man
(Robin Hardy, 1973)

not an attack on contemporary religion, but a comment on it[1]

one of the strangest films ever to come out of Scotland[2]

To See or Not to See? The Importance of Distribution

Distribution is perhaps the most overlooked aspect of the film industry. On the one hand, it appears prosaic in comparison with film-making itself. On the other hand, it lacks the familiarity of exhibition. It is probably safe to assume that every reader of this book has had the experience of seeing a film in a cinema, or of watching one at home, but the routes via which films reach screens are not widely known. Distribution has, however, always been central to the development of the film industry. The dominance of the Hollywood studios was built on its control: Paramount, which produced *The Ten Commandments*, began as a distributor.[3] Today, many films rely on revenues generated by television, video and DVD distribution to break even. The current drive to introduce improved home viewing formats (HD-DVD or Sony's 'Blu-ray' disc) is partly motivated by the need to revive the tiring revenues generated by DVD, on which many studios have come to depend. When conventional channels are closed to film-makers, new distribution methods continue to emerge: 2003 saw the first simultaneous distribution of a feature film, *This is Not a Love Story* (Billie Eltringham, 2003) both in British cinemas and by live stream over the Internet.

It is impossible to discuss *The Wicker Man* without reference to distribution. Its notoriety and status as a piece of 'cult-like' (I discuss the appropriateness of this term later) fascination are due partly to its tortuous distribution history. Moreover, the demands of distributors have impacted the film's content and its presentation of the fictional encounter between Christian policeman Sergeant Howie and the pagan inhabitants of Summerisle.

When *The Wicker Man* (director, Robin Hardy) was filmed in 1972 its prospects looked good. Writer Anthony Shaffer had authored the Broadway hit *Sleuth* and Alfred Hitchcock's *Frenzy* (1972). British Lion, the company backing the film, was an established rival to the conglomerates dominating British cinema, such as Rank, which owned the large Odeon cinema chain. However, by the time *The Wicker Man* reached post-production (the processes of editing, sound-mixing and the adding of special effects), British Lion had been sold to EMI. In the face of a marked lack of enthusiasm from the new company executives, Hardy, Shaffer and Christopher Lee (who played Lord Summerisle in the film) struggled to negotiate *The Wicker Man* through the distribution bottleneck and secure its release. Producer Peter Snell's on-set affair with Ingrid Pitt (the partner of Rank's head of exhibition) is rumoured to have contributed to the failure to win favour at Odeon. The film *was* sold for American distribution to National General, but they immediately went bankrupt; Warner Bros. inherited the rights but was reluctant to invest in publicity.[4] As the possibility of full-blown release as a feature film receded, *The Wicker Man* eventually appeared as a B-movie, the second feature on a double bill with *Don't Look Now* (Nicholas Roeg, 1973). In order to fit the B-movie format, the 102-minute Director's Cut was drastically re-edited. The resulting 84-minute film condensed the narrative, and deleted its opening sequence, which was crucial in terms of establishing Howie's character motivations (his Christian commitment) and articulating the reasons for his journey to Summerisle.

For many years, this version of *The Wicker Man* was the one most widely available. That it circulated at all was due partly to the personal efforts of Hardy and Lee, who remain significant figures in the film's promotion. (Hardy, for example, appeared at a Glasgow University *Wicker Man* conference in 2003.) It steadily gained a following of art-film goers and students, until in 1977 a group of Louisiana fans, headed by local television presenter Stirling Smith, formed Summerisle Films and raised funds to restore some of the missing footage. Their 96-minute version met with some success, stimulating a special issue of *Cinéfantastique* (a journal devoted to fantasy and science fiction film), but a rights dispute signalled the end of its run (and Smith's company). It also emerged that the original negative of the film had been lost (one theory is that it was used as infill during the construction of the M3 motorway). On the back of these tribulations, an article in *Film Comment* recounted *The Wicker Man*'s fate as a case study in how not to do things, distribution-wise.[5] For devotees of the film, however, *The Wicker Man*'s chequered history adds to its attractions. For its fans it possesses, like *Jeanne*, a special status as a hard-to-find film, a hidden masterpiece, something 'they' didn't want you to watch: 'there is boundless fascination ... for the calamitous horrors which constitute *The Wicker Man*'s misfortunes.'[6]

This chapter discusses the 2002 incarnation of *The Wicker Man*, created for DVD release by Warner Bros. and Canal+. Although labelled as a Director's Cut, this is a marketing ploy: the film is not that which Hardy assembled in 1973. However, this 99-minute version includes footage taken from a print that survived in the offices of Roger Corman – the producer and distributor whose suggestions originally led to the creation of the B-movie. I have chosen this version of *The Wicker Man* for three reasons.

First, it is readily available. Second, it illustrates the way in which the DVD format has begun to change the experience of film viewing, and the concept of the film 'text' itself. The superior data storage capacity of DVD means that in addition to a film, 'special features' or 'extras' can be stored on the disk. Indeed, the provision of such material is now so common that a popular name ('vanilla') has emerged to designate those disks that carry the feature film *only*. From the marketing perspective, including extras entails a host of opportunities. Regular fans and students alike can be persuaded of a need to buy again films that they already own on video, or could see on television. In keeping with this trend, *The Wicker Man* DVD offers a choice of two versions of the film, a commentary with the director and lead actors mediated by Mark Kermode (a leading British film reviewer and writer specialising in the horror genre) and a host of other promotional matter. Provision of these 'extras' both satisfies and stimulates the desire to consume *The Wicker Man*.

Third, and more importantly for this book, much of the restored footage is concerned with establishing Howie's character and the role of Lord Summerisle in the island's ritual life. In other words, this version of the film attends more carefully than its predecessors to the definition of religious commitment, thereby heightening the clash of beliefs at the heart of the drama.

Christianity as Tomorrow's Paganism?

A plot outline indicates the centrality of the Christian–pagan encounter for *The Wicker Man*. The film's opening sequence, set in fictional Ullwater in the Scottish highlands, introduces Sergeant Howie (Edward Woodward), establishing him as a committed Christian. We see him in church, reading from the Bible (1 Corinthians 11:23–6, on the institution of the Lord's Supper) and receiving communion; we also learn that he is a virgin who has not slept with his fiancée, Mary. On receiving an anonymous letter from Summerisle, Howie travels there to investigate the reported disappearance of a girl, Rowan Morrison. His enquiries uncover little. Pagan imagery is everywhere: a flag depicts a sun face; an eye is painted, apotropaically, on the harbourmaster's boat; and the islanders' names are all those of plants and trees. In the rowdy Green Man pub (Howie's lodgings) the mystery deepens: on an island famed for agriculture, Howie is offered canned food. He goes for an evening walk, only to discover groups of people having sex on the grass. Back in his room, he kneels to pray, but hears voices outside. Lord Summerisle (Christopher Lee) has brought Ash Buchanan for his sexual initiation with the landlord's daughter, Willow (Britt Ekland). As their ecstatic moaning increases, the film cuts first to the distressed Howie, then to the bar, where the drinkers are also listening, but joyfully.

The next morning, Howie continues his investigation at the schoolhouse. En route, he passes a maypole dance: it is May Day Eve. The air of conspiracy and sense of ideological distance grows. Howie finds Rowan's name on the school register (the islanders had denied her existence), and suspects murder when Miss Rose (Diane Cilento) suggests Rowan has 'returned to the life-forces in another form'. She tells Howie the islanders are pagans, believers in the transmutation of souls: Christianity is studied merely as 'comparative religion'. Conversations with other islanders support this.

Howie visits Lord Summerisle and dialogue further exposes their differences. When Howie castigates the islanders' 'fake biology, fake religion', Summerisle retorts that Jesus was 'the son of a virgin impregnated ... by a ghost'. He explains that pagan rites were re-instituted in 1868 by his agronomist grandfather, as a way of galvanising the then poverty-stricken peasants.

Exhumation reveals that Rowan's grave contains only a hare, and an old photograph reveals the failure of last year's harvest. Howie speculates that Rowan may be alive, but destined for sacrifice on May Day. He determines to return to the mainland and alert the authorities but must pass another night in the pub. Willow seductively dances naked in the next room; Howie hears her singing and slapping the wall but resists temptation.

The next morning is May Day. Howie, whose seaplane will not start, researches paganism in the library; his findings reinforce his suspicions as to Rowan's intended fate. He attacks the pub landlord, steals his fool's costume and joins the festivities, disguised. At some standing stones, a mock sacrifice is enacted. On the beach, Summerisle offers a beer libation, then announces that it is time for a 'more dreadful rite'. As Howie expects, Rowan is produced. He runs to her, and she suggests an escape route. However, Rowan leads him not to safety but to 'the appointed place'. She is part of a wider conspiracy: *Howie* is the intended sacrifice. Summerisle reminds him that the islanders need to appease the gods to ensure good harvests. After careful research, they have identified Howie as the ideal offering: a willing, king-like, virgin-fool. Stripped and anointed by Willow and the librarian (Ingrid Pitt), Howie is shut inside the wicker man – a towering structure that will be the sacrificial pyre. As the fire is lit, Howie preaches to the islanders, sings 'The Lord is My Shepherd', and prays. The crowd sings joyously. A closing shot sees the wicker man's head fall to the ground as the sun sets in the distance.

In its depiction of Lord Summerisle, the cultured, 'enlightened' pagan, and a modern-day community willing to practice human sacrifice, *The Wicker Man* suggests that a thin line separates civilisation from barbarity. This theme, and the depiction of Howie's unease at being an outsider in a community whose values differ from his own, play on established horror conventions. But *The Wicker Man*, more unusually, suggests parallels between Christianity and paganism. Both are presented as, at least in part, social constructs. Lord Summerisle describes how his grandfather revived paganism because the community's spiritual and psychological needs – and his own requirement for a motivated workforce – were seemingly unmet by Christianity. Summerisle's 'Old Religion' is a recent imposition on a newly acquired territory. Howie's faith also appears as colonising, and dependent on human agency and power. When he speaks of Scotland as a 'Christian country' this is always in the context of a desire to assert the authority of the mainland over the island community.

The presentation of sacrifice also implies similarities between paganism and Christianity. Howie's murder forms an *inclusio* with the film's opening. He sings the same hymn in each scene, and his death as an offering to sun-god Nuada[7] echoes Jesus' sacrifice, which he has previously commemorated in Holy Communion. Indeed, the film's somewhat inconsistent construction of Howie's religiosity seems driven by a desire to comment on the nature of sacrifice. For, whilst his strict morality and abhorrence of the pub might suggest a Presbyterian or other Calvinist disposition, he is shown participating in an Episcopalian service, led by a surplice- and cassock-wearing priest, and (in words borrowed from Sir Walter Raleigh's last speech) describes himself as dying 'unshriven'.[8] This high-church sensibility enhances the suggestion of parallels between the islanders' mystical understanding of Howie's body and blood as a sacrifice on their behalf, and *his* faith in Jesus' atoning death.

Critics disagree as to whether *The Wicker Man* relativises, upholds or ridicules Christianity. For Krzywinska, the film implies that 'all religions are subject to fashion and expediency', whilst Jones sees it as studiously presenting both worldviews as 'valid social constructs rooted in supernaturalism'.[9] The later novelisation of *The Wicker Man* lends some support to this position, referencing Disraeli's claim that 'Man is born to believe. And if no church comes forward ...to guide him, he will find altars and idols in his own heart and his own imagination'.[10] Some viewers nevertheless discern a more sympathetic attitude towards Christianity. Brown notes that some conservative Christians have regarded the film as a stimulus to reflection.[11] Certainly, the film shows Howie's faith as steadfast. He resists Willow's sexual overtures, and in some respects dies a martyr ('no matter what you do ... I believe in the life eternal as promised to us by our Lord Jesus Christ'); there is a defiant note in his suggestion that if the crops again fail, next year may see Lord Summerisle having to assume the role of sacrifice. Whereas Howie's Christianity fuels his desire to rescue Rowan, the logic of Summerisle paganism leads inexorably to the undermining of human value and the wicker man atrocity (the novel progresses this idea, likening the onlooking crowd to those at the Nuremberg Rallies).[12]

However, the film's attitude to Christian belief is not straightforward. When Howie kneels each night to pray, it is not clear whether this posture indicates religious inclination, or exhaustion, or both. If the latter, are we intended to regard human weakness as a precondition for faith? Should this be regarded as a positive recognition of the true human condition (as traditionally posited in Christian theology) or as an atheistic sideswipe at religion as a 'crutch' for the weak and infirm?

As Bartholomew notes, Christianity's representative in *The Wicker Man* is a man falling into confusion, teetering on insanity's edge.[13] Whilst the islanders' beliefs fuel murderous intent, Howie's Christian morality contributes to his downfall: sex with Willow would have rendered him unacceptable as a sacrifice. And although Summerisle's religion is presented as a Victorian construct (evoking that era's paternalistically motivated recreations of 'Merrie England'[14]) the ancient standing stones on the island imply that Christianity's presence there, evoked by a ruined church building in which Howie attempts to erect a makeshift cross, is a mere interruption within the flow of a much longer pagan history.

During Ash's initiation, Lord Summerisle recites a Walt Whitman poem, ridiculing Christian piety as a peculiarly human problem:

> I think I could turn and live with animals, they're so placid and self contain'd,
>
> I stand and look at them long and long.
>
> They do not sweat and whine about their condition,
>
> They do not lie awake in the dark and weep for their sins,
>
> They do not make me sick discussing their duty to God ...[15]

In keeping with these sentiments, the Summerislanders seem more at ease with themselves and their environment than does Howie. Whereas the establishing shots of Summerisle (aerial shots, as if seen from the seaplane) present it as fertile and verdant, the mainland is a built environment dominated by concrete and tarmac, and devoid of greenery. It is significant, perhaps, that when Howie reaches Summerisle, he requires technology (a loudhailer) to communicate with people on the shore, but they are able to call to him across the water, unaided by any device.

An assessment of Christianity's place in *The Wicker Man* must also attend to the question of Howie's position in mainland society. Christian faith is presented as alienating him from Ullwater life, much as it does from Summerisle. When in one early scene Howie enters the station room, the constable and postman talking there fall suddenly silent; this motif is reused in a later scene in Summerisle's Green Man pub, inviting viewers to draw parallels between the two incidents. We are shown only interior shots of Howie's spiritual home, the church, and the dialogue in this scene is a hymn and a reading from the King James Version of the Bible – visual and verbal indicators constructing Howie's faith as claustrophobic and time-worn. In scenes with work colleagues, he appears inflexible (even his clothing is highly fitted) and outmoded ('Get your hair cut, McTaggart!'). Alone amongst the

film's characters, he never jokes. In these ways *The Wicker Man* hints
that just as happened previously on Summerisle, so on the mainland;
Christianity is losing its attraction and relevance. In the early
1970s, the age of the advent of the contraceptive pill, it is Howie's
celibate sexuality that is emerging as deviant, or non-normative. His
commitment seems out of step with modernity. The implication is
that Christianity is on the way to becoming tomorrow's paganism,
the 'old religion' of the future.

The likening of Christianity to paganism is a crucial theme implicit
in an important source text for *The Wicker Man*, James Frazer's *The
Golden Bough*. Since its publication in 1890, *The Golden Bough*
has remained in print, and although long-regarded as suspect
academically, is one of the most well-known and emotionally
persuasive accounts of magic and religion. Hardy and Shaffer read
all twelve volumes of the book. Part of *The Wicker Man*'s appeal –
the satisfying, convincing nature of its paganism for some viewers
– stems from its evocation of Frazer, or of Frazer as mediated in, for
example, popular explanations of folk customs as surviving elements
of fertility rites.

Frazer drew connections between Greek and Roman mythology,
the rituals of tribal societies worldwide (as reported by Western
observers) and the practices of European peasants. Much of the
interest value of his work lies in the examples catalogued, and many
of these appear in *The Wicker Man*. On May Day Eve Howie watches,
disgusted, as May Morrison places a frog inside the mouth of her
younger daughter, Myrtle, to cure a cough (an English folk-cure).[16]
When Howie opens Rowan's school desk he discovers a beetle
attached by thread to a nail. As the beetle crawls around, it coils
the thread about the nail, gradually ensnaring itself. According to
Frazer, this was a form of imitative magic used to secure the return of
runaway slaves in North Africa; in the film it can function similarly,
as a charm to entrap Howie, or it may be simply a visual metaphor
for his journey towards death.[17] When Howie investigates the island
graveyard he notices that trees, to which umbilical cords are tied (like
Frazer, the gravedigger calls them 'navel-strings'), are planted on the
graves. Frazer describes various indigenous peoples' traditions of

burying umbilical cords beneath trees, or of tying them to branches, in the hope that the child whose cord it is will grow strong like the sapling.[18] On a more gruesome note, Willow and her father deploy a hand of glory (a torch made by settling alight a dead man's hand) against Howie on May Day morning – a magical practice intended to induce deep sleep in victims.[19]

As these examples suggest, *The Wicker Man*'s approach is eclectic, juxtaposing customs from diverse times and places. This strategy is not completely at odds with Frazer's: given his conviction that all societies evolved through similar stages of magic and belief, he was willing to infer that practices observable in one location could - or indeed must –have also occurred elsewhere. Moreover, the film's account of Summerisle religion as a revival serves not only to explain to Howie (and the audience) how a pagan community can persist in 1970s Scotland, but also to license such inconsistencies.

In addition to a host of incidental detail necessary for the construction of a plausible pagan society, *The Wicker Man* derives from *The Golden Bough* the underlying motif or principle of Summerisle religion. Frazer argued that 'primitive' societies were organised around the concept of the sacred king, a ruler-priest who had to be killed and replaced when growing weak or old, because his virility was mistakenly associated with the success of cereal and other crops. He saw traces of this tradition in Druid culture (the class of priests, teachers and judges among the ancient Celts) as described in Julius Caesar's *Gallic War*:

> The whole nation of the Gauls is greatly devoted to ritual observances ... employing the Druids as ministers for such sacrifices. They ... use figures of immense size, whose limbs, woven out of twigs, they fill with living men and set on fire, and the men perish in a sheet of flame.[20]

Frazer also believed that echoes of the belief in a temporary king who was required to die survived in a range of later British and Irish folklore, including the Beltane fires, lit in the Scottish Highlands as late as the eighteenth century, and other May Day ceremonies.[21] Like *The Golden Bough*, *The Wicker Man* blends aspects of reported Druidical practice with later spring festivities – dancers plaiting ribbons around the Maypole, a sword dance culminating in a mock execution, and including the characters of the Fool and the Teaser or Betsy (a man dressed as a woman) and a hobby horse procession.[22] But whilst Frazer was cautious about the *exact* purpose of the wicker man sacrifice, the film prefers the explanation of German scholar W. Mannhardt (dismissed by Frazer in later editions of *The Golden Bough*), that the Druid custom of burning living offerings inside wickerwork cages was a magical ceremony to secure sunshine needed for crop growth.[23] A sun-god image on the postmark of the letter received by Howie is the initial clue to the island's culture, and Lord Summerisle's closing invocation connects the burning pyre and the coming year's harvest.

The film's confident exposition of the wicker man ritual is a reminder that, just as it is inappropriate to assess *La Passion de Jeanne d'Arc* or *The Ten Commandments* purely in terms of their fidelity to a written source-text, so *The Wicker Man* is not a direct translation of Frazerian theory to the screen: creativity and the medium exert their own demands. The film's departure from Frazer allows it to present a climactic visual spectacle cohering with the film's account of paganism as a function of agrarian society.

Finally, a consideration of *The Wicker Man*'s use of Frazer also has implications for an assessment of its presentation of the relationship between Christianity and paganism. Although Frazer's account of dying and replaced/reviving rulers does not mention Jesus explicitly, it is clear that Christianity was a target of his researches:

> ... we cannot but wonder at the singular powers which the human mind possesses of transmuting the leaden dross of superstition into a glittering semblance of gold. Certainly in nothing is this alchemy of thought more conspicuous than in the process which has refined the base and foolish custom of the scapegoat into the sublime conception of a God who dies to take away the sins of the world.[24]

The Golden Bough's argument is that Christianity ('a glittering *semblance* of gold') is barely removed from paganism and the – in Frazer's eyes – primitive practices of indigenous or illiterate peoples. Belief in the salvific power of the crucifixion is, therefore, a piece of faulty logic, rooted in ancient humans' resort to magical manipulation of a world they struggled to control and understand. Christopher Lee, quoted at the head of this chapter, has described *The Wicker Man* not as an attack on Christianity, but as a commentary on the potential for all religions to be exploited by despots. This theme is present in the film, but at the same time its dependence on Frazer's text means that *The Wicker Man* inevitably participates in his scepticism.[25]

The Wicker Man may, then, be characterised as an example of the playing out of a particular theory of religions on the screen. It is notable for its attempt to image (or to imagine) a believable, not idealised pagan society, and, like the work of Frazer on which it draws, it offers space for viewers to consider generally the meanings and nature of religious community and experience, as the variety of responses to the film attests. However, Frazer's text is not determinative in its influence on *The Wicker Man*, and discussion of the film's relation to his theory does not exhaust its meanings.

Scotland the Movie

In its portrayal of a living paganism, *The Wicker Man* depicts many customs and rituals not linked historically with the Western Isles. Notably, the hobby horse procession is based on the Morisco dance-drama staged each May in Padstow, Cornwall, and the sword dance on those of Northumbria. Given these realities, and the lack of Scottish personnel amongst the acting and senior production teams, two questions emerge: why is the drama located in Scotland, and why are viewers convinced by this essentially 'inappropriate' setting?

At the time *The Wicker Man* appeared, most 'Scottish films' were largely external creations. Made by personnel based in London or Hollywood, they reflected a perception of the country – which was both geographically removed from the industry's headquarters and commercially insignificant as a film market – as a distant hinterland.[26] This trend was not inevitable: Danny Boyle, the director of *Shallow Grave* (1994) and *Trainspotting* (1996) – films credited with ushering in a new era of more complex, gritty Scottish films – was born in Manchester. But influenced by stereotypes derived from nineteenth-century literature (including such writers as J.M. Barrie, Ian

MacLaren and S.R. Crockett) and the music hall, most films engaged little with the realties of modern Scottish life. Describing common themes in mid-twentieth-century screen images of Scotland, Craig has termed them 'Tartanry' (the figure of the kilted Scot – either a romantic, noble Highlander or a parodic red-nosed, drunken, mean figure) and 'Kailyardism' (the conception of Scotland as a country of small towns, populated by 'characters' with a propensity to wry smiles and wise sayings).[27] Scotland frequently appears more as an imaginary construct than a physical entity. As such, Petrie suggests, it becomes a territory onto which a host of concerns and ideologies may be mapped:

> Scotland tends to be represented as a picturesque, wild and often empty landscape, a topography that in turn suggests certain themes, narrative situations and character trajectories. Central to this is the idea of remoteness – physical, social, moral – from metropolitan rules, conventions and certainties. Scotland is consequently a space in which a range of fantasies, desires and anxieties can be explored and expressed; alternatively an exotic backdrop for adventure and romance, or a sinister and oppressive locale beyond the pale of civilisation.[28]

How far *The Wicker Man* is expressive of psychological or social anxieties and desires will be explored later. However, aspects of the film support Craig's and Petrie's general assertions. In keeping with popular stereotypes, Howie is dour and humourless, whilst his opponents are presented as canny, quick-witted and willing to consume alcohol – and don tartan – at (almost) every available opportunity. In the film's opening scene, Howie's conversation with McTaggart reveals that both know little about Summerisle, save the fact that it is an isolated place with no licensing laws and where singing and dancing take place on Sundays. These remarks identify both the Summerislanders and Scots more generally as Others: as mainlanders Howie and McTaggart find Summerisle enigmatic, but they also live in a society structured by a religious code not shared by the film's implied audience. Sabbath observance, including the abstention from song, dance, and other forms of worldly entertainment, is one of the distinctives of the Scottish Presbyterian churches.

The film's opening title card reads as follows, giving the impression of an ethnographical interest in its subject:

> The Producer would like to thank The Lord Summerisle and the people of his island off the west coast of Scotland for this privileged insight into their religious practices and for their generous co-operation in the making of this film.

This is an ironic touch, simultaneously encoding and ridiculing the discourse of Frazerian anthropology; its presence conjures up images of fantasy and otherness reinforced later in the work.[29] When Howie arrives at Summerisle, he is initially rebuffed by a harbour master, reluctant to let him ashore without Lord Summerisle's permission. These early scenes establish Summerisle as a place both alien and familiar, in line with *The Wicker Man*'s efforts to present a society at once normal and monstrous. Commenting on the film's use of folklore, Hardy described its strategy thus:

> What we hoped would fascinate people is ... that they would recognise an awful lot of these things as sort of little echoes from either out of childhood stories and nursery rhymes or things they do at various times of the year.[30]

By analogy, the Scottish setting emerges as less inappropriate than it might initially appear. In popular parlance Druids are commonly associated with both human sacrifice, the climax of the film's drama, and Scotland – although they actually inhabited a wide area of western Europe, and Caesar's account of their wicker man occurs in a book describing what is now France. Moreover, the 1970s witnessed a burgeoning interest in folk culture, and the beginning of the contemporary fascination with Celtic culture and spirituality. Such impulses lie behind the film's use of music and lyrics derived from British folksongs as a way of evoking a pre-modern society (many of the thirteen songs are also narrative devices, expounding the islanders' theology) and enhance the plausibility of the film's narrative premise, since the Celtic nations were, and still are, popularly believed to preserve more elements of the ancient past than those that survive in England. Like the 'little echoes' triggered by *The Wicker Man*'s use of the maypole and other folklore, its Scottish setting resonates with audience pre-knowledge of ritual sacrifice and the persistence of the ancient past within the Celtic present.

In addition to these factors, other more prosaic concerns probably feed into both the setting of *The Wicker Man*, and audiences' willingness to suspend disbelief and accept its construction of Scotland. The Findhorn community in north-east Scotland attracted hysterical press coverage in the early 1970s. Like the Summerislanders, Findhorn's residents are primarily horticulturalists, growing herbs, flowers and vegetables (including, famously, 40-pound cabbages). The tabloids took great interest in community members' unorthodox lifestyles, and their attempts to blend horticulture with spirituality: daily meditation was a key part of Findhorn life in its early years and the founders (who began the project in 1962) believed that their gardening successes were in part attributable to the assistance of nature spirits.

Although Findhorn philosophy is more New Age than pagan (it draws inspiration from several world religions, especially Hinduism and Buddhism), its media profile helped to sustain notions of rural Scotland as the site of distinctive sub- and counter-cultures. The subsequent development of the Celtic heritage industry has reinforced this perception. Similarly, some critics, noting that campaigners for independence were highly active in the 1970s, have detected echoes of Scottish nationalism in *The Wicker Man*. Bruce argues such overtones 'are difficult to avoid', given what he claims is a strong connection between nationalism and the occult.[31] However, he does little to establish widespread belief in this link and over-interpretation is a possibility, given the fact that the conflict in *The Wicker Man* is essentially intra-Scottish.

Finally, as mentioned earlier, *The Wicker Man* is locatable within the history of screen images of Scotland. Many films depicted their stereotypical Scots gaining the upper hand – like the Summerislanders – over arrogant, patronising incomers. Just as Howie's efforts to exert his authority are outwitted, so in *Whisky Galore!* (Alexander Mackendrick, 1949) the officious and uncompromising Captain Waggett finds himself beaten by the amoral experience of the Todday islanders, who steal, hide and consume a shipwrecked liquor cargo.[32] Some viewers' expectations and assessments of *The Wicker Man* are shaped by knowledge of other 'Scottish' films: Bruce's assessment of the film as 'one of the strangest ... ever to come out of Scotland' implies this kind of viewing experience.[33] Reception history is explored later, but it is necessary first to examine the function of stars within *The Wicker Man* and its relationship to the horror film, which is simultaneously one of the most popular and the most disreputable of the film genres, as well as one that draws overtly on religious and spiritual discourses.

English Horror(s)

As touched on in Chapters III and IV, stars contribute to films in numerous ways. Their profile may be used to secure funding and distribution, or to promote a film to potential audiences. Stars function as organising principles for film-makers and consumers, because they bring with them to the screen sets of ancillary meanings or connotations (typically based on previous roles or on widely known details of their personal lives). These meanings may cohere with the narrative construction of their character in a given film. For example, Colin Firth's identification with the role of Mr. Darcy in the BBC television adaptation of *Pride and Prejudice* contributed to expectations and the reception of his appearance as Mark Darcy in *Bridget Jones's Diary* (Sharon Maguire, 2001). Alternatively, a star's connotations may perform a more disruptive but equally significant function within a film. Firth's established image as a figure of troubled but benign heterosexual masculinity enhances the ambiguities of Vince Collins' character in *Where The Truth Lies* (Atom Egoyan, 2005).[34]

Several actors brought (and bring) distinctive subtexts to *The Wicker Man*. In the 1970s, British television audiences knew Edward Woodward through his appearance as a British counter-intelligence agent in the popular series, *Callan*. His role in *The Wicker Man*, like later television performances in *The Equalizer*, plays on his association with the crime-thriller. Whilst Howie is more conventional than the embittered, liminal Callan, he is the only character who directly engages in violence (the attack on landlord Alder Macgreagor), hinting that beneath the starched uniform he possesses the capacity for cruelty.

Christopher Lee is by far the best-known cast member. His performances in *The Curse of Frankenstein* (Terence Fisher, 1957) and *The Horror of Dracula* (Terence Fisher, 1958) helped to launch the successful series of Hammer horror films, and linked him irrevocably with the genre. By early 1972, Lee wished to stop 'Draculating'[35] but in *The Wicker Man*, as more recently in Peter Jackson's *Lord of The Rings* trilogy, he again assumes the role of a sinister aristocrat, orchestrating behind-the-scenes conspiracy.

Several of the film's female actresses also possess noteworthy subtexts. Although she was by then a mother in her mid-thirties, the film's American publicity emphasised Britt Ekland's reputation as 'the quintessence of a Swedish girl – blond hair, blue eyes, a luscious figure,'[36] and her character's narrative function as Summerisle's own Aphrodite figure plays on this. Ingrid Pitt's reputation, like Lee's, was inseparable from horror. Her previous roles included a lesbian vampire in *The Vampire Lovers* (Roy Ward, 1970), and a countess with a penchant for bathing in the blood of virgins in *Countess Dracula* (Peter Sasdy, 1970). In *The Wicker Man* a conservatively dressed Pitt at first appears to have been cast against type, but her reputation, acknowledged in a brief nude shot (afterwards the camera halts on black lingerie, hanging from the bathroom door), disrupts the connotations usually attached to the occupation of librarian and fosters suspicion of Summerisle society.

Similar factors feed into the casting of mime artist and choreographer Lindsay Kemp, whose protégés include David Bowie and Kate Bush, as landlord of the Green Man. Kemp's performance was criticised as unconvincing by some early reviewers. But to regard his exaggerated facial expressions and intonation (reminiscent in a 1970s context of *Carry On* acting styles) as failed efforts at realism is surely to misread a piece of high camp. (Camp, historically associated with closeted homosexuality, is definable as an excess of style; it highlights incongruities between what an object or person *is* and what it *looks* like.[37]) The stagey gestures, and Kemp's presiding over a pub that falls into a stereotypically sudden and sinister silence on Howie's entrance, are consciously artificial to the point of parody. As such, they are important markers of *The Wicker Man*'s self-conscious negotiation with established horror conventions.

Shaffer and Hardy were Hammer fans, who wanted to 'give their audience something a bit tastier to chew on.'[38] Thirty years after its release, *The Wicker Man* may strike today's viewers as a conventional horror film. It deploys a number of genre clichés. Howie is in many respects simply a modification of the professional vampire hunter of earlier films – an investigating outsider, equipped with special knowledge (as policeman and Christian) but frustrated by organised evasion in an isolated community. Like the vampire hunter, his speeches have a didactic quality, and he erects a protective cross in a ruined churchyard. In other stock horror moves, he journeys by carriage to Lord Summerisle's castle ('his Lordship is expecting you,' is the doorman's greeting) and participates in the night-time exhumation of a coffin.[39]

However, whereas classic British horror shows graphic images of sex and violence, *The Wicker Man* exercises a degree of visual restraint.[40] In making Howie and not Rowan the sacrifice it also turns away from normative horror presentations of the woman as victim – a point reinforced by the striking directness of the female gaze in Willow's naked dance scene, and the fact that women are shown as active, 'on top', sexual beings in Summerisle.

Significantly, the horror of Summerisle paganism is not overcome at the film's end. Despite its increasing sensationalism, Hammer horror, like the Victorian Gothic novels on which it drew, was ultimately confident in the capacity for rational thought (with which Christianity was assumed to cohere) embodied in the scholar or cleric, to overcome evil. *The Mummy* (Terence Fisher, 1959, remade by Stephen Sommers in 1999), in which a family of British archaeologists battle 'primitive' forces in the shape of an Egyptian mummy seeking revenge for the disturbance of a royal tomb, is a good example of this. By contrast, in *The Wicker Man*, the 'old religion', sustained by feudal social structures, triumphs. Howie cannot defeat a community that is willingly subservient to Lord Summerisle. This depiction of paganism victorious departs from horror conventions, but accords with a growing trend in the late twentieth and early twenty-first centuries (initiated by *Psycho* (Alfred Hitchcock, 1960) and catalysed by *The Exorcist* (William Friedkin, 1973)) to refuse viewers the security of narrative closure by leaving the forces of Christian law and order less than triumphant at the end of the film.

The Wicker Man's rejection of a clear demarcation between paganism and Christianity is also in keeping with 1970s trends. No clearly definable monster appears on the screen, rather, we are presented with a society that is itself monstrous, having being organised around a worldview that brings out the dark impulses of otherwise normal people. A large part of the horror of *The Wicker Man* therefore lies not in the behaviour of the 'others', but in Howie's experience of otherness itself.

For many contemporary critics, the increasingly diffuse construction of horror and eschewal of resolution in films like *The Wicker Man* are symptomatic of a wider shift in Western culture. They reflect failing confidence in the ability of rationalism to deliver happiness and security, and an increase in moral and cultural relativism. (In this respect *The Wicker Man* simultaneously draws on Frazer whilst also challenging his belief in the evolutionary progress of human societies from magic, to religion, and eventually science.) This interpretation of horror films suggests they can be explained in relation to contingent factors – that their narratives work through shared anxieties and so are barometers of social change. Thus a feature like *The Exorcism of Emily Rose* (Scott Derricksen, 2005) in which viewers are asked to accept the validity, if not the reliability, of a supernatural explanation of Emily's condition over that suggested by medical professionals, embodies postmodern relativism and an unease surrounding the claims of scientific discourse. The medical professionals who argue that the now-dead Emily suffered from a psychological illness are presented as cold and unfeeling. Audience sympathies lie with Emily's priest, not so much because he can provide empirical evidence in support of his Catholic belief but because of the strength and sincerity of his conviction that she was demon-possessed.

Such readings react against the tendency of early studies to evacuate horror of historical and social significance. For interpreters like Ivan Butler, writing in the late sixties, horror films fulfil a function previously served by religion. Whilst in the face of technology and the (albeit not unchecked) rise of the scientific world view, religions decline in their ability to deal credibly with 'the immanent fears of mankind [*sic*]: damnation, demonic possession, old age, death', screen horror provides a new vehicle for the basic human need to explore anxieties, desires and inhibitions.[41] There is some merit in Butler's account: part of the *frisson* of watching horror films lies in the experiencing of feelings relating to taboo agendas,[42] and psychological and psychoanalytical approaches are vital for understanding some well-known films, such as the consciously Freudian *Psycho*. However, in addition to the difficulties that beset any theory assuming secularism as a given, and the criticisms of Freudian discourse described in Chapter III, the previous discussion of *The Wicker Man* has revealed the limitations of any interpretation that ignores the *contexts* in which it was – and is – made and watched.

What social and historical factors feed into *The Wicker Man's* variation on the horror theme? Some of these have been identified already. They include its actors' subtexts, and Frazer's account of religion and magic. Additionally, the Englishness of *The Wicker Man* is apparent not only in the handling of the Scottish setting, but also in the qualities of the horror envisioned. The characters of Lord Summerisle and his grandfather are probably informed by the figure of Alastair Crowley, a libertine-philosopher who attracted a large personal following in the early twentieth century, and stimulated modern interest in the occult.

The presentation of Lord Summerisle's relationship to the island's belief system also assumes a stereotypically English quality. Summerisle is an *English* Lord of a Scottish island, establishing him as a quasi-colonial figure. Paternalistically, he suggests that whilst the ruling elite may understand and appreciate religion's real character, it holds simpler comforts for ordinary folk:

> Parthenogenesis ... reproduction without sexual union ... Who can blame them? What girl would not prefer the child of a god to that of some acne-scarred artisan?

> ... What my grandfather started out of expediency, my father continued out of love. He brought me up the same way, to reverence the music, the drama and the rituals of the old gods.

This understanding of religion as the glue that binds society and encourages individuals to accept and fulfil hierarchically structured roles evokes stereotypical English public school attitudes, as does the film's dependency on Frazer (himself disparaging of 'peasants') and the Latin classics. It is interesting to note that Shaffer was educated at St. Paul's and Cambridge University; fellow Cambridge graduate Hardy was the son of a colonial official; and Lee was a classics scholar at Wellington College.

Nevertheless, Summerisle's account of the island's history reveals that his is not a historic title – he is in fact nouveau riche, his grandfather having bought the island for commercial reasons: 'What had attracted him, apart from the profuse source of wiry labour that it promised was the unique combination of volcanic soil and warm gulf stream which surrounded it.'

In a sense, the film's focus on a crisis point in the island's history – the wicker man sacrifice is a desperate attempt to prevent a repetition of a disastrous crop failure – could be regarded as a commentary on the ultimate insufficiency of world views constructed on the basis of market economics. Discussing the conflict between paganism and Christianity in 1970s horror, including *The Wicker Man*, Chibnall and Petley also see refracted in such narratives the debates associated with the fracturing of the postwar consensus in English politics, and an attempt to mediate the social upheavals of the 1960s and the 1970s conservative backlash epitomised by the Heath government's law-and-order agenda.[43]

This view holds some attractiveness. The film is ambivalent in its attitude towards authority, and towards the social and sexual mores of both Howie and the islanders. However, although borne out by some initial reviews (see later), from a cultural studies perspective such readings, like psychological exegeses, fail to do justice to the goal of engaging with a film through its entire life cycle, rather than simply in relation to its context of primary production. This task assumes an even greater urgency in the case of a film like *The Wicker Man*, which has a complex distribution history, and has itself become the focus of intense and creative fan activity.

Reception and the 'Cult' of Fandom

In a 1977 issue of *Cinéfantastique*, David Blake, who had some years earlier sold *The Wicker Man* to National General for American distribution, described the film as 'marginally well ahead of its time' – a slightly contradictory assessment, which reflects its initial failure to excite either company executives or the critics.[44] There were very few reviews of the film in 1973–4 (chiefly because, as Margaret Hinxman noted in the *Sunday Telegraph*, there was no press screening[45]) and those that did appear were at best lukewarm. Reviewers for the *Financial Times* and *Monthly Film Bulletin* (David McGillivray) judged that Shaffer's 'superb' and 'cleverly dovetailed', screenplay had been let down by Hardy's direction, resulting in 'a case of fascinating ingredients that do not quite blend', so that it was not hard to see why the promoters 'had second thoughts about their product'.[46] Patrick Gibbs felt that Shaffer had also failed to 'properly digest' *The Golden Bough* (Dilys Powell in *The Sunday Times* also references Frazer[47]), questioned (incorrectly) the accuracy of the depiction of palm trees in the Western Isles and judged the film 'merely…an interesting failure'.[48]

Equally scathing was Alexander Stuart's assessment in *Films and Filming*, which highlighted the colonial overtones of the imposition of paganism on Summerisle but regarded the depiction of the islanders as ridiculous, Woodward's acting as 'rather dull' and the burning of Howie as 'pointless, ritualistic'. Echoing the *Financial Times* reviewer, Stuart suggested that Hardy seemed 'uncertain as to whether he was making a travelogue, a television thriller, a horror film or a sex romp'.[49]

Several common threads emerge in this material. Significantly, a number of the readings are intertextual, lending weight to the earlier suggestion that knowledge of Frazer, or popular mediations of his thought, are important for some viewers' assessments of the film. But whereas in the early 1970s *The Golden Bough* was a pre-text, knowledge of which audience members brought to the film, for some more recent fans *The Wicker Man* is the stimulus for interest in Frazer's thesis and other theorisations of British folklore, as is discussed later.

In later studies, the film's distribution history (already noted by some commentators in 1973) became an increasingly significant reference point, as did the growing body of *Wicker Man* fans. By the mid-1990s, the fan culture developing around the film had become interpolated into the film text itself. *The Wicker Man* ranked sixtieth in *Classic Television*'s readers' top 100 British Films of all time – ahead of such features as *Don't Look Now* (the film it supported as a B-movie in the 1970s), *The English Patient* (Anthony Minghella, 1996), *Gregory's Girl* (Bill Forsyth, 1980) and *Withnail and I* (Bruce Robinson, 1986).[50] Stephen Appelbaum in *Film Review* introduced the film as 'one of the most highly regarded cult movies', and in 2003 *The Times Higher Education Supplement*'s Olga Wojtas characterised its fans' attitude as 'a burning passion that's close to worship'.[51] But what *is* the nature of *Wicker Man* fandom? Where does the film's appeal lie, and what sorts of fan activity does it stimulate? Is it accurate to characterise appreciation of the film as religious?

Part of *The Wicker Man*'s appeal for its fans, attested by reviews in *Cinéfantastique* and *Flesh and Blood*, is its distinctiveness when compared with other horror films of the period – its bending of genre conventions and the above-average quality of acting, script and design.[52] The film's lack of narrative closure also enables it to sustain multiple readings. In the period since 11 September 2001, for example, Chris Pizzello, writing for *American Cinematographer* (a leading technical periodical), has suggested that, 'in the light of the polarized religious climate that exists around the world, a fresh viewing of … *The Wicker Man* takes an added resonance'.[53] This elasticity of meaning contributes to the film's longevity. However, published reviews and academic critiques cannot provide a direct or full account of the fan culture surrounding *The Wicker Man*. During the past decade or so, an increasing number of film theorists have adapted cultural studies approaches and applied them to film in order to investigate how fans actively interpret, enjoy, and derive meaning from what they see and hear.[54]

In popular stereotypes, fans are people (particularly young adult males) who are excessively and uncritically devoted to a particular book, television programme or film. They queue for hours to attend a screening of the latest *Star Trek* or *Star Wars* film, for example, because they are easily duped social misfits, unable to sustain healthy relationships with their families and peers. Cultural theorists challenge these assumptions. For Henry Jenkins, fans are 'a group insistent on making meaning from materials others have characterised as trivial and worthless'.[55] This definition does not pathologise fans, nor does it regard them as passive consumers. It suggests instead that they constitute an alternative community, which creatively appropriates and manipulates texts in resistance to the 'dominant' readings proposed by professional critics and other elites. Why do fan cultures develop around some films and not others? Umberto Eco explains this with reference to the properties of the cult films themselves:

> the work must be loved... but this is not enough. It must provide a completely furnished world so that its fans can quote characters and episodes as if they were aspects of the fan's private sectarian world ... I think that in order to transform a work into a cult object one must be able to break, dislocate, unhinge it so that one can remember only parts of it, irrespective of their original relationship to the whole.[56]

Read against this account, this chapter's discussion of *The Wicker Man* is suggestive of various reasons for the film's particular appeal. As the film's distribution history illustrates, a vulnerability to dismemberment and reassembly, which for Eco is a precondition for fan interest (without it there is little scope for the work of active manipulation that lies at the heart of fan culture), is intrinsic to *The Wicker Man*. Moreover, the film's narrative points beyond itself (will the coming year's crops succeed or fail? What will happen when Howie's colleagues investigate his disappearance?), as do the unusual casting choices (how did the non-Scots, like the librarian, arrive on Summerisle?). The film's excessive qualities – in particular the wealth of detail inspired by *The Golden Bough* that is used to evoke the island's culture, but is in many instances extraneous to the development of the film's plot – also make space for speculation and debate. Jenkins speaks of fans exercising a 'popular "expertise" that mirrors in interesting ways the knowledge-production that occupies the Academy'.[57] Fans of *The Wicker Man* find in the film's inconsistencies, in its playing with horror conventions, and in its troubled history, a rich stimulus to their own 'research' and 'teaching' activities.

The active fan culture surrounding *The Wicker Man* takes many forms. Probably the most striking example is that of Stirling Smith and the other American fans who restored some of the missing footage and were largely responsible for the revival of the film in the late 1970s. Far from being passive consumers of *The Wicker Man*, they became actively engaged in its production. In a different vein, British heavy metal band Iron Maiden's 2000 album, *Brave New World*, featured a track inspired by the film and bearing its name, whilst the depiction of the town of Royston Vasey (motto, 'you'll never leave!') in BBC television's Gothic comedy *The League of Gentlemen* owes much to *The Wicker Man* and might loosely be regarded as fan activity on the part of the writers. Other less dramatic but significant forms of creativity and activism include a number of appreciation societies and fan publications (some now defunct) including *Summerisle News* and *Nuada*, published in England by Gail Ashurst. Fans also make journeys retracing the film's locations, especially the Burrowhead site of the wicker man's burning and the Ellangowan Hotel, Creetown, which was the location for the Green Man public house. In 2002 a festival celebrating cult music and cinema, the focus of which is a bonfire reminiscent of that in *The Wicker Man*, was launched in Scotland. (A similar event has been held in San Francisco, and latterly in Nevada, since 1986.[58])

Since the 1990s, cultural studies has begun to consider seriously the impact of the Internet on popular cultures and subcultural fangroups.[59] The Internet is now a major site of film promotion, exhibition (especially of short films) and reception. In particular the potential for exchange of information and ideas across national boundaries enhances the viability of fan communities that develop around individual productions, directors and stars. Googling (the verb itself attests to the Internet's cultural impact) *The Wicker Man* yields approaching a quarter of a million results, although this is an approximate figure, given the ephemeral nature of Internet resources.

Notable sites include 'Nuada, The Wicker Man Journal', 'The Wicker Man, Settling the Score' (reflections from Gary Carpenter, the film's Associate Musical Director) and 'The Wicker Man Trail' (one of numerous guides for film fans who wish to visit locations in south-west Scotland).[60] Although not all these sites are constructed exclusively or primarily by fans, most comment at some point on the film's reception and offer opportunities for fans to share their thoughts; some are created specifically for this purpose. The Wicker Man Yahoo Group, founded in 1999 and with over 400 members, is one such forum 'for discussion about the cult 1973 classic *The Wicker Man*.'[61]

Are these sites idealising in their approach to the film? The answer is both yes and no. The Yahoo Group contributors' readings of the film, for example, tread a line between warm affection and critical distance. On the one hand, aspects of the film and the careers of its acting and other personnel are charted in intimate – not always approving – detail. The appearance of Geraldine Cowper (who played Rowan Morrison) as Rosie Miller in the BBC soap opera *Eastenders* was one comment-worthy event in 2004. Some fans share their memories of seeing the film for the first time and its impact on them; others upload photographs taken on visits to the film's locations. Bearing out Jenkins' notion of fan community, many contributions imply a sense of collaborative endeavour. Internet postings may begin with the phrase 'Any thoughts on this one?', or end with 'What does anyone else think?'. Festive greetings are circulated seasonally, especially around May Day, when the film's action is set: some fans re-view the film, or describe themselves as participating in 'rituals' at that time – although it is not clear whether this activity has been stimulated by an interest in the film, or vice versa.

On the other hand, *The Wicker Man* emerges as a point of debate. The different versions of the film – especially the mis-selling of some versions as director's cuts, and the manipulation of its aspect ratio (some fans object to the film's being 'forced' into widescreen on the new DVD) – are both a source of pleasure (a certain amount of enjoyment is entailed in discussion of *The Wicker Man*'s dismemberment and reconstitution) and of frustration, both in fanzines and online. In 2004 and 2005 a more urgent source of concern was the remake of the film, directed by Neil LaBute and due for release in 2006. Group members were largely dismissive of the decision to relocate the film's action in

America (and to transform the island into a matriarchy, headed by Lady Summerisle). Fears were expressed by some about the casting of Nicholas Cage in the role of Sheriff, and there was speculation that the film would fall into the trap of over-explaining the details of pagan culture and belief. This latter concern is perhaps unsurprising, given the importance of excess and redundancy as characteristics of the cult film. In relation to Cage's credentials, and regarding 'Hollywood' generally (does the studio system foster or stifle creative talents?) differences of interpretation and opinion also emerge, although open arguments rarely erupt. Positions are likely to be concluded with the suggestion that opinions are subjective, or with self-deprecating remarks ('I could be talking absolute rubbish, of course').

In short, *The Wicker Man* fandom emerges as a complex set of activities. To describe it as 'cult-like' is a neat piece of hyperbole, constructed by commentators looking for easy parallels between the film's depiction of the Summerislanders and those who regularly review and rehearse those images. *Wicker Man* fans are not, as in the popular understanding of 'cult', slavish or uncritical in their response to the film. Whether it is meaningfully described as 'religious' also seems doubtful. Certainly, fan culture combines both the internal-personal and the external-communal. It provides a context for individuals to recall their own experiences and shape their own interpretations of a film, whilst also allowing for the public dissemination of ideas, within the fan community and more broadly with film industry professionals and corporations. In other words, fandom may share qualities with, and perhaps even shed light on the processes associated with, a range of religion's dimensions. But this is not the same as saying that film fandom *is* a religion, nor that its participants (mis-)perceive it in such terms.

Finally, it is important to note that whilst cult film fans are not conformist dupes, specific elements of *The Wicker Man's* reception also caution against an overly idealising account of the radical or alternative nature of fandom. When Yahoo Group members express scepticism surrounding the ability of 'Hollywood' to remake the film effectively, they are voicing concerns similar to those dominant within the Academy, which, despite the growth of (popular) cultural studies, remains distrustful of commercial cinema. Moreover, they rely on commercial systems and spaces to communicate with one another. And last but not least, the intricate relation between fandom and academia is further evident in the work of figures like Ashurst, a prominent figure within fan discourse on *The Wicker Man*, who is currently completing a PhD on the role that personal mythopoesis plays in creating and sustaining that same fan culture.[62]

VI

My Son the Fanatic
(Udayan Prasad, 1997)

I am interested in all sides of the argument[1]

love and religion are ... timeless absolutes[2]

Cinema and Diaspora

National cinema is a key organising concept in film studies. From this perspective, films (especially those perceived as 'quality' films) produced within a given territory may be understood as indicative of a national spirit or character. However, in the past 20 years or so, national cinema studies have come under considerable pressure. Many of the reasons for this are implicit in this book's earlier chapters. The Dane Carl Theodor Dreyer's making of *La Passion de Jeanne d'Arc* illustrates how many film professionals work across state boundaries; *The Wicker Man*'s treatment of Scottishness raises questions about the national qualities of British cinema. Globalisation – the growing extent and pace of the exchange of information, people and technologies – also demands the rethinking of national cinema, a challenge with which both academia and industry wrestle. In 2001, for example, the Academy of Motion Picture Arts and Sciences rejected Britain's nomination of the Hindi language film *The Warrior* (directed by Asif Kapadia) as its entry to the Oscars. Many Britons speak either Hindi, or the closely related language Urdu, but the Academy ruled the film ineligible on the grounds that Hindi was not an indigenous British language.[3]

If the concept of national cinema has become problematised and de-centred in the early twenty-first century, that of diaspora is increasingly to the fore. Originally referring to the scattering or dispersal of Jews outside of the land of Israel, it is now readily applied to a range of migrations (African, Armenian, Caribbean, Irish, and so on.). In cultural studies diaspora also functions metaphorically, to refer to notions of identity that challenge essentialist thinking and emphasise 'journey over arrival, mobility over fixity, routes rather than roots'.[4] In a seminal article on the subject Stuart Hall summarises the approach by suggesting that 'we should think... of identity as a "production", which is never complete, always in process, and always constituted with, not outside, representation ... Cultural identity ... is a matter of "becoming" as well as of "being".'[5]

The concept of diaspora provides a useful way of interrogating *My Son the Fanatic*'s (Udayan Prasad, 1997) treatment of religion. The film's subject matter – the conflict between Parvez (an Asian migrant, played by Punjabi actor Om Puri) and his son Farid (Akhba Kurtha) who embraces a militant form of Islam – places it in modern Britain, a key locus of the South Asian diaspora. (The British Asian community has its origins in the pre-modern era but developed rapidly after the Second World War, when Britain was keen to fill a gap in its labour market, and the strife accompanying the partition of India and Pakistan encouraged migration to the former colonial power). At approximately one-and-a-half million people, Britons with personal or familial roots in India, Bangladesh and Pakistan today constitute the country's largest diasporic or ethnic 'minority' community.[6]

More specifically, *My Son*'s writer,[7] Hanif Kureishi, is an author well known for his fictional treatments of inter-ethnic and queer sexualities. In *My Son*, Kureishi's treatment of sexuality centres on prostitution and Parvez's relationship with Bettina, a sex worker (played by Rachel Griffiths). A key aspect of Kureishi's public persona is his own dual heritage (as the son of an English mother and a Muslim father who left India on the eve of partition). Pakistan-born director Udayan Prasad's previous projects include the 1996 *Brothers in Trouble* (in which Om Puri also appears), about a group of illegal immigrants living in the North of England in the 1960s.

Hall's account of diaspora as intertwined with representation and identity-in-process also highlights themes important for this study. Significantly, Hall's work in this area singles out *My Beautiful Laundrette* (Stephen Frears, 1985), also written by Kureishi, as exemplifying the kind of new ethnic identities coming to the fore in diaspora. He suggests that *Laundrette*, which depicts a gay relationship between a British Asian and a white punk, is 'one of the most riveting and important films produced by a black writer in recent years'. Its 'refusal to represent the black experience as monolithic, self-contained, sexually stabilised and always "right-on"'[8] signals a move beyond the output of earlier minority film-makers, who had felt pressurised to depict idealised images of Asians or Afro-Caribbeans to counter the racist stereotypes that appeared elsewhere in the media. The ambiguous identities of many characters in *Laundrette* demonstrate the extent to which new generations of film-makers like Frears and Kureishi are able to break free of colonialist ('us' and 'them' or 'good' and 'bad') polarities and to define their own agendas and interests. In short, it embodies a diaspora aesthetic, foregrounding complexity and contingency, hybridity and hyphenated identity.

As this chapter explores, *My Son the Fanatic* adopts a similar approach in its depiction of 1990s Britain. The film challenges popular understandings of inter-generational conflicts in minority communities, especially regarding religion. It explores the constructedness of culture and the dynamics of 'fundamentalism'. Whilst neither unsympathetic to religious commitment, nor uncritical of liberalism and assimilation, it ultimately prefers the kind of culture-blending activities associated with diaspora aesthetics as evoked by Hall.

Finally, the locating of *My Son the Fanatic* vis-à-vis the concept of diaspora again emphasises the extent to which film meanings are not intrinsic but are always formed within particular moments. *My Son* was made in collaboration with BBC Films and funded by the Arts Council of England, suggesting a synergy between the film-makers' concerns and the needs or interests of the (cultural) establishment.

An important aspect to consider will be how far the film departs from, or coheres with, the 'Othering' of Muslim 'fundamentalists'; a trend in public discourse which has accelerated in the years since *My Son*'s release. At the same time, institutional support of film-makers has sometimes been felt to create or exacerbate an expectation that the resulting films should speak for particular groups, making visible the truths of their experiences. (Kobena Mercer has dubbed this the 'burden of representation'.[9])

Whilst diaspora films themselves perhaps no longer reflect such a mindset, some viewers may approach *My Son the Fanatic* with the expectation that it will be documentary, or quasi-documentary, in its treatment of Islam in contemporary Britain. Such elision of fiction into fact in the responses to *My Son* will be discussed in the chapter's final section.

Filming Fundamentalism

The production and public funding of *My Son the Fanatic* can be understood as part of a larger trend towards the incorporation of South Asian influence on films, music and fashion within mainstream British, and latterly, North American, culture.[10] The growing visibility of British Asian culture is attributable to various factors including increased affluence within the Asian diaspora, the launch of Channel 4 television (which has screened Hindi films since its inception in 1982) and the ongoing importance of film consumption as a social focus and identity marker for Asian expatriates and their descendants.[11]

However, the film differs in several respects from many of its companions. In *Bend it Like Beckham* (Gurinder Chadha, 2002) Jess's love of football is threatened by familial efforts to impose traditional gender roles; the Sikh community appears closed and conservative in its attitude towards women. *East is East* (Damien O'Donnell, 1999) takes these impulses further, showing (albeit it not without affection) the efforts of George Khan (a role also played by Om Puri) to exercise abusive and sometimes violent control over his family. Like *Anita and Me* (Metin Hüseyin, 2002) *East is East* is set in the early 1970s. Sets, costumes and music all create a retro feel that resonates with images of South Asian cultures as backward or dated. *My Son the Fanatic* offers a contrasting account of British Asian life. Whilst *East is East* centres on second-generation Muslim children rebelling against their father's conservative values, *My Son* depicts the son of a liberal father who finds meaning and purpose in Islam.

The earlier part of *My Son* is principally occupied with Farid's journey into religion as observed by Parvez, whose confusion is evoked stylistically by the use of a hand-held camera, and unusual shots that place him (like Dreyer's Jeanne) outside the golden third of the frame.[12] As presented in the film's opening scene, Farid stands, literally and figuratively speaking, on the threshold of the English middle classes: taxi driver Parvez, along with Farid and Minoo (Parvez's wife) are seen visiting the country home of Farid's white fiancée, Madeleine. A conversation between Parvez and Madeleine's father, Police Inspector Fingerhut, indicates that Farid is to become an accountant. However, Farid breaks the engagement and begins selling his possessions. At first Parvez suspects that he is using drugs – a move suggestive of the quality of what Farid later terms 'spiritual thirst' – and asks Bettina to describe the signs of heroin misuse. (Later in the film we see Bettina snort coke with a client.) It is soon clear, however, that Farid's obsession is with a new-found faith. At home, the sounds of Parvez's jazz records are punctuated by those of Arabic prayer. Later Parvez follows Farid, who has swapped Western clothes for a *salwar kameez* and *kufi* hat, to the mosque and sees him clash with community elders.

The strategy of mediating Farid's religion in piecemeal fashion, through Parvez's perspective, is significant. First, it positions the viewer with Parvez. Since each stands outside the world into which Farid is moving, audiences are encouraged to empathise with his father, as co-observers of the process. Second, the progressive distancing of Farid from Parvez, which is concomitant with Farid's incremental adoption of religious rituals, emphasises the constructedness of 'fundamentalist' Islam. It represents a break from his immediate heritage. In a telling move, Farid learns to pray in Arabic via the medium of modern technology, in the form of an instructional video cassette.

Two extended dialogues articulate the core of Farid's philosophy. In the first, he explains the reasons for his broken engagement:

FARID: Can you put keema with strawberries? In the end our cultures, they cannot be mixed.

PARVEZ: Everything is mingling already together, this thing and the other.

FARID: Some of us are wanting summat more besides muddle ... belief, purity, belonging to the past. I won't bring up my children in this country.

And later, when Parvez tries to convince Farid to return to his former lifestyle, Farid responds with:

They tell us to integrate, but they live in pornography and filth and tell us how backward we are ... Their society's soaked in sex ...

Accountancy ... is capitalism and taking advantage ...

It is you who have swallowed the white and Jewish propaganda that there is nothing in our lives but the emplty accountancy for things.

Here, Farid's Islam is positioned as separatist (a stance undermined linguistically by his Yorkshire dialect), linked to a desire for clarity and the rebuilding of a connection with the imagined past. It offers an alternative to the ideologies of assimilation and capitalism, and is antisemitic.[13] When a *maulvi* (religious teacher) from Lahore comes to stay in the family's home, a violent potential within Farid's faith is realised. There is initially some warmth in the presentation of the *maulvi*, who is shown laughing at television cartoons over breakfast. But later, when he runs up large utility bills that Parvez must struggle to pay, banishes Minoo to the kitchen and then expresses the desire to remain permanently in Britain, he appears as a self-serving hypocrite. Under the *maulvi*'s encouragement, Farid and his friends launch a campaign against the local sex workers, including Bettina. This spills over into the firebombing of a brothel-house, which forms the dramatic climax of the film.

As this summary indicates, the film envisions 'fundamentalism' as rupture or innovation. In cultural studies terms, it is created by the processes of bricolage, as older symbols, ideas and behaviours are adopted and adapted by young men like Farid in order to articulate a new social identity. Thus when Farid speaks about his faith over a meal in a restaurant, his language has a stilted quality: the Qur'an is seemingly more icon than message. Some critics have regarded the unnaturalness of Farid's words in some dialogues as a weakness in the film,[14] but it may be interpreted as suggestive of the inorganic *agree* nature of his newly-learned philosophy. Notably, it contrasts with the freer, intimate exchanges between Parvez and Bettina in the same restaurant later in the film.

However, the film is not entirely unsympathetic towards Farid. In one scene, he selflessly carries Parvez into the house in order to prevent his feet from getting cold. Later, although despising his father's drunkenness, he drives him safely home. There is also some truth in the allegations he levels at Parvez. Moreover, whilst it rejects 'fundamentalism's' self-understanding, *My Son* does offer an account of its attractiveness for men like Farid.

If Farid's choice, like Parvez's liberalism, is thoroughly modern, it is also presented as an *intelligible* reaction to a young British Asian man's experiences of exclusion in a late capitalist society. The lukewarm response of Madeleine's parents to the couple's engagement sets the tone for the racism, by turns overt and insidious, that pervades British society in the film, suggesting that the barriers to integration are not exclusively or primarily of Farid's own making. *My Son* suggests too that in his desire to assimilate, Parvez (who in the early interactions with his son and wife, typically speaks much of material security and advancement, and rarely of values or feelings) has repressed much of *Obvi.* his own self, and in doing so has failed to offer Farid the inner resources that might have enabled him to deal effectively with inequality and prejudice. In one exchange with Bettina, Parvez expresses regret that he prevented Farid from pursuing his early interest in music. Militant Islam thus appears, in part, as that which emerges to fill a spiritual vacuum in Farid's life. In other words, as Kureishi suggests in an essay about his travels in Pakistan in the 1980s:

> 'fundamentalism' – Islam as a political ideology – was filling a space where Marxism and capitalism had failed to take hold….

This kind of Islam resembled neo-fascism or even Nazism: an equality of oppression for the masses with a necessary enemy – in this case 'the West' – helping to keep everything in place.[15]

The logical response to such a diagnosis of the 'fanatic's' condition is that (as Bettina urges Parvez), 'you need to give him [Farid] a better philosophy'. But what, if any, philosophy does *My Son* advance?

As its title implies, the film is structured (narratively and stylistically) around Parvez's point of view. In contrast to Farid, Minoo and Madeleine, who are afforded little activity or subjectivity, Parvez is a compelling, energetic creation, by turns concerned for his son, egotistical, and playful. Crucially, he has no certainties to counter Farid's. Although the film's deliberately open ending suggests that happiness lies not in easy answers but in an ability to balance personal desires and expectations with those of others (in the penultimate scene, he negotiates future plans with Bettina), for much of the film Parvez, like many of Kureishi's protagonists,[16] is a socially disengaged individualist. Whereas Farid visits fellow Muslims in prison, a move which also emphasises the volte-face from his engagement to a policeman's daughter, Parvez's place within the community is uncertain.

Particularly in earlier scenes, he refuses to identify with others. When Minoo wants to use the lavatory in the Fingerhuts' house, Parvez forbids her, lest their hosts 'think we are Bengalis'. His remark at once evokes white racist assumptions, and the persistence within the British Asian community of the divisions between Bangladeshis (Bengali speakers) and Pakistanis. Describing himself to German businessman Schitz as a 'gentleman', he dubs the other taxi drivers 'low-lifes', and 'barely educated'. In short, whilst he treats Bettina as a human being rather than a commodity, Parvez is a snob.[17]

The development of a doubly transgressive romance with Bettina, a white sex worker, is the vehicle for Parvez to transcend his life with Minoo and Farid. When confronted by restaurant owner Fizzy about the affair, Parvez for the first time voices his own needs: 'What is there for me, yaar, but sitting behind the wheel without tenderness? That's it for me, is it, until I drop dead and not another human touch … Minoo has never given me satisfaction.'

If Farid seeks an alternative to 'the empty accountancy for things' in religion, his father finds it in physical love. But the significance of Parvez' relationship with Bettina lies not simply in its offering a parallel to the passions consuming Farid. *My Son* posits intimate relationships as a redemptive *answer* to the dogmas of conservative Islam and assimilationism. In an important dialogue with Bettina, Parvez recalls his childhood in Pakistan. The harsh methods and intolerance of the *maulvi* who taught him that his best friend, a Hindu, must go to '*kafir* ['unbeliever'[18]] hell' meant that Parvez 'said goodbye to next life…and said hello…to work.' In depicting both Parvez's unhappy marriage and the fate of Farid, however, *My Son* argues for the unsatisfactoriness of Parvez's initial response: it is only through love that humans can overcome cultural and religious divides. In a later essay, Kureishi has suggested that,

> If both racism and fundamentalism are diminishers of life – reducing others to abstractions – the effort of culture must be to keep others alive by describing and celebrating their intricacy, by seeing that this is not only of value but a necessity.[19]

This call to recognise the political character of intricacy or intimacy between and with 'others' lies at the core of *My Son the Fanatic*'s ideology, and at the heart of diaspora aesthetics as envisioned in contemporary cultural studies.

From a religion and film perspective, what this analysis reveals is that *My Son*'s 'message' is overwhelmingly secular. In presenting Islam only as lived by young militants like Farid – or rather, only as this lifestyle is perceived by his non-observant parent – the film unwittingly perpetuates stereotypes of Islam as monolithic and of young Muslim males as dangerous extremists. This indirect and partial handling of religious commitment indicates that essentially *My Son* is not concerned primarily with Islam per se, but rather points towards one of the classic dilemmas facing pluralist societies: how do they respond appropriately to groups who would reject the very values on which they claim to be based? However, the film has been regarded by many critics as being 'about' militant religion – which makes it important to give some further consideration to its treatment of Islam.

115

Diversity within the Muslim community surfaces briefly, when Parvez (who has to be reminded to remove his shoes at the mosque entrance) witnesses an altercation between Farid's friends and other worshippers. According to one of the elders:

> These boys are not welcome ... They think everyone but them is corrupt and foolish ... They are always fighting for radical actions on many subjects ... It is irritating us all here, yaar. But they have something these young people – they're not afraid of the truth. They stand up for things. We never did that.

Aside from this speech, the film offers no other interpretation of Islam to act as a foil to militancy. Even here the implication is that, despite the elder's opening comments, Farid and his friends are representatives of a purer, more committed form of religion. In this way, by offering no sustained Muslim critique of militancy, *My Son* participates in the elision of 'Islam' into 'fundamentalism' in contemporary popular Western discourse, feeding into what might be termed, following Stanley Cohen's classic definition,[20] the 'moral panic' surrounding young Muslims in the West today. The perception that they are the least assimilable and the most dangerous of minority groups has crystallised around events like the Salman Rushdie Affair (1989), and more recently, the terror attacks on the USA on 11 September 2001 and in London on 7 July 2005.

My Son the Fanatic's interpolation into the responses to these atrocities will be discussed in more detail later. For now it is important to note that, whilst Kureishi professes interest 'in all sides of the story',[21] it is clear that, taking their cue from the partiality of its makers, some of *My Son*'s viewers have found some 'sides' of the story 'more interesting' than others. In this sense, perhaps, *My Son the Fanatic*'s credentials as an articulation of diaspora aesthetics are shaky. The film attempts to use the folk devil of the 'fundamentalist' Muslim to deconstruct the logic of racism, but its disinterest in Islam per se leaves open the possibility that it will in fact reinforce 'us-and-them' thinking.

It's Different for Girls

Mapped onto *My Son the Fanatic*'s handling of Islam is its treatment of gender. Bettina and Minoo are the two main female characters in the film, of whom Bettina is the most complex. Most obviously, she is in more than one sense a 'working girl' and her occupation reflects and questions the significance of modern shifts in relations between the genders.

As discussed in Chapter VII, feminist critics have argued that film, like other cultural practices, reflects a set of predominantly male, heterosexist understandings of sex and gender. Heterosexuality is central to the representation of women on screen, and more specifically images of working women (particularly those of the sex worker or prostitute) are associated with sexual(ised) performance.[22] *My Son the Fanatic* acknowledges and underlines these connections by emphasising sex work as performance: as Parvez begins to find solace in his nightly conversations with Bettina the camera films his (optical, as well as libidinous) point of view as she removes her make-up and wig in the taxicab at the end of a night's work. Later, as the couple becomes closer, Bettina reveals her real name, Sandra, and permits Parvez to use it when they are alone.

As Parvez' confidante-turned-lover, Bettina appears as a feisty character, who jokes and trades insults with her clients and fellow workers. When German businessman Schitz reifies her, asking Parvez (who has introduced him to her as a potential client; there is truth in Farid's denunciation of his father as a 'pimp who organises sexual parties') 'Couldn't you just kiss every part of her?' she retorts, 'Couldn't you just kick every part of *him*?' In this respect, and in contrast to Minoo, who waits at home for Parvez's wages, Bettina is an empowered career woman who does not let emotion inhibit her ability to earn an income. She takes a similarly defiant approach when Parvez comments on the bruises on her body, although the tone is more defensive, and their presence suggests a different story.[23] On several occasions, she tells Parvez that she likes his 'taking care' of her. Dialogue also reveals that Bettina did not choose prostitution, but was forced to abandon her early hopes of becoming a teacher after her mother's death.

The visual organisation of *My Son* around a male character, Parvez, and the ambivalent portrayal of Bettina's experience, raise questions about any notion of the film's establishing of a repressive–liberal/ religious–secular distinction. These are thrown into sharper relief when considering the portrait of Minoo, Parvez's wife.

Tantalisingly, the film acknowledges but does little to develop the idea that experiences of migration and assimilation are different for women and men. Apart from the opening visit to the Fingerhuts', Minoo is never seen outside the family home. She appears as a stereotypically submissive wife, cleaning her husband's clothes and preparing food, first for her family, and later for the *maulvi* and his pupils. These activities, and Minoo's tacit support of Farid's conservatism, raise important but unexplored issues about what life in Britain means for immigrant women.

Interestingly, the film's screenplay includes two scenes that do not appear in the final work, but which would have pursued this angle further. In one, the normally isolated Minoo is shown enjoying the company of other women, as she prepares food for the *maulvi* and his students on the day of the riot. In another, Parvez attempts to rape Minoo, which makes her eventual decision to leave for Pakistan more intelligible.[24] In one final outburst, Minoo tells Parvez that 'I hate this dirty place! The men brought us here and then left us alone!', but her exit from the story at this point signals both the film's privileging of Parvez's position (it neatly resolves difficult questions about the continuation of his affair should Minoo remain) and its lack of interest in female subjectivity.

More emphasis is placed on attitudes *to* women in Farid's circle. Justifying his abandonment of accountancy on the grounds that such a career would entail mixing with women, Farid tells Parvez, 'Many [women] lack belief, and therefore reason.' Other elements of the film lend support to the implication of this phrase – namely, that *My Son* constructs Islam as patriarchal and chauvinistic. When the *maulvi* comes to stay in the family home, gender segregation is introduced and Minoo takes her meals alone in the kitchen. Symbolically, as

[handwritten note: formally- I don't think it's coherent - the color comes from nowhere. -even though that's kinda what they're going for]

Bettina/Sandra's clothes in her scenes of intimacy with Parvez are increasingly colourful (red tones predominate; when Parvez and she make love, the screen is flooded with red) Minoo's dress becomes more and more muted. Together with the climactic images of Muslim youths firebombing a house and then beating up the fleeing women (seemingly, the prostitutes' male clients are not targeted), Minoo's fate in *My Son the Fanatic* lends support to images of Islam as being bound up with the violent subjugation of Muslim and non-Muslim women.

Hit the North

The action in most of Kureishi's work that has been adapted for the screen – such as *My Beautiful Laundrette, Sammy and Rosie Get Laid* (Stephen Frears, 1987) and *The Mother* (Roger Michell, 2003) and the 1993 television series, *The Buddha of Suburbia* – is located in London. Contrastingly, *My Son the Fanatic* is set in what the screenplay describes as 'a northern city', unnamed but certainly Bradford, West Yorkshire. Although London is the most ethnically diverse settlement in Britain, the Yorkshire and Humber region has a larger proportion of British Asians than the capital (around one fifth of the total British Asian population).[25]

More specifically, Bradford is an important centre within the Asian diaspora, numerically (around 90,000 residents are of Asian heritage) and culturally speaking. In the mid-1980s, when local head teacher Ray Honeyford notoriously argued that schools should emphasise social cohesion over multiculturalism, and that the preservation of the distinct cultural identity of ethnic minority communities was solely a private matter for individual migrants and their descendents, it became a nexus for debates surrounding education, identity and public policy. Following the burning there of Salman Rushdie's *The Satanic Verses* in January 1989, and riots in summer 2001, Bradford's status as an icon of British Muslim resistance and 'fundamentalism' was ensured. Indeed, there is some truth in Robert Young's observation that, '"Bradford Muslims" has become a generic description not of Muslims who happen to live in Bradford, England, but of what are considered "fundamentalist" Muslims in the west.'[26] Less controversially, the town was the site of the first full-time Asian cinema in Europe, and its National Museum of Photography, Film and Television hosts 'Bite the Mango', a festival with a heavy emphasis on South Asian and other diasporic films.

Kureishi visited Bradford in the 1980s, and wrote an essay of the same name about his experiences. Much of the detail of Parvez's life is evocative of this earlier text; for example, 'The taxi driver had a Bradford-Pakistani accent, a cross between the North of England and Lahore, which sounds odd the first few times you hear it.'[27] More specifically, events in Bradford in the summer of 1995 form an important context for *My Son the Fanatic*. The film's subplot – the campaign against the sex workers – unfolds in a manner resembling the rising tensions that culminated in riots in the city's Manningham district. As in the film, the vigilantes were primarily young Muslims; whilst the organisers cautioned against violence, several women were attacked and a café used by sex workers was firebombed. Such correspondences suggest a relationship of dependence between the film and contemporary events. They also form a thematic counterpart to the aesthetic realisms (the use of hand-held camera, the emphasis on Parvez's point of view) that characterise the film.

My Son's drawing on events in Bradford's recent history is not evidence of a simple desire on Prasad's or Kureishi's part to create a work that 'mirrors' reality, although it does contribute significantly to the film's realism. Chapter V discussed the ways in which several films imagine Scotland as a territory conventionally as well as geographically distant from metropolitan London. Similarly, *My Son*'s depiction of Bradford taps into screen images of 'the North' of England as a terrain wherein a range of fantasies and anxieties may be projected and explored.

The mid-1990s saw the release of a number of popular films, set in the North of England, in which common themes can be traced. First, there is a tendency to depict 'the North' as dated, in political and social terms. This assumes a generally positive, nostalgic character, where strong familial and communal ties are depicted between people who live and work alongside one another: even redundancy cannot break the bonds between former steelworkers in *The Full Monty* (Peter Cattaneo, 1997). Conversely, it acquires negative connotations when associated with racism and restrictive ideas about gender roles. In *Brassed Off* (Mark Herman, 1996), Gloria's wish to join Grimley colliery band is mocked because she is a woman; the family of *Billy Elliot* (Stephen Daldry, 2000) will not countenance the idea of a boy learning ballet. Second, the North of England is typically presented as a site of economic depression and decline: in the films named above, industries are either threatened (in *Brassed Off* Grimley's pit faces closure; *Billy Elliot* develops against the backdrop of the 1984 miners' strike) or already gone, as in *The Full Monty*.

My Son's presentation of 1990s Bradford sits firmly within this framework. As discussed earlier, the emergence of conservative Islam is presented as an indictment of the racism experienced by men like Farid. In the only scene to depict non-Asian 'community', Parvez accompanies Bettina and Schitz to the 'Manningham Nightclub', where a white audience, including local police officers, enjoy a turn by a stand-up comic who unleashes a string of sexist and racist jokes. Parvez quickly becomes the butt of the comic's 'jokes' ('If you fuckers all left town on the same day, we'd have two hours extra bleeding daylight') until Bettina leaps to his defence; the three leave the venue after a scuffle.

The cultural impoverishment of white Bradfordians in *My Son* echoes, like Parvez's accent, Kureishi's account of the town a decade earlier:

> The clothes [white] people wore were shabby and old; they looked as if they'd been bought in jumble sales or second-hand shops. And their faces had an unhealthy aspect; some were malnourished.

> At the bar, it was mostly old men. They sat beside each other. But they didn't talk.[28]

In general terms, Bradford appears as a largely deserted, post-industrial town, inhabited by the marginalised and the alienated – be they youths like Farid, or sex workers like Bettina. The once dominant textile mills are closed, and have been replaced by a soulless consumerism, embodied variously in those who buy the services of prostitutes, Parvez's friend Fizzy and his restaurant empire, and the amoral Schitz, who privately despises the town but hopes to cash in on its poor fortunes by building a profitable retail mall on the site of a disused factory.[29] Within this bleak urbanscape, least sympathy is reserved for the town's white population. Kureishi may be distant from the 'fundamentalism' of young men like Farid, but his stereotyping of white Bradfordians leaves audiences with little option not to regard them as negative Others.

Specifically in relation to religious matters, *My Son*'s location in Bradford may be probed further. Since the late twentieth century, ethnic and religious diversity have been increasingly problematised in Britain. The three Labour Governments elected since 1997 have expressed a commitment to a pluralist society and actively sponsored the development or protection of particular kinds of religious identities (through the promotion of 'faith schools' and measures to ban incitement to religious hatred, for example). There has been a shift in public discourse from the notion of 'ethnic minorities' to 'faith communities', which in turn impacts British Asian self-understandings.

However, the simultaneous construction of 'Islamic civilisation' as a threat to 'the West', which has been mobilised by fascist organisations such as the British National Party, also shapes the rhetoric and policies of the mainstream political parties (for example, the proposal to introduce linguistic and other tests for foreign religious teachers wishing to enter Britain) and media. Particularly since the 2001 disturbances in Bradford, Burnley and Oldham, and the 7 July 2005 bombings in London (three of the four bombers were from Bradford's neighbouring city, Leeds) a recurring feature of public debate has been the identification of the North of England as an area of racial, ethnic and religious segregation, where isolated and socially conservative communities jostle alongside one another in the competition for scarce economic resources.

In this context, *My Son* unsurprisingly displaces racism onto 'the North', a location outside the centres of political power, film production and criticism,[30] in which uncomfortable problems can be worked through, or sidelined. Similarly, the location of the film in the North of England – a region in which, stereotypically, traditional familial and gender roles remain firmly in place ('Yorkshire women... always have dinner on the table when you get home'[31]) – also legitimates the film's handling of gender relations in ways that privilege male action and subjectivity.

This interplay between religious identities and the representation of place in contemporary Britain is foregrounded in two scenes in *My Son*. As he drives Schitz from the airport to his hotel, Parvez introduces him to Bradford:

> You see that chimney, it's so tall it can be seen from Ilkley moor … Even the Ayatollah Khoumeni wore a robe made in this city in a mill over there – actually you won't see it because it was demolished some years ago.

In a parallel scene, Farid introduces Bradford to the *maulvi* in virtually identical fashion. Unlike Parvez, however, he seeks to explain the mill closures in religious terms; the chimney is not a source of pride, but a sign of the arrogance of ungodly industrialists. These modifications both emphasise the differences between father and son, and reinforce the notion that Farid's return or conversion to Islam is essentially a swapping of one set of pat slogans for another. At the same time, they highlight the film's own constructedness, particularly in relation to its rehearsal or staging of the declining North.

The Burden of Representation

Despite the criticisms that some British Asians levelled against *East is East* for its mocking portrayal of Islam, the film attracted large audiences and was one of the most commercially successful British films of the 1990s, while *My Son the Fanatic* slipped into relative obscurity.[32] Unlike *My Beautiful Laundrette*, which was originally intended for television but crossed over into mainstream cinemas, it remained firmly in the art house. The reasons for the differences between these three films are various. Poor distribution was a factor inhibiting the initial progress of *My Son the Fanatic*,[33] but it was also one offset in part by the power of the Hanif Kureishi brand. The concept of the film auteur is most usually linked with the role of the director, as discussed in Chapter IV, but in the case of *My*

Son Kureishi's reputation as a provocative writer who has produced significant work in a range of forms (essays, novels, plays and films) secured the film its first, or second, viewings.

Most early reviewers agreed that the romance between Parvez and Bettina was the most compelling and artistically successful dimension of the film. David Parkinson, writing in *Empire*, suggested that, 'Kureishi overdoes the grim-up-North aspect of the film, but is successful in his portrait of romance between Parvez and Bettina', whilst for *Screen International* Sheila Johnston similarly felt that 'the film really scores when it focuses on Puri and Griffiths as their relationship develops'.[34] The film gained early approval insofar as, like *East is East* and *My Beautiful Laundrette*, it reflected a contemporary (post)modern ethic, privileging romantic love and individualism over religion and community.

The same feature that probably made *My Son the Fanatic* initially less attractive to mass audiences than *East is East* or *Laundrette* has increasingly come to the fore in the film's reception. Whereas *East is East* leavens its exploration of weighty issues with a large dose of slapstick humour, and *Laundrette* (with its celebration of romance between British Asian Omar and reformed racist Johnny) is optimistic about the possibilities inherent in ethnic diversity and eclecticism, *My Son* pursues a more unsettling line, eschewing a happy ending and problematising the hybrid himself – the ultimately unassimilable Farid, with whom multiculturalism cannot cope.

Writing on *My Son* has increasingly de-centred Parvez and Bettina's relationship, concerning itself instead with Farid's story. Why might this be? Earlier in this chapter, I suggested that BBC and Arts Council funding of *My Son the Fanatic* implied a synergy between the film's concerns and those of the (cultural) establishment. Indeed, Kureishi himself has described it as 'almost a legacy of the 1960s and 1970s, when one of the purposes of the BBC was to make cussed and usually provincial dramas about contemporary issues like homelessness, class and the Labour party'.[35] Setting aside Kureishi's othering language (the us-and-them distinctions implied in words like 'provincial') these remarks emphasise *My Son*'s implication from the start in social and political discourse. And particularly since

2001, the film has been invoked in discussions of many of the actual and aborted terror attacks that have taken place in the anglophone world.

Various articles draw links between the fictional story and the willingness of some young men to engage in violent jihad. A 2002 article by Matt Seaton about Richard Reid (a British man who tried to blow up a plane by igniting a shoe-bomb) and John Walker Lindh (an American Taliban fighter) in the *Guardian* newspaper was titled '*My Son the Fanatic*'.[36] Dohra Ahmad's work on Salman Rushdie's 1996 novel *The Moor's Last Sigh* references Kureishi's story as an example of recent fiction that can 'teach us about fundamentalism' after 11 September 2001.[37] More recently, one essayist has dubbed *My Son* 'The First 7/7 Movie' and presents the film as answering 'the big question' posed by the London bombings: 'How could apparently assimilated, British-born Muslims end up stuffing bombs into their backpacks and murdering dozens of their compatriots in the Tube and on a London double-decker bus?'[38]

Whilst the broad trend in such writing is to evaluate the film positively, regarding it as a source of information and insight on British Islam, other critics bemoan the film's handling of religion. Ruvani Ranasinha criticises the failure to show positive images of (Muslim) community.[39] Maya Jaggi and Akbar Ahmed also protest the film's rehearsal of 'tired stereotypes' of 'fanatics and book-burners'.[40] Despite their differences, however, these two families of approaches to *My Son* have in common an assumption that film is, or should be, in some way descriptive or documentary of reality. This kind of approach is not unique, of course, to the reception of British Asian cinema. (Chapters III and IV described analogous concerns in relation to film treatments of Jeanne d'Arc and the exodus; the privileging and invocation of 'historical accuracy' over other dramatic factors forms the core of the pre-release controversy surrounding *The Da Vinci Code*.)

In this instance, however, the complaints of Ranasinha *et al.* assume an added dimension. Whilst recognising the social dimension of meaning, they nevertheless foist on to Kureishi, Prasad and other British Asian film-makers the burden of representation, requiring that their images serve political ends and shore up both liberal multiculturalism and a minority community that feels itself to be embattled.

The limitations of any approach that regards film as straightforwardly 'about' things have been emphasised throughout this book. The recognition that audiences play a significant role in meaning-making – that to understand a film one must move the discussion beyond the sounds and images as they appear on screen – reveals the weakness of positions that require British Asian film-makers (or others who would address questions of religious and ethnic politics) to 'do everything' within a given film.

Tellingly, in relation to the build up to the 1995 Bradford riots (the events that inform the presentation of the young Muslims' campaign in *My Son the Fanatic*) it has been observed that:

> Tension mounted when the television series *Band of Gold* [in which the principal characters were a group of sex workers] focused nationwide attention on prostitution in Manningham, bringing in coach loads of sightseers on their way to Haworth and Emmerdale country.[41]

In a move that highlights the intricacy and inseparability of text and context, tourist activity stimulated by a television programme provokes events that themselves become the basis for a screenplay that is (mis)perceived as offering quasi-documentary insights on reality.

Arguably, however, in the case of *My Son the Fanatic*, aspects of the film itself invite audiences to 'burden' its makers, suggesting that viewers regard it as a bearer of insight into 'fundamentalism'. The preface to this book noted briefly the perspective of Adorno and Horkheimer, whose 1944 *Dialectic of Enlightenment* is highly sceptical of the cinema. They believed that film's nature as a mass-produced cultural form associated it with the dulling of critical consciousness, the breaking down of individuality, and – they were both refugees from Nazi Germany – the rise of totalitarianism. In a similar vein Gillian Rose has suggested an inherent sympathy between representation and fascism. For Rose, that which is represented is by that act fixed, bound and confirmed as 'other' than ourselves.

There is an element of hyperbole in Rose; her text deliberately assumes a playful, provocative tone.[42] But there is also (particularly given Kureishi's previous associations with the notion of a diaspora aesthetic) much of worth in its implications, namely, the suggestion that the 'problem' with *My Son the Fanatic*, the aspect of the film which ultimately underlies the critical unease surrounding it, is not so much that it fails to document the full diversity of British Islam, but rather that it is too documentary, too realist in its approach.

Whereas *My Beautiful Laundrette* blends realism and fantasy, *My Son* consistently seeks to establish its realist credentials on multiple levels. Narratively, the story's referencing of events in British history (particularly the Bradford riots of 1995, but also other examples of 'militancy' by young Muslims) fosters this view, which is reinforced by the *mise-en-scène*. In effect, the audience are passengers in Parvez's taxicab, encouraged – like Schitz and the *maulvi* – to recognise the (sets and settings as accurate evocations of) actual places. (In this sense, it matters little whether viewers identify these as Bradford, or simply as 'the North'). The use of a hand-held camera and numerous subjective point-of-view shots (described earlier) also give the film an air of psychological or emotional realism. Taken collectively, these aspects are suggestive of an assumption on *My Son*'s part of the authority to narrate 'the Muslim'. The burden of representation is, then, not so much something that has been foisted onto the film, as it is a mantle that the film has willingly, perhaps dangerously, assumed.[43]

if it is funded by Bits – not surprising.

Finally – The film seems unfinished to me,

VII

Keeping the Faith
(Edward Norton, 2000)

a substantive discussion of faith[1]

a frothy... lightweight comedy[2]

Reception: Once More, With Feeling

Poorly distributed and commercially disappointing, *My Son the Fanatic* continues to find favour as the object of scholarly, and on occasion even political, attentions. By contrast, Edward Norton's directorial debut[3] *Keeping the Faith*, which opened on more than 2000 American screens in April 2000 and features a Catholic priest and a Conservative[4] rabbi amongst its lead characters, has received scant critical treatment from scholars of religion and film, or more broadly within film and cinema studies. Like *The Ten Commandments*, *Keeping the Faith* is usually held to belong to a category (it is a popular film, made by Touchstone Pictures, a division of the Walt Disney Company) and a genre (romantic comedy) assumed to be incapable of sustaining the weight of critical analysis.

A brief survey of some early review material supports the notion that it is sentimental, schematic, and locatable firmly within Hollywood conventions – and may, therefore, readily be dismissed. For *Empire* Ian Freer adopted a knowing tone: 'There's something delightfully old school about *Keeping the Faith*. Playing like a romantic comedy from Hollywood's golden era...'. Ahead of Anwar Brett's dismissal of the film as 'frothy' (reproduced at the head of this chapter) *Variety's* Emanuel Levy deemed it a 'schematically constructed romantic comedy', linking a formulaic approach on the screen to Stuart Blumberg's (the film's writer) early career as an investment banker.[5] Such remarks at once place the film as an 'artefact' or piece of Hollywood 'product', rather than a serious work of 'art' or avant-garde cinema. They also position the reviewer, whose assessment of *Faith* signals an ability to identify and see through 'Hollywood', and more specifically, the emotional manipulation within the film itself.

This book has already questioned (see especially Chapters II and IV) the use (value) of the art/multiplex distinction and the notion that the popular consumption of a film is in itself an indicator of its vacuity. More specifically, popular films like *Commandments* and *Keeping the Faith* are not necessarily disqualified from serious study just because they are, in many respects, 'easily' viewed. Charles Affron, drawing on Stanley Fish's arguments about the complexity of supposedly 'transparent' literary texts, has tellingly observed that 'easy fictions contain a complexity of gears whose smooth meshing conceals how they come together and how, once they are engaged, the reader is also engaged in the functioning of the mechanism'.[6]

Arguably, perhaps, whilst a film like *La Passion de Jeanne d'Arc* foregrounds its constructedness, and in doing so facilitates a certain kind of critical distance, one like *Keeping the Faith*, which is filmed so as to enable the spectator to watch with little conscious effort, demands the practice of 'readings of resistance' in order to explore fully the film's interest in complex questions of religious, ethnic and sexual politics.

A Priest Walks Into a Bar...

...and sex, laughter and misunderstanding ensue. The opening scenes of *Keeping the Faith* acknowledge and subvert Hollywood conventions. High-angle long shots of a famous skyline immediately establish that New York is the context for the film's action. As the opening credits fade (in keeping with the film's strong sense of place, the font used for these is 'New Yorker') the camera moves from the generalities of the cityscape to the specifics of a particular Manhattan neighbourhood, and Brian Finn (played by Edward Norton), jacket closed over his dog collar, emerges from (or is thrown out of) The Blarney Stone and enters Peter McManus' bar. Reluctantly at first, he begins to tell the Irish bartender his problems, a device repeated later on, to form an *inclusio* or envelope around the film's core.

Brian's relationship with his best friend, Jake Schramm (played by Ben Stiller), has been thrown into chaos. The two men are caught in an erotic triangle, rivals for the affections of an old childhood friend, Anna Reilly (Jenna Elfman[7]) who has recently returned to the city. Such images and narrative fall safely within the usual parameters of classical Hollywood. But at the same time, *Keeping the Faith* exhibits a markedly postmodern turn. The initially world-weary response of the bartender dismisses Brian's story as one he (and the audience) have 'heard before', acknowledging the film's appeal to convention. It soon emerges, however, that the rivals are a rabbi (Jake) and a Catholic priest (Brian).

In pursuing Anna, each man is defying the ideals of his religious community – Jake because Anna's name immediately defines her as a non-Jew (someone, therefore, not regarded in *halakhah* (religious law) or *minhag* (custom) as an appropriate partner), and Brian because Catholic priests take a vow of celibacy. Stereotypes are further disrupted by the revelation that the bartender, whose badge enjoins readers to 'Kiss me, I'm Irish', is in fact Pakistani.

In its efforts to hold in tension convention and innovation, *Keeping the Faith* typifies a mode of film-making sometimes referred to as 'New Hollywood'. The definition, and the very 'newness' of New Hollywood are contested; the concept is applied to a number of trends discernible in the film industry from the late 1960s onwards.[8] Some of these shifts are industrial. Since the successful saturation-marketing of *Jaws* (Steven Spielberg) in 1975, studios have attempted to generate profit from a film in as short a time frame as possible, by advertising extensively in anticipation of an opening at multiple locations. Companies increasingly rely on a small number of astronomically successful 'event' movies (typically large-scale spectaculars like the recent *Lord of the Rings* trilogy, or – as explored in this book's conclusion – *The Passion of The Christ*) to break even. Other hallmarks of the New Hollywood phenomenon may be deemed stylistic, although cultural studies' awareness of the cinema as simultaneously industry and art form is a reminder that attempts to delineate factors clearly from each other must always be at some level artificial.

In the 1960s Hollywood production staff for the first time began to be drawn in large numbers from the ranks of film school graduates. Such figures include writer and director Paul Schrader (whose scholarship on religious film has been discussed earlier in this book) as well as figures like Martin Scorsese (who also studied in a Catholic seminary), Francis Ford Coppola and George Lucas, who all embarked on their professional lives well versed in the techniques of their predecessors (particularly European directors like Ingmar Bergman, Alain Resnais and François Truffaut, but (visibly in Lucas' case) also American creatives like DeMille) and in the critical discourse of auteurism, which was introduced in Chapter IV. The result was a cinema of rich citation or intertextuality; one that blended 'special grace notes for insiders, appoggiatura for the cognoscenti, and a soaring, action-charged melody for the rest'.[9]

Like other New Hollywood productions, *Keeping the Faith* is a knowing film, rife with allusion. An early scene establishing the childhood friendship between Anna, Brian, and Jake deliberately references an incident in Truffaut's 1962 *Jules et Jim*. Like Catherine (Jeanne Moreau) in one of the earlier film's most memorable sequences, Anna dons male dress (a baseball uniform) and runs a race with the two boys. Stylistically, Norton finds in Truffaut's film a simple visual evocation of youthful freedoms, but the citation also hints (for those who identify it) at the difficulties that lie ahead. Like Jules (a German Jew) and Jim (a Frenchman), Brian and Jake are destined to have their relationship torn open by the encounter with a free-spirited and unconventional woman.

In a similar vein the casting of Miloš Forman as Father Havel, the adult Brian's mentor, evokes the off-screen role of Forman (who directed Norton in his breakthrough role as Alan Isaacman in *The*

People vs. Larry Flint (1996)) in developing Norton's career, whilst the name Havel in turn is a deliberate nod to Václav Havel, the playwright and political activist who served as the first President of the Czech Republic (Forman's birthplace) from 1993–2003.

In a crucial later scene, *Faith* directly foregrounds its sense of the importance of cinema history. When Jake and Anna begin dating (a secret they hide from Jake's community and from Brian) they visit a film theatre, but risk the discovery of their romance when the President and other members of the synagogue arrive. In the auditorium, Jake ignores Anna – a concrete marker of the inviability of their relationship as it is currently organised. At this moment of intense unease, the film they are watching is *When A Man Loves a Woman* (Luis Mandoki, 1994) and Andy Garcia is saying, 'Jesus Christ, I'm in a crisis here, I need some help'. Although quite different from *Keeping the Faith*, Mandoki's film (which is about a woman's battles with alcoholism, and the difficulties with her husband (played by Garcia) in negotiating the necessary change in their relationship) is also about a struggle to reintegrate a 'returning' woman. Both the helplessness and the controlling nature of Garcia's character offer implicit comment on Jake's behaviour.

Discussion of New Hollywood fails to address the question of whether, in keeping with other developments, the cinema's treatment of religion has also shifted in recent years. However, New Hollywood does provide an important context for assessing and understanding some of the more innovative screen treatments of the Jesus story (note, for example Scorsese and Schrader's collaboration on *The Last Temptation of Christ*) and more generally of religious identity. Francis Ford Coppola's *Godfather* trilogy (1972–90), for example, is widely hailed as the definitive Mafia film, but it is also inventive in its presentation of Catholicism. The depiction of Italian-Americans overturned the earlier Hollywood tendency to elide Catholicism into Irish ethnicity. It also exploited the affective and visual powers of ritual in new ways, in famous sequences like that in *The Godfather* (1972), which intercuts scenes of the baptism of Michael Corleone's nephew with those of his men as they prepare to slaughter the Corleone family's rivals.

Keeping the Faith is a quite differently animated production but it, too, is unusual in its interest in exploring several dimensions of religion. In contrast to the depiction of religious leaders and institutions in many of the other films considered in this book (the senior theologians and priests in *La Passion de Jeanne d'Arc*; the *maulvi* in *My Son the Fanatic*; the pagan culture on Summerisle) both Bryan and Jake are presented as sympathetic, positive figures.

The film reserves its harshest treatment for secular characters like Ali Decker, a woman Jake dates briefly in an attempt to satisfy his congregants, who expect a rabbi to be married. Although the *mezuzah* fixed to her doorpost might be held to signal some kind of religious observance (in fact, it may just as well be an ethnic marker),[10] Ali quickly reveals that exercise is 'like a religion' to her. What appear to be antique books on the shelves in her sitting room are in fact fakes, discreet covers for a library of fitness videos. When Jake, responding to Ali's overly insistent invitations to test her strength, punches her and knocks her to the floor, the hollowness of her 'faith' is emphasised – a point underscored on the ethical plane later in the evening, when she uses her purse to beat a homeless man who has approached the couple as they dine at a pavement café.

Eschewing the unspiritual and vacuous Ali, *Keeping the Faith* prefers to construct New York as a web of faiths and ethnicities. (An Asian American karaoke salesman's performance of immigrant identity provides one particularly memorable scene, but Jake and Brian also shoot basketball with a group of African and Latin Americans, and Brian hears confessions in English and Spanish.)

Much of its early interest centres around the religious growth and developing vocation of the two male characters. The film handles the material as an opportunity for visual, slapstick humour: Brian's early efforts with the thurible (censer) are disastrous, and Jake faints during a circumcision ceremony. But more importantly, it seeks to establish the closeness of the two men and their similarities. In an important early sequence editing creates a montage of two scenes – Brian preaching in his church, Jake addressing the synagogue on Shabbat – to establish parallels between the men and their roles as progressive, charismatic leaders.[11] This device, like the film's main subplot (Brian and Jake's efforts to build a Catholic/Jewish seniors' centre) suggests that what they, and their respective communities, hold in common is more significant than that which divides them. Brian's remark to the bartender, that the pair's approaches to worship soon had them 'playing to packed audiences' also suggests that religious leadership is a kind of performance.

Functional parallelism is again evident in the crisis prompted by the inevitable public exposure of Anna's and Jake's relationship. Although the outcomes are in each case different – Brian learns that his commitment to God and the celibate life is not a one-off decision but must be made afresh each day, whilst Jake uses his *Yom Kippur*[12] sermon to declare his love for Anna – both men face and meet the challenge of reconciling individual desires with communal expectation.

The film's attention to duty and aspects of religious ritual is fairly unusual, and has been noted favourably by some commentators. For the United States Conference of Catholic Bishops, Brian's 'vow of celibacy and his accompanying doubts are dealt with in an earnest manner that does not undermine his priestly commitment', whilst Donna Bowman, for *The Journal of Religion and Film*, finds 'Norton's decision to treat the problems of his characters seriously – as seriously as the characters themselves do – ...refreshing.'[13]

However, *Faith's* practice of its own form of 'comparative religion' risks ignoring the specificity of religions' distinctive content. The parallels it draws between the roles of priest and rabbi inevitably heighten the functional similarities between the two men's roles, at the expense of other dimensions. Just as *Prince of Egypt* (see Chapter IV) seemed more interested in belief itself than it was in the object of religious devotion, so at times the structuring of narrative in *Keeping the Faith* suggests that 'keeping faith' (with celibacy in Brian's case; with love for Anna in Jake's) is ultimately more important than the content of any one belief system.

Jewish/Christian Romance at the Cinema

In naming its rabbi 'Jake', *Keeping the Faith* taps into a distinctive subgenre of the romantic comedy, namely the Jewish/Christian romance. As most students of film history are aware, *The Jazz Singer* (Alan Crosland, 1927), released a year before Dreyer's *Passion*, was the first film to include spoken dialogue as well as musical numbers, and it turned Al Jolson into a star. What is less frequently remembered is that a romance between Jewish singer Jake (Jolson) and a Christian girl, Mary, is central to the plot. Indeed, *The Jazz Singer* was also the first anglophone picture to use the Yiddish term for a gentile woman, *shikse*.[14] *Faith*'s acknowledgement of this heritage extends beyond a simple choice of name. *Yom Kippur*, the day on which Jake finally uses his sermon to declare his love for Anna, is also the day of crisis for the older film's protagonist. In keeping with the integrationist preoccupations of early twentieth-century America, however, the final scenes of Crosland's film saw Jake swap the culture of his Jewish parents for the twin prizes of happiness with Catholic Mary and stardom in the musical theatre. Narratively speaking, in a move that set the pattern until the rise of New Hollywood, *The Jazz Singer* suggests that Jewishness is a flawed or problematic state, to be resolved through assimilation to Christian norms.

Keeping the Faith's more recent predecessors have become less 'optimistic' than *The Jazz Singer* about the possibilities for romance and marriage between Jews and Christians. Significantly, the cinematic trend cuts against statistical evidence: since 1990, a majority of American Jews have married non-Jewish partners (a majority of which self-identify as Christian), with similar patterns emerging throughout the Jewish diaspora.[15] This shift in approach can be positioned in relation to a number of broader ideological contexts, and is variously exemplified by Woody Allen's *Annie Hall* (1977) (a story of 'nervous romance' between WASP (White Anglo-Saxon Protestant) Annie and Jewish New Yorker Alvy Singer) and *Crossing Delancey* (Joan Micklin Silver, 1988) in which the protagonist Isabella has two unsuccessful relationships with non-Jews before finding happiness with Sam Posner, a pickle-seller (the food is a quintessentially Jewish one) whom she first meets through a *shadchen* (matchmaker) hired by her *bubbie* (grandmother).

In contemporary discourse, ethnic difference is intrinsic to American identity. In the wake of the failure of assimilation (the ideology reflected in *The Jazz Singer*) to be truly inclusive, plurality has been naturalised as typically American. Within this discourse intermarriage often functions specifically as a synonym for the (now negatively viewed) erosion of Jewish identity through assimilation. Thus its performance in the cinema has become increasingly problematic.

On first impression, *Keeping the Faith* might be thought to buck this trend. It depicts strong friendships across religious boundaries between the pre-adolescent Anna, Brian and Jake, and an ongoing relationship into adulthood between the two men. More significantly, the development of Jake and Anna's relationship allows the film to touch on the question of Jewish/Christian intermarriage. Before Anna and Jake become lovers, it is revealed that Jake's family has disowned his brother Ethan, because he married a gentile. Throughout the film Ethan and his wife remain unseen, hovering behind the drama. On the one hand, their absent-presence is highly evocative: they are 'lost' to the family, a haunting precursor of the fate (perhaps) awaiting Jake and Anna. On the other hand, it also lets *Keeping the Faith* off a difficult hook. For, whilst it celebrates pluralism in modern American society, the film appears deeply ambivalent about the blurring of identities and of inter-communal boundaries that is, arguably, one of pluralism's inevitable consequences.

This ambiguity is most apparent in the film's final scenes. As described earlier, Jake uses his *Yom Kippur* sermon to place his own personal fulfilment above the demands of communal expectation and declare his love for Anna. However, just as *The Ten Commandments* manages to invoke the iconic power of the divine law, whilst also sidestepping any requirement to depict the demanding realities of a life lived according to its demands, so the tricky personal and professional implications of Jake's love for a non-Jew need not be addressed. It is revealed soon afterwards that Anna has in fact been secretly attending conversion classes: Jake will, after all, marry a Jewish bride. The film suggests, therefore, in somewhat idealistic terms, that if one keeps faith with one's feelings and emotions, a rewarding dissolution of life's problems will swiftly result.

Also significant here is the film's (non-)portrayal of Anna's journey into Judaism. Although her character is the only one to move significantly (in geographical and spiritual terms) during the course of the film, its engagement with her is minimal in depth. Anna's surname implies that she is descended from an Irish Catholic family, but this aspect of her history is unexplored. Whereas Jake is regularly portrayed in familial contexts (at a Shabbat meal; in family photos; during a visit to the Cloisters; by his mother's sickbed) and Father Havel supports Bryan, Anna appears rootless. Significantly, she is depicted several times with Jake's mother, but never with family or friends of her own. Whereas Jake and Bryan are settled, spiritually and physically, in New York, Anna lives in temporary accommodation. *Keeping the Faith* thus presents religious conversion as a rather simplistic joining of a community or acquiring of an identity, with little acknowledgement of the pain or difficulties that may be associated with leaving another one behind.

In its ideological distance from *The Jazz Singer*, *Keeping the Faith* is expressive of the problematics of religious and ethnic diversity in contemporary America. Whereas the liberal rhetoric of an earlier age advocated the image of American society as a 'melting pot', the current mood is more cautious or pessimistic about this ideology's effectiveness as a strategy for managing a diverse population, and typically prefers the 'salad bowl' metaphor of cultural pluralism.

Keeping the Faith struggles with these two competing models. In exploring the obstacles facing Jake and Anna's interfaith relationship, it recognises the existence of different and boundaried communities. Yet in its treatment of both Anna's projected conversion, and the synagogue's welcoming response to it, it argues that these boundaries are readily permeable – that identity and belonging are largely matters of individual choice. In this sense, *Keeping the Faith* speaks enticingly to a post-assimilationist generation of Americans, who wish to reassert the discourse of difference, whilst continuing to reject the problematic ideology of race in which it was previously grounded.

A 'Women's Picture'?

As a romance, *Keeping the Faith* also stands in the tradition of the 'women's picture', typically defined as a film centred around a female character, marketed to and consumed by female audiences, and

The Jews prob. wouldn't be so accepting

concerned with evoking emotional responses to 'women's issues' such as heterosexual romance, domesticity and motherhood. Feminist theorists disagree as to whether women's films should be understood as irredeemably conformist and problematic displacements of structural inequalities into problems of personal relations, or whether they can in fact speak genuinely to social conflicts.[16] Drawing on the perspective of cultural studies, however, Janice Radway's ethnographic study of the readers of romantic fiction in 'Smithton' has emphasised that the effects on consumers of literary texts (and other media) cannot be deduced from the analysis of the texts themselves. For Radway, 'romantic fiction... ultimately reconciles women to patriarchal society and reintegrates them within its institutions', yet at the same time, these qualities do not preclude the possibility that readers may develop self-esteem and assertiveness in the process of its consumption.[17]

Like the 'women's picture', *Keeping the Faith* both foregrounds and ultimately domesticates a character whose activity transgresses normative social definitions of female roles. At the beginning of the film, Anna is a tomboy and the dominant personality within the children's group. On her return to New York, her independence and her active pursuit of a high-powered career in corporate mergers again pose a threat to gender boundaries, a point underscored by a number of narrative and stylistic touches. In the work environment, Anna's wearing of trouser suits and her voyeurism (she uses binoculars to watch a businessman in the opposite tower block have sex with his secretary) suggest that she is 'masculinised'. In the scene when she and Jake temporarily break up (because Anna is 'not Jewish', 'not spiritual') he is seated, whilst Anna stands, placing her in a position of dominance or power. The disruptive grammar of this shot is highlighted by humorous dialogue; at first, she is about to walk out of her own apartment. Yet by the end of the film Anna's conversion domesticates her, placing her (literally and ideologically) within Jake's embrace. She will accept the conventions of his faith and take 'a break from this exciting life', turning down a chance of promotion.

Arguably, however, heterosexual romance is not the prime concern of *Keeping the Faith*. In a pre-release interview, Norton (in typical New Hollywood style) likened the film to *The Philadelphia*

Story (George Cukor, 1940) in which James Stewart and Cary Grant play two men competing for the affections of a wealthy Philadelphia socialite (Katherine Hepburn). Tellingly, he suggested that 'Jenna Elfman is Cary Grant in our movie in the sense that Cary Grant is there to be perfect and look great in suits and for us to know from the minute he walks into the room that that is who Katherine Hepburn is supposed to be with', whilst Ben Stiller is 'like' 'bronze goddess' Katherine Hepburn, and his own character, Brian Flynn, is 'like' Jimmy Stewart.[18]

Read alongside the narrative subjugation of Anna, Norton's remarks – which imply that Anna and Brian are rivals for Jake's love – are suggestive of the convergence that Eve Kosofsky Sedgwick and others have identified between 'the suppression of the homosexual component of human sexuality' and a 'system whose rules and relations oppress women'.[19]

Sedgwick's starting point is René Girard's insistence that in any erotic triangle, the bond that links the two rivals is as intense and potent as the bond that links either of the rivals to the beloved. Applying this to English literary tradition, she argues that the conceptualisation of the *ménage à trios*, or erotic triangle, is also structured by two additional factors. The first of these is the modern Western construction of sexuality, which is heterosexist (or homophobic) and establishes a 'radically disrupted continuum … between sexual and nonsexual male bonds'.[20] The other is patriarchy: in a society run by and in the interests of men, women function primarily as a means of cementing the bonds of men with men. Under these conditions, narrative structures are created in which the threatening potential for homosocial activity (male bonding) to merge into homosexual desire is worked through and supplanted by the outcome of an ideal heterosexual coupling.

Sedgwick's work is not without criticism, particularly because it relies in part on totalising theories like that of Freud, and it positions gay culture as an object of speculation rather than as a vibrant and living reality. But when *Keeping the Faith* is read against these concepts, new aspects of the film are illuminated. The bond that links Brian and Jake *is* more intense than that which links either of them to Anna. Whilst her relationship with Jake is one factor diminishing the likelihood of desire between the two men, its 'threat' is only fully defused after Brian's sexual 'death' – his decision to reassert his commitment to celibacy. In the film's final scene (a karaoke party to mark the opening of the seniors' centre) reconciliation between the two men is the vital precursor to Anna's arrival at Jake's side. The closing shot – an image of a photograph taken at the party by Jake's mother – depicts Anna looking ahead, and the two men gazing into each other's eyes.

Anna, whose subjectivity is of comparatively little interest to the film, can, then, be read quite convincingly as a device intended to moderate and legitimate the relationship between Brian and Jake. Interestingly, in the first draft of the screenplay, Anna was Brian's sister. If this characterisation had survived the processes of revision, the theme of competition for her love would (presumably) not have been so clearly present in the film. Even so, its very presence at the script's inception underscores the argument that the narrative is structured primarily around the relationship between the two men.

In short, there is more to *Keeping the Faith* than frothy, lightweight comedy. Read this way, the film's nostalgia for the cinema of the past also assumes the character of a hearkening back to older certainties, a symbolic recovery of male power. Despite its seeming celebration of diversity, the film is not interested in the substantive aspects of religions, either separately or in relation. Rather, it offers a conformist fantasy, a suggestion of the wonderful things that can happen when religious structures and heterosexual love are able together to overcome the problematic of male homosocial desire.

VIII

Lagaan
(Ashutosh Gowariker, 2001)

film is especially important for the student of Hinduism[1]
another innovative ploy for feting the nation[2]

Hooray for Bollywood

Chapter VI touched on issues surrounding British Asian identity as inscribed in 1990s cinema. Since that time, Hindi film has emerged as Britain's fastest-growing foreign language cinema, fuelled by growing awareness of Asian cultures amongst non-Asians, a rise in inter-ethnic marriage and British-born Asians' own interest in constructing hyphenated identities that blend the experience of life in Britain with nostalgia for a perhaps never-visited motherland.[3] Changes in film exhibition practice towards the end of the twentieth century also facilitated this rise: programming space for Hindi film has been easier to find in the multiplexes that are now ubiquitous features of the British cityscape. Thus in November 2004 – its release timed to cater for *Diwali* and *Eid* audiences – *Veer Zaara* (Yash Chopra) entered the UK box office charts at the record-breaking position of number four. The fascination for 'Bollywood' (the popular name for the Mumbai-(Bombay-)based industry, producing chiefly Hindi and Urdu features) has in turn influenced Hollywood practice. *Moulin Rouge*'s (Baz Luhrmann, 2001) blend of genres and rich visual style evokes Hindi film, whilst *The Guru's* depiction of cross-cultural confusion gently satirises Western constructions of Indianness (Daisy Von Scherler Mayer, 2002). Gurinder Chadha's 2004 *Bride and Prejudice*, featuring the Bollywood superstar Aishwarya Rai, was funded by the Miramax Corporation.

For students of religion and film, Bollywood presents distinctive problems and rewards. It provides a route into the visual culture that is vital for understanding Hinduism. Conversely, its unique narrative and visual style are a stumbling block to interpretive methods that rest on mistakenly universalised, culturally specific (Christian, Western) assumptions. Drawing a sobering analogy between academic discourse and colonialism, Paul Willemen observes that 'scholars formed within the paradigm of Euro-American film theory are rushing to plant their flags on the terrain of... Indian film'.[4] Cultural studies approaches to film attempt to resist these tendencies and concentrate on interrogating, and being led by, the specific cultural formations (including religious ones) implicated in a particular film.

This chapter, therefore, tries to approach *Lagaan* on its own terms. However, as religious studies students have long been aware, it is unhelpful for any commentator to pretend that she can somehow 'fuse' with the world view of others. *Lagaan's* depiction of Indian village life, its referencing of Hinduism's sacred texts and other stock motifs establish it as a Bollywood film; how readily can viewers steeped in other cinemas appreciate its character? At the same time, the film is modelled partly along Hollywood lines, and enjoyed international success, including an Oscar nomination in 2002. Its narrative structure and period setting allow Western audiences a point of access to *Lagaan* and through it (perhaps) to Indian cinema.[5]

Lagaan is set in central India, in 1893. The villagers of drought-stricken Champaner are required to pay double *lagaan* (tax) imposed by Captain Russell (Paul Blackthorne), the capricious head of the nearby British cantonment. The situation worsens when he catches a young farmer, Bhuvan (Aamir Khan) mocking his beloved game of cricket. Russell decrees that the whole province must now pay triple *lagaan*, unless they can field a cricket team to defeat his own, in a match to be played in three months' time. Victory for the villagers will see their *lagaan* waived for three years. Despite opposition from within Champaner and the wider province, Bhuvan, watched admiringly by his sweetheart Gauri (Gracy Singh) assembles a team. Russell's sister Eliza (Rachel Shelley), impressed by their courage and attracted to Bhuvan, teaches them the game.

When the cricket match is finally played, things begin badly: the British use unsporting tactics, including bodyline bowling and sledging. The villagers spend the eve of the final day's play in prayer at the temple. Numerous twists of fate – or workings of divine providence – inaugurate a reversal in fortunes. Bhuvan scores the winning runs, and the tax is repealed. The much needed rains arrive. Bhuvan marries Gauri, and the final scene shows the British abandoning the cantonment, with Captain Russell headed for an unattractive posting in the African desert.

Clearly, *Lagaan* cannot be readily described using Western genre categories. Essentially, it is a melodrama, with a strong romantic subplot. But it is also a historical film. The villagers' efforts to master cricket offer pretexts for comedy, and the action is punctuated by song and dance sequences. Such blending of entertainments is typical of Indian films.

In Western discourse, melodrama (drama involving the passions of the on-screen characters and the audience, who are addressed primarily on the affective level) is sometimes dismissively conflated with the 'women's picture', but it is fundamental to Bollywood. Vijay Mishra proposes that Hindi film is 'primarily … sentimental melodramatic romance'.[6]

Typically, in *Lagaan* the conflict between good and evil is depicted through characterisation and shot structure. Bhuvan's and Russell's first encounter, in which Bhuvan tries to save the life of a deer that Russell wishes to shoot, delineates the characters and their conflictual relationship. An eyeline match, with Russell aiming a rifle suggests at first that Bhuvan is his intended victim. The Englishman's sadism is swiftly underlined by a verbal threat to kill Bhuvan, and by his casual shooting of a rabbit. The logic of this presentation is that the irredeemable villain must be utterly defeated; he (occasionally, she) is often also ridiculed at the moment of downfall. Thus at the end of the cricket match Russell mistakenly believes that he has caught Bhuvan's winning shot (he has actually taken the catch after stepping over the boundary), and his misplaced, premature celebrations heighten his humiliation.

Such polarisation of good and evil is one factor behind the frequent critical dismissal of Indian film as unrealistic.[7] This assessment is too simplistic. Hindi cinema audiences are not naive: only a small proportion of Bollywood films succeed each year.[8] Whilst the sudden transition from spoken dialogue to song – a practice unfamiliar to many Western viewers, and consequently experienced by them as disruptive of film narrative – is less apparent to Indian audiences, the latter are more likely to apply criteria of verisimilitude to a film's moral universe. Behaviour contravening *dharma* (norms), especially kinship codes, may be dismissed vocally as incredible.[9] In *Lagaan*, as Bhuvan faces the crucial final ball, he is strengthened by memories of loyal Gauri, and his mother – the archetypal foundation of Indian society.

Sexuality is also distinctively encoded in Hindi cinema. Until recently, kissing on screen was unacceptable, and physical intimacy between characters largely taboo. Some of the latest blockbusters (like *Jism*, Amit Saxena, 2003) have been less coy about matters sexual, but many films continue to deploy elaborate visual signs in order to circumvent the 'rules' and suggest an encounter between lovers. In the infamous 'wet sari' device, a sudden rainstorm wets the heroine's costume, revealing her body. (*Monsoon Wedding* (Mira Nair, 2001), popular recently with Western audiences, cleverly exploits the rainy season's erotic associations.) Dream sequences license the depiction of forbidden pleasures, and the 'behind the bush' motif, in which a couple disappear behind a bush or similar object and reappear with the woman rearranging her clothes or hair, or wiping her mouth, also indicates that intimate contact has occurred.

Lagaan deploys these stylistic techniques. Bhuvan and Gauri's relationship encounters its toughest obstacle when Eliza declares her love for Bhuvan (in English words he cannot understand), a statement coinciding with another development that threatens Gauri – the arrival of the final member of the cricket team, from which she, as a woman, is excluded. The subsequent song, 'O Rey Chori' exploits the similarity between 'Gauri' and *gori* (Hindi for 'white woman') and fantasy sequences depict first Eliza, dressed in Gauri's clothes and frolicking with Bhuvan, and then Bhuvan, clothed as an English officer and partnering Eliza at a ball. It is the visual highpoint of the first half of the film. The next sequence reassures viewers as to Bhuvan's feelings for Gauri, by suggesting a physical encounter between them. Gauri (whose braided hair now falls loosely about her shoulders) and then Bhuvan, are shown rising from (importantly, *not* lying together in) a pile of straw. The song's lyrics underline the visual's significance:

GAURI: Should someone ask,
           I will tell them what's happened to me
           My every limb is fragrant because you touched me.

BHUVAN: Your fragrant body
           Your flaming beauty
           You are the rose I see
           How can this allure not awaken my desire?

This section has located *Lagaan* in relation to key aspects of Bollywood cinema, particularly melodrama and romance, the polarisation between good and evil, and song and dance. It has stressed the importance of approaching Indian cinema on its own terms. Film scholarship has rarely taken Bollywood seriously. Arguably, this holds for Indian commentators as much as for Western ones.[10] More recently, scholars (such as those referenced in this chapter) have tried to analyse the origins of Hindi cinema's distinctive character, its representational strategies and its implication in Indian national identity. Commonly identified roots of Indian cinema include Classical (Sanskrit) theatre, which was highly stylised and episodic in structure, placing emphasis on visual spectacle; Parsi (Zoroastrian) theatre, which blended song and dance with action-comedy, and was often castigated as 'melodramatic'; and the Sanskrit epic texts, the *Ramayana* and the *Mahabharata*, which have a long tradition of performance and re-presentation and are foundational for Hindu consciousness.[11]

The influence of the epics, discussed later, is particularly interesting for students of religion and film. *Lagaan*'s recourse to the *Ramayana* for development of theme and ideology is both significant and overt. However, historically speaking there are difficulties associated with theories that over-emphasise the connections between the birth of Indian cinema and indigenous performing traditions, as if there is an essential, timeless 'Indianness', that simply transplanted itself into the new medium; many early film-makers were international in education or outlook.[12]

From a cultural studies perspective, it is also interesting to note that the typically episodic, genre-bending character of Hindi film is closely linked to Bollywood production practices. A feature is normally shot over several periods of a few weeks, which may stretch across a time frame of three years or so. Schedules are subject to funding, in turn dependent on the availability of stars who may work on a dozen films at any given time. Dialogue and background sound are dubbed in a studio after the shoot, and narrative detail, usually undecided at the beginning, emerges gradually during production. A film's character is, then, a reflection of its construction from a set of pre-assembled parts, as much as a distinctive Indian 'heritage'.[13] It is noteworthy that for financial reasons *Lagaan*, which has a much tighter structure than the typical Hindi film (see later), was shot in a single schedule. It also uses synchronised sound (the songs alone are dubbed by playback singers).[14] The importance of considering film as both art form and industry is ever apparent.

Seeing and Believing

Constitutionally India is a secular democracy, but religious traditions shape national identity and the lives of most citizens, especially those in rural areas (nearly three-quarters of the population).[15] Pluralism is a hallmark of Indian society:

> The vast majority of Indians may be Hindus, but we have more than a hundred million Muslims ... we have more Sikhs than any other country, more Jains too, more Parsis as well; India has had Christians for over fifteen hundred years ... and while the number of Indian Buddhists today may be small, ours is the birthplace of Buddhism.[16]

This diversity is reflected in the cinema. For example, Aamir Khan is a Muslim, as is A.R. Rahman (*Lagaan's* music director); Gracy Singh is a Punjabi Sikh. However, Indian film is informed primarily by Hinduism.

The first Indian feature, made by *Brahmin*[17] Dhundiraj Govind Phalke, was *Raja Harischandra* (1913), a screen life of Krishna (the central character of the *Mahabharata*, regarded as an incarnation of the deity Vishnu and the object of many forms of *bhakti* (devotional worship). Phalke was influenced by an early film of the life of Christ, and a strong belief that Hindu mythology must be retold in ways relevant to the modern age.[18]

The 'mythological' continues to enjoy mass appeal in India, as do films portraying the lives of pious individuals. Beginning in 1987, the state television channel, Doordarshan, screened an 87-week serialisation of the *Ramayana*, reflecting and enhancing its familiarity, and coinciding with the escalation of efforts to erect a Ram temple on the site of a mosque in Ayodhya.[19] In a different vein, the presentation of the relationship between a deity and her suffering devotee in *Jai Santoshi Ma* (Vijay Sharma, 1975) established Santoshi Ma as a popular *devi* (deity) among working-class women in urban centres, which are rapidly growing and where knowledge of traditional rituals is decreasing.[20]

Many productions mine the *Ramayana* and the *Mahabharata* for narrative, themes and ideology. The *Ramayana* (*c*.400 BCE–400 CE) is a story of good's triumph over evil as revealed in the life of the Ayodhan prince Rama. Rama is worshipped as an incarnation of Vishnu (one of the most important Hindu deities, the protector-sustainer of the world). As a heroic warrior, conscientious son and noble ruler he also models *dharma*, whilst his consort, Sita, is the ideal selfless wife. The *Mahabharata* (*c*.400 BCE–300 CE) is the longest poem in the world. Ostensibly, it relates an internecine conflict between two royal families, the Pandavas and the Kauravas, but it contains numerous excurses in the form of parables and statements on cosmology, ethics, law, ritual and statecraft. Its most famous passage, the *Bhagavad Gita*, is set on the eve of a great battle, at which moment Krishna (charioteer to Pandavan prince Arjuna) reveals himself as an incarnation of Vishnu, who has descended to

Earth 'for the protection of the good and the destruction of evil-doers'. Krishna's speech emphasises the importance of fulfilling one's *dharma*, and selfless action as the path to spiritual freedom. The *Gita* is widely used as a devotional text and Krishna is worshipped, often with his consort, the *gopi* (milkmaid) Radha.[21] In *Lagaan*, Champaner's temple is dedicated to the couple, simultaneously invoking ideals of devotional lovers and the human soul's quest for union with the divine.

Whilst 'Hinduism' is an umbrella term embracing a plurality of beliefs and ritual practices, the *Ramayana* and *Mahabharata* may justifiably be regarded as universal texts. They are variously transmitted and consumed – performed on stage and screen, and read in many Indian languages. 'They are critiqued, their values challenged, their structures destabilised, even parodied, but they remain foundational nevertheless.'[22] Appeal to these shared myths is one aspect of Bollywood's allure. As film star Amitabh Bachchan, the narrator in *Lagaan*, observes, 'leading men in Hindi cinema are modern manifestations of the great heroes from our two great epics, the *Mahabharat* and the *Ramayana*. They are always invincible and they always win in the end.'[23]

The Radha-Krishna tradition found in the *Mahabharata* and subsequently developed in such works as the *Bhagavata Purana*, is an important intertext for *Lagaan*. For example, in a scene emphasising the Gauri-Bhuvan-Eliza triangle, the three join village celebrations of Krishna's birthday. At first, they all appear in the shot, standing at the temple entrance. Bhuvan explains to Eliza (her curiosity also functions as a vehicle for the mediation of Indian culture to *Lagaan's* Western audiences) that Krishna and Radha were married to others, but their deep love is regarded as an ideal: they are eternally neither united nor separated. At this point, the camera pans to Bhuvan and Eliza alone, implying their identification with the divine lovers, a melodramatic association underlined by the film's closing reference to Eliza (who, the narrator states, will never marry) as 'Bhuvan's Radha'. The following song, however, sees a flute-wielding Bhuvan playing Krishna to *Gauri's* Radha. Whilst she protests his flirtatious behaviour, he says she is his only love, even though he stirs the heart of 'the fairest [whitest] damsel'. This ambiguity resonates, like 'O Rey Chori', with traditional conceptualisations of Krishna's care for his devotees. According to legend, the music of Krishna's flute attracted a crowd of *gopis*. He demonstrated the infiniteness of his love by appearing to dance with each of them individually, paralleling the possibility for any devotee to enter into union with god.

It is not only in relation to romance that *Lagaan* invokes Hinduism's sacred texts. The narrative's links to Sanskrit tradition, and the association of its hero with Krishna, establish the Hindu in a position of authority over the diverse Indian community.[24] However, before considering such aspects of *Lagaan* it is important to discuss the concept of *darśan* in relation to Hindi cinema, and the screen representation and mediation of religious experience.

Darśan – experiencing the presence of the divine through the act of seeing an image of a god or saint – is an important form of Hindu worship. Crucially, *darśan* is a 'two-way look'. In Hindu thought, the deity presents itself to be seen in its image, and so 'gives' *darśan* as well as receiving it. For the devotee's sake, the deity 'dwells' in an image, helping the worshipper to grasp the infinite.[25]

Hinduism is, then, an image-making tradition, with relatively little notion of the divine as being beyond representation. Whereas early Western film-makers encountered difficulties in portraying a moving Christ, Hindi cinema does not have such problems – some temples have statues of gods with moving limbs and voices. In addition to helping explain the relative confidence of film-makers in approaching mythological subjects, the concept of *darśan* illuminates various aspects of the popular Indian cinema experience.[26]

Like some other human figures (especially kings and religious leaders), film stars may give and receive *darśan*. This happens most obviously when actors appear in the role of deities, or play characters iconographically or ideologically equated with gods (such as Bhuvan in *Lagaan*). The potential in such instances for the distance between sign and referent (that is, the actor and the deity to which they refer) to collapse (so that a star's own personality is popularly invested with qualities attributed to the deity) is one factor contributing to the successful careers of some actors as political 'heroes', especially in South India. It is not unknown for such careers to be launched by campaigns during which the star-candidate dresses as a mythological figure, although few have temples dedicated to their deified selves, as happened posthumously to Maradur Gopalamenon Ramachandran.[27]

More generally, actors are implicated in *darśan* to the extent that, like deities, they are active agents, inviting and permitting the audience's gaze. Such an understanding of the screen image as a benevolent power-holder contrasts with many Western theorisations of 'the gaze' or 'the look,' which typically associate the position of the audience with voyeurism and emphasise the potential for actors to be objectified or reified by the camera. *Darśan*, as dynamic, *mutual* exchange, suggests that the meanings of screen images are negotiated between parties.

There are other senses, too, in which *darśan* is relevant for a consideration of the screen representation and mediation of religious experience. The question of a transcendental cinematic style, or a religious aesthetic, has been a recurring theme in this book; a critical tendency to equate spirituality with sparse visual style has been regularly observed. In Chapter III this position is associated with the writing of Paul Schrader, and in Chapter IV with critics who have castigated the genre of the Hollywood biblical epic. A similar position is outlined in Coates's study of the impact of Romantic ideas about religion in Polish cinema.[28] *Darśan*, with its stress on the capacity for the visual to stimulate rather than subdue the religious imagination, differently proposes that,

> spectacle is not…in itself a derogatory category. Its sensuous, visual, evocative quality definitely has the potential to convey pleasure of an aesthetic, emotional, and even mental-intellectual kind. In its cinematic form and combined with a rigorous, historical, social and cultural insight, spectacle can communicate the truth of human experience in vivid, perceptual and cognitive terms.[29]

Such statements are reminders of the dangers associated with interpretations that generalise from the particular, and highlight the need to investigate films in relation to their own differentiated contexts of religious (and other) meaning-making.

Unity and Diversity

Hindu tradition is influential in *Lagaan*, but Bhuvan's cricket team is drawn from an assortment of religions and castes, and might be interpreted as advocating pluralism. How are these potentially contradictory impulses managed in the film?

Questions about the relation of religion and national identity are at the forefront of contemporary Indian politics. In 1984, campaigns for an autonomous Sikh state resulted in the Golden Temple siege at Amritsar; Indira Gandhi's decision to use the army against the militants triggered a wave of killings, and her own assassination. Since 1990, violence between Hindus and Muslims has increased (especially conflict generated by the Ayodhya controversy, and disputes over Kashmir) as have anti-Christian assaults, prompting some to fear for India's secular democracy and religiously plural culture.[30]

Thus contextualised, *Lagaan* emerges as an assertion of a moderate, optimistic vision. The members of Champaner's cricket team represent various interdependent population groups. Of particular interest is Ismail, the potter. At first sceptical, he joins the team, having recognised the survival of the whole community to be at stake. Dialogue emphasises his Islamic piety and loyalty, and prefigures his willingness to take to the crease in the final match, despite injury, as he asserts:

> It is Allah's command. We must be with him [Bhuvan].
> I swear by God ... I am with you.
> It is the word of a man of prayer.

Similarly important is Deva Singh Sodhi. A Sikh, his joining the team signals a turning point in its fortunes, since having served in the British army he has played cricket before. The articulation of Ismail's and Deva's personalities and contributions in part reflects narrative conventions. The foregrounding of the special skills brought to the team in turn by each member – Hindu, Sikh or Muslim – plays out a cliché popularised internationally by *The Magnificent Seven* (John Sturges, 1960) and its inspiration, Akira Kurosawa's *The Seven Samurai* (1954). It also has political overtones. *Lagaan's* inclusion of

Sikh and Muslim argues that inter-religious cooperation has deeper roots than the current geopolitical tensions might otherwise suggest. The interdependence of faiths is not a modernist fiction, or a dilution of identity, but the historical basis for Indian success.

The issue of caste, the inherited and hierarchical (but not static) status categories to which Indians traditionally belong, is interwoven with that of religion.[31] Historically, one's caste was determinative of education, employment and other life chances. Since independence, India's constitution has outlawed the disabilities associated with caste, but inequalities persist and positive discrimination in favour of members of lower and 'unscheduled' castes or *dalits* ('down-trodden'; formerly, *shudras* or 'untouchables') are controversial. Hinduism and caste are inextricably linked (for example, as noted earlier, public interpretation of the Sanskrit scriptures was formerly the preserve of *Brahmin* castes) but not coextensive. Non-Hindu Indians also belong to castes. So, caste conflicts are sometimes displaced onto religion, and vice versa.

The relation of caste and religion is too complex and sensitive a problem for *Lagaan* to address directly in detail. But in the figure of Kachra, *Lagaan* deploys the supreme icon of caste oppression – the 'untouchable'. Kachra suffers social and physical disability. He is first seen on the margins of the community, and since his right arm is partially paralysed, he embodies the inequalities conferred by his caste status. However, Bhuvan accidentally discovers that Kachra's disability makes him a natural spin bowler. Like that of team member Goli, whose bowling action is based on his experience with a slingshot, Kachra's character is probably inspired by well-known and highly successful Asian spinners like Bhagwhat Chandreksekhar, who was disabled by polio as a child, and Muttiah Muralitharan, a Sri Lankan bowler cited for throwing (and subsequently cleared), whose unusual action is attributed to a congenital condition.

In the *Lagaan* match, Kachra takes crucial wickets and turns the fortunes of the game on its final day. His role within what is a proto-independence movement resonates with much mainstream Indian rhetoric in which statehood has been posited as a solution to caste-linked problems.[32] Yet initially, skills are not sufficient to win Kachra's entry to the team. Led by Lakha (who later emerges as a traitor) the others refuse to play with him, citing fear of ritual pollution.

Significantly, Bhuvan justifies Kachra's inclusion in a speech blending contemporary rights discourse and reference to Hindu mythology:

> You brand people untouchable and pollute humanity. You choke the air in our village with this caste division. Is it right to shatter hearts in the name of skin colour? Then why worship Ram, who ate a tribal's half eaten berries? The Lord himself was ferried by a low-caste boatman, and yet you talk of untouchables!

Tradition is at once questioned and upheld; *Dharmik* values are challenged by appeal to Hindu conservatism's iconic text.

However, is *Lagaan's* vision straightforwardly pluralist? Whereas the film depicts numerous different, more-or-less rounded Hindu characters, rooting them in domestic contexts and relationships (Gauri and her father; Bhuvan and his mother), Ismail and Deva are described in superficial terms, and are more (stereo)types than individual personalities.[33] Ismail's identity is defined by his name, his wearing of the white *hajji* hat, and a vocabulary marked by references to prayer and Allah's will. Before Deva's name and face are known, the Five Ks that identify him as a *keshdhari* Sikh are fetishised. The camera pans slowly upwards, from his feet and bangle-clad wrist (revealed as he stoops to pick up the cricket ball) to his legs and torso (as he straightens his body) and finally to a dagger neck-pendant, a beard and a blue turban. It is only some time later, after bowling a ball that shatters the stumps, that Deva speaks.

This presentation, like his declared desire 'to be in every battle against the British', suggests taciturn, controlled aggression and plays on popular associations of Sikhism with militarism. Its roots are partly historical: deeming Sikhs a 'martial race' innately suited to fighting, the British used them as agents of control, and many joined the army during imperial rule.[34] However, just as Ismail remains two-dimensional, in the absence of further development of Deva's personality, *Lagaan* does not critique, but participates in, the colonialist othering of a religious minority.

Similarly, *Lagaan* critiques caste-based inequality, but never really moves to depict Kachra as an autonomous agent. Bhuvan does not invite Kachra to join the team, but declares him to be a member. When other players rebel, it is Bhuvan who exhorts them to work together. The earlier quotation from his speech catches its flavour, and reveals *Lagaan's* tendency to project wider political and social debates onto the issue of untouchability. From a critical perspective, the denial of Kachra's voice is especially striking given that today *dalits* provide the clearest example of a group that has become acutely conscious of its history, and seeks to articulate a distinct identity.

The film's preference for Bhuvan over Kachra (or Ismail or Deva) is indicative of the former's pivotal role within *Lagaan*. Throughout, Bhuvan appears as a leader and a reconciler of differences. Arguably, it is not religious or cultural pluralism per se that *Lagaan* celebrates, but Bhuvan's openness and flexibility. It is his acceptance of Russell's wager that draws the villagers into the cricket match – a dangerous gamble, but also one promising relief from punitive taxation – and it is he who finally scores the winning run. Between these two moments, Bhuvan's personality is the force drawing his fellow Indians together. His creativity enables him to seek out some team members, and welcome others, recognising in each their potential contribution. He is a moderating presence when he corrects Deva's condemnation of all Britons, telling him that Eliza is on the villagers' side. And when Lakha's treacherous collaboration with Russell (motivated by Lakha's desire to destroy Bhuvan and win Gauri's love; reminiscent of contemporary cricket match-fixing scandals) is discovered, it is Bhuvan who restrains the angry mob of villagers and negotiates a solution. Significantly, this scene is set in the temple, with its garlanded terracotta figures of Krishna and Radha in prominent view.

Repeated associations of Bhuvan with the Sanskrit epic heroes, and his appearance at the temple at key narrative moments, underline the extent to which, despite the attempt to offer in *Lagaan* a celebration of the human spirit,[35] the film privileges a Hindu perspective. Bhuvan's character presents Hindu identity positively, as a blending of conservativism (illustrated by his honouring of kinship ties and his occupation as a farmer, a profession linking him literally and symbolically with the land) with the ability to adapt creatively to new situations. The film does not portray the different religious and social groups in equal terms, but celebrates the integrative capacity of the Hindu. In short, it offers him to viewers as the icon of integral nationalism.

It's Not the Taking Part, It's the Winning That Counts

'My films are *Swadeshi* ['home-grown', literally 'own country'] in the sense that the capital, ownership, employees and stories are all *Swadeshi*.'[36] Phalke's famous dictum highlights the interrelation of film text and context, and more specifically, the cinema's importance for Indian national expression. The birth of the Indian film industry coincided with that of modern nationalism in the country, and its post-Second World War boom, with the acquisition of statehood. Perhaps inevitably then, many films explore questions surrounding Indian-ness and 'belonging'.

A preoccupation with national politics is readily apparent in the many 1950s films that lionise individuals who sacrifice personal happiness for the greater good. In *Mother India* (Mehboob Khan, 1957) poverty-stricken Radha kills her lawless son for the sake of the community. Similar themes may be detected in more recent productions. The eponymous *Mr. India* (Shekhar Kapur, 1987) is both Indian 'everyman' and a superhero who thwarts an attempt to destroy his country with nuclear weapons. The controversial 'social' film, *Bombay* (Mani Ratnam, 1995), is a story about the lives of a mixed Hindu-Muslim family, during the intercommunal violence of 1992. *Pardes* (Subhash Ghai, 1997) compares the experiences of Indians living in India and North America, and, in its narrative preference for a chaste 'love match' over an unsuitable arranged marriage, intersects with contemporary debates about women's rights. Similar themes emerge in *Monsoon Wedding*'s treatment of love and family.

As a period drama about a group of Indian villagers who use the colonials' own game to defeat them – or rather, defeat them after realising that the 'game' is nothing more than their own *golli danda* (a well-known street game) in a different idiom – *Lagaan* is inevitably a political film. Although its narrative is fictional, the 1890s was a decade of famine-related suffering, during which some rural Indians withheld their taxes.[37] For the historically aware, *'lagaan'* remains a resonant term, especially in the north of India.

Lagaan's portrayal of the Raj is comparatively unusual for Hindi film, which generally eschews costume drama, whilst its presentation of the point of view of the colonised distinguishes it from the imperial visions projected by British and Hollywood films of the 1930s and 1940s.[38] (In more recent decades this once popular genre was parodied for Western audiences in *Carry on ... up the Khyber's* story of British attempts to guard India's north-west frontier (Gerald Thomas, 1968) and was differently inverted in *Gandhi* (Richard Attenborough, 1983).)

Lagaan presents the colonials as an alien presence on Indian soil. In the opening minutes of the film, the occupier–occupied distinction is quickly constructed with reference to the temple, the literal and ideological centre of Champaner. The first image of Champaner's residents shows them leaving the shrine, and establishing shots organise the village along a single main track running from the bottom to the top of the frame, and leading up to the temple. When the British troops first appear in Champaner, they march from right to left across the frame, disregarding the village (and the logic of the shot). As they pass, village children call, 'lippit, ret, lippit, ret', a parodic counterpoint to the army drill ('left, right, left, right') which underscores colonialism's lack of fit with the rhythms of Indian life.

As *Lagaan* develops, the images of villagers' dignified poverty contrasts with British decadence and self-indulgence. Russell first doubles the *lagaan* after failing to force the Maharajah to eat meat, an incident revealing his sadism yet also prefiguring his ultimate impotence in the face of Indian tradition, exemplified here by dietary habits. Eliza, although a positive figure, breaks Indian and Victorian British mores by disobeying her brother, and declaring her love for Bhuvan. None of the British characters display any sympathy for religion, save Eliza who, as discussed earlier, is briefly a participant-observer in a Hindu temple rite.

The film also hints critically at colonialism's motivations. The images that begin the opening title sequence evoke the themes of chance and gaming; they also link political ambition with financial expediency. A rupee coin, spinning on a map of India, lands 'heads' side up to reveal a picture of the British Queen and the phrase 'Victoria, Empress'. This motif, and its associations, recur later in the film. The coin reappears in the toss at the start of the cricket match, with Russell calling 'heads'. When Lakha plots with Russell in his study, the camera (evoking Lakha's point of view) dwells on a model ship that bears a plaque identifying it as a gift from the East India Company, and a medium close-up shows Russell's head and shoulders against a backdrop filled entirely by a union flag hanging on the wall.

It is on the cricket pitch, where Russell's side are consistently unsporting, that the film's anti-colonialism is played out most consistently. The British indulge in sledging, and they bowl bodyline, although this technique was only introduced much later, in the 1932–33 Ashes series. At one point, Russell instructs bowler Yardley to 'knock his [Lakha's] bloody head off', and Bhuvan himself is injured on the ear.

However, just as notions of *swadeshi* have shifted, so that even the Hindu rightist Bharatiya Janeta Party (BJP) leader Atal Bihari Vajpayee redefined it as 'anything that promotes ... [strengthening] India's economic base',[39] so *Lagaan's* anti-colonialist rhetoric is pretty modest. This may be a reflection of the relative lack of real animosity to the British in India today. It also helps to account for the successful reception of the film internationally, and may owe something to a growing awareness of the importance of the Western box office.

The British umpires are determinedly neutral in exercising their duties. The contrast between their concern for fair play and Russell's all-consuming desire to subjugate the villagers implicitly suggests that the colonial project is as much a threat to British values as it is to Indian ones. Eliza's support for Bhuvan's team is motivated by similar ideals, at least initially. Finally, a scene in which Russell is summoned to appear before three critical senior officers suggests that they consider his behaviour at best irregular: during the cricket match, they politely applaud the Indian successes.

The film's pragmatic approach to colonialism has its counterpart in *Lagaan's* blending of elements of Hollywood and Hindi film style.

Although it is a multi-genre picture, *Lagaan* is less episodic than most Bollywood films, and is in some respects not far removed from features discussed elsewhere in this book, as in *The Ten Commandments* or *Keeping the Faith*. The narrative is a linear sequence of events organised according to the logic of cause-and-effect. The songs are more thoroughly integrated into the narrative than is usual, and most serve to communicate the thoughts and emotions of characters, or to underline dramatic themes, as one might find in a 1950s Hollywood musical. Because of the decision to shoot the film using synchronised sound, the dialogue is more realistic in tone, with the actors 'doing very little in front of the camera'.[40] Finally, *Lagaan* is notable for its efforts to show the passage of time in fashion and other aspects of material culture: in many Indian films, characters wear contemporary clothing even when the action is set in the past.

Significantly for religion and film work, *Lagaan*'s pragmatic blending of Hindi style with Hollywood extends to its treatment of the supernatural.[41] The film's narrative offers competing accounts of the villagers' success that are intelligible and acceptable in terms of both popular Hindu and secular elite and/or Western expectations. The villagers' cause is aided by a series of unforeseen events, which become increasingly frequent as the cricket match progresses. Thus, in the final over, Bhura seems to lose his wicket, but the umpires rule that he has been caught off a no-ball; Russell catches Bhuvan off the final ball, but only after stepping beyond the boundary line.

From a secular perspective, these events may be read as simply fortuitous. Moreover, the team's success is at least partly attributable to its preparation for the match, which has been characterised by rational process: its members are recruited on the basis of their possession of appropriate skills, and they have all participated in a three-month programme of fitness and cricket training. However, the film also acknowledges Bollywood conventions, creating the potential for moments of good fortune to be read as instances of divine intervention. On the eve of the final day's play, with five wickets lost and 323 runs needed for victory, the villagers turn to Krishna in prayer:

BHUVAN'S MOTHER: O Saviour
O Pure of Essence
Our dearly beloved
O Saviour
O Pure of Essence
We have no one but you
Ease our troubles O Lord
We have no one but you

GAURI: You alone are our sole support
You alone are our protector
We have no one but you

These opening verses accompany a shot structure that reflects the activity of (and invites the audience to participate in?) *darśan*. Alternating shots show first the images of Krishna and Radha (as if from the point of view of the women worshipping at the temple's entrance), and then return the gaze to the women themselves. The song lyrics stress the villagers' absolute dependence on their divine protector. From a secular standpoint it articulates their desperation, but it also paves the way for more traditionally minded viewers to interpret the match result as the answer to prayer.

As in its handling of political and religious issues more generally, *Lagaan* negotiates a careful middle path in relation to faith and miracle. The film attempts to hold in tension unity with diversity, myth with history, and the supernatural with the rational.

Reception

Lagaan won awards in eight categories at the 2002 Indian National Film Awards (including Best Popular Film Providing Wholesome Entertainment), received a nomination for the Best International Film Oscar, and was popular at home and overseas. In the UK it took more than $1.4 million in its first month.[42] These facts are remarkable, given the lack of recognition typically accorded to popular Hindi cinema in the West, the early financing difficulties – stemming partly from the unusual subject matter, and partly from Gowariker's reputation as a director whose career was 'going nowhere' – that dogged the film's production,[43] and the obscurity of cricket in the American market. To investigate why the film succeeded it is necessary to gain a fuller sense of *Lagaan* as a cultural artefact, by looking at its international reception.

All the major Indian newspapers publish regular reviews and other film-related articles. Writing in *The Hindu* in June 2001, reviewer Ziya Us Salam suggested that the film would be popular because it was a canny exploitation of Bollywood convention. Whilst *Lagaan's* plot was 'paper thin', it made 'the best possible use of three factors which guide our nation – cricket, patriotism and romance. All these woven to tuneful music.'[44]

Similarly positive but differently oriented evaluation was offered in India's film magazines. Film periodicals have been published in India since the 1930s. As Rachel Dwyer notes, some of the most well-known ones are written in English, a characteristic that reflects marketing needs and resonates with their presentation of Hindi cinema as a site of glamour and aspiration. The magazines appeal to the upwardly mobile middle classes, who either speak English as their first language or aspire to speak it fluently. Their language follows its own conventions, with a heavy emphasis on humorous wordplay relating to the themes of desire and love, but the magazines ultimately convey a chaste, essentially conservative message about family values and the work ethic.[45]

Articles on *Lagaan* that appeared in *Cinéblitz* (launched in 1974; circulation 80,000) illustrate these tendencies effectively. For example, a promotional interview with Gracy Singh is titled, '"I was passionately involved...": Gracy on Aamir and *Lagaan.*' The headline suggests an off-screen romance between the lead actors, paralleling the one between their characters in the film. Such a relationship would be transgressive, since Aamir Khan was married to Reena Datta at the time (the couple subsequently divorced).[46] But the content of the article, in which Singh describes the experience of filming in rural Bhuj, her status as a newcomer to the film industry, and extolls the virtues of Khan as a meticulous film-maker, are far less remarkable.

Sensationalism and bourgeois values are also juxtaposed in Purnima Lamchhane's 'Aamir's Crazy Obsession'. In this article,

Khan is identified with the values and qualities to which *Cinéblitz* readers might be expected to aspire: he is a family man, a lover of good food and someone who treats his employees with decency. Like many other Indian pieces, Lamchhane's also stresses the challenge of filming *Lagaan* in the 'barren desserts' [*sic*] of Bhuj. Although the film itself encourages viewers to regard Champaner as a figure for the nation as a whole, for *Cinéblitz* readers the Indian village is, ideologically as well as geographically speaking, far removed from their urban, internationalised context.[47]

Although *The Telegraph*'s reviewer described the film as anti-British and said that Khan should be ashamed about his involvement,[48] this was not typical of mainstream review responses. Most responded positively, and the box office figures in Britain suggest that it was also popular with audiences, but inevitably the film was interpreted in ways differing from those outlined by the Indian sources.

Contrary to the intention of the film-makers, British audiences, for example, were consistently amused by the sight of Rachel Shelley miming a playback singer's voice in 'O Rey Chori'.[49] (Interestingly, the Indian actors are also dubbed, but their performances did not meet with a similar response.) Because of the general lack of knowledge of Hindi (and other Asian) film in the West, most commentators inevitably touched on *Lagaan's* efforts to position itself in relation to the international as well as the domestic market. Two reviews in *Sight and Sound*, for example, noted the film's blending of Bollywood with Western film convention.[50]

A similar approach characterises North American reviews. Roger Ebert described *Lagaan* as 'a memory of the films we all grew up on'. In *Village Voice*, Ed halter likened Gracy Singh to a 'silent-era starlet' and argued that '*Lagaan* may be high-concept Bollywood but it plays like well-crafted old Hollywood' – remarks that at once praise the film and position Indian cinema as backward or outmoded.[51] Discussion of *Lagaan* frequently elided into general comments on Hindi cinema as, say, non-realist or 'genre-mangling', a practice that may support the suggestion made earlier in this chapter: namely, that the film functions as an entry point to Bollywood for non-Indian viewers.[52]

In 2002, the initial flurry of coverage surrounding *Lagaan's* release in the latter half of 2001 was succeeded by publicity associated with its nomination for an Academy Award. In a subtle piece of pre-Oscars analysis, Ajit Duara suggested,

> No one can resist a Radha-Krishna love story with a beautiful Englishwoman as Radha ... Also, the tragic Victorian ending to the possible romance...would be reassuring to the traditionalists in the audience. Attraction between races is one thing, the cultural consequences of a relationship quite another.[53]

There is an ironic and ambivalent edge to this assessment: on the one hand, *Lagaan* is seen as a reworking of a narrative with universal appeal; on the other hand, its culturally specific nature is acknowledged ('no one can resist ... with a beautiful Englishwoman'). The film's ambiguous attitude to religious and cultural pluralism is described as echoing that of the largely North American Academy members: as Duara notes, like *Keeping the Faith*, *Lagaan* flirts with, but does not realise, the idea of inter-communal romance.

After the ceremony, Indian commentators also discussed the reasons for *Lagaan's* failure (a film about the Balkan conflict, *No Man's Land* (Danis Tanovic, 2001), eventually took the Award for Best International Film), and acted to reassert the film's qualities. Comparing *Lagaan* with other Indians who did not receive the highest levels of recognition internationally, Shiva Kiran asked, 'Does Gandhiji need Nobel? Does Sachin need a Wisden certification? No, a Nobel needs a Gandhiji, Wisden needs Sachin, national awards need Aamir. So, *Lagaan* does not need an Oscar. An Oscar needs a *Lagaan.*'[54]

Kiran's placement of *Lagaan* alongside a pantheon of Asian greats – Mahatma Gandhi, cricketer Sachin Tendulkar and Aamir Khan himself – touches on a theme crucial for an understanding of the film's resonances for modern Indian audiences. *Lagaan* has a nostalgic quality, not simply because it deals with the past, but also because of the values it espouses, its appeal to cricket (a sport still popular in South Asia, but not as phenomenally as was the case a generation ago) and its celebration of the Indian village.

Whereas many contemporary Hindi films reflect the problematisation of Indianness in the modern state, *Lagaan* evokes a more confident age, when the threats to communal integrity were primarily external ones, and Hinduism exercised an integrative function, rather than a potentially divisive one. As Gowri Ramnarayan observes, '*Lagaan* renewed the nation's hope and faith in itself'.[55]

IX

Conclusions

The screen is dominated by a close up of Jesus' (Jim Caviezel's) face, its flesh criss-crossed with lacerations. One eye is swollen shut, and the other bloodshot after numerous beatings. Jesus is lying on the ground. About him, a mob rages. With a rasping breath, he reaches out towards the cross, which lies close by. His cherishing touch suggests a tactile pleasure is to be found in its surfaces. His blood mingles with the dust on the ground and the grain of the wood. Jesus strains forward and embraces the cross: it is a moment of sensuality and intimacy, before the deathwards journey resumes.

This brief, striking scene is emblematic of *The Passion of The Christ*. The film invites viewers to embrace, visually and emotionally, the horror of Jesus' final hours, in a way that is perhaps more akin to the days of silent cinema than to the intellectualising positions of recent Jesus films such as *The Last Temptation of Christ* (Martin Scorsese, 1988) or *Jesus of Montreal* (Denys Arcand, 1989). Its style and the use of ancient languages (Aramaic and Latin dialogue, learned phonetically by the actors), which forces most viewers to rely on subtitles, bespeak a commitment to the visual, 'to telling the story with pure imagery and expressiveness as much as anything else'.[1]

Gone from this cinema of attractions is the gospel picture of Jesus as a prolific teacher and healer. In its place the scourging of Jesus, passed over in a single clause by the Synoptic Gospels, occupies around 20 of *The Passion*'s 126 minutes, during which the camera's attention alternates between the lacerations inflicted by the canes and *flagrum* (cat-o'-nine-tails), the enjoyment of the increasingly blood-splattered soldiers, and the mixed reactions of those who make up the crowd of onlookers.

From pre-production onwards, scholars of religion and interfaith activists alike were quick to voice doubts about *The Passion*. As noted in Chapter II, central to their concerns was the film's violence, and more specifically its participation in antisemitism, a charge fuelled by Mel Gibson's refusal to criticise in public his father Hutton Gibson's claims that the Holocaust was exaggerated, and his own traditionalist Catholicism (which celebrates the Latin Tridentine Mass and rejects the Second Vatican Council and with it *Nostra Aetate*, the promulgation that sought to reverse the Church's ancient 'teaching of contempt' for Jews and Judaism).[2] *The Passion* was also criticised by lesbian and gay groups, for its portrayal of Herod Antipas as a decadent and effeminate homosexual. Yet audiences flocked to see the film. At the time of writing it is the tenth highest-grossing film and the highest-grossing R-rated film of all time in the USA.[3]

What was it about *The Passion* that appealed to viewers? Narrative analysis of the kind still dominant in religion and film (and in the distinct but related field of theology and film) alone cannot provide the answer to this question. Gibson's film did not secure its audiences on the basis of a Christian storyline. As recently as 2003 another faith-motivated production, Philip Saville's *The Gospel of John*, narrated by Christopher Plummer, made little impact.

Similarly, whilst in popular discourse this is often the standard against which to measure a biblical film (see Chapter IV) *The Passion* was not characterised by 'fidelity' to the gospel texts' accounts of Jesus' trial and death, nor to the teachings of a large religious movement. Mel Gibson openly acknowledged that his film addressed the New Testament through the meditations of Anne Catherine Emmerich, an eighteenth-century German mystic.[4] And whilst Gibson belongs to a traditionalist Catholic church, the film found popularity with mainstream Catholics, Protestants and other Christians. To those engaged in religious studies in Western higher education contexts, some of the significance of this 'ecumenism' may be lost. But it is important to note that amongst the vocal champions of *The Passion* were conservative evangelical individuals, and publications in whose pages one might ordinarily expect to find denunciations of the Catholic church as non-Christian.

Gibson's successes in exploiting as a marketing point the furore surrounding the film's participation in antisemitism has been well documented.[5] Arguably, another factor in *The Passion*'s commercial success was its acknowledgement of the importance of seeing for believing – an awareness that experience and identity is constituted with (and not outside) imagery, and one that takes us to the heart of religion-film relationships, as elucidated in this book.

The Passion of The Christ is not simply 'about' the final 12 hours of Jesus of Nazareth's life. At times, it does assume a didactic stance: an experienced soldier's need to instruct his juniors on the correct method of nailing a man to a cross is a narrative innovation serving to license the audience's 'education' on the same subject.

However, the film's dominant preoccupation is with the importance of witnessing and bearing witness to what, for Gibson, is the saving suffering of his God. Accordingly, whilst the film borrows many flourishes from the horror genre[6] – the full moon and smoky sky in the opening Garden of Gethsemene scene; the monstrous children who hound Judas to suicide – it departs from classic horror conventions in its determination not to suggest, but to display in long takes (punctuated by dialogue with lessening frequency as the story moves towards the crucifixion itself), the detail of the various tortures inflicted on its central character. Many of its specifics (the various falls; the encounters with Mary, Veronica and so on) are derived from Catholic tradition, including the Stations of the Cross and the Sorrowful Mysteries of the Rosary.[7] The ways in which events are depicted also owes much to these rituals. Thus each fall scene is dialogue-free and shot in slow motion, lending the screen images an iconic quality. They become, like the Stations, a series of pictures or tableaux intended to elicit a response of faith.

If Gibson wants audiences to look at suffering, he also wants to suggest to them the importance of the gaze. This is, above all, modelled for viewers in the activity of Mary. One of the most important features of *The Passion* is the way her face continually changes and reacts to the events. Other figures from Christian, particularly Catholic, tradition are also shown patterning the look, especially Veronica (who is shown mopping Jesus' face with her handkerchief on the way to Golgotha – she also models the veneration of relics) and Simon Peter, as does Antipas' African servant, who seemingly 'recognises' Jesus as the Christ in one exchange of glances.[8] The scene in which the importance of the look is most obviously encoded is the deposition from the cross. A dialogue-free image, styled as a classic *pietà*, invites the audience not just to see Mary cradling the dead body of Jesus but to be seen by her, as she gazes directly into the camera. The striking and overtly reciprocal nature of the look in this scene implies an exchange between viewer and viewed that possesses a dynamic quality akin to that of *darśan*. *this is a stretch*

The importance of the look for *The Passion* touches on what has been a recurring question throughout this book: what constitutes a 'religious film'? Some treatments of this question, acknowledging the limitations of narrative as a criterion, have attempted to isolate a particular visual quality, which, it is argued, imputes sacredness to a film. As described in Chapter III, Schrader advances the notion of a transcendental style based on an aesthetics of sparsity. He suggests that austerity in the cinema may bring viewers to a sense of the limitations of their own subjectivities, and point suggestively towards that which lies beyond (the transcendent). Coates similarly links sacralisation with anti-realism, specifically a rejection of a desire to represent the details of religious experience or (in a Christian context) salvation history.[9]

Realism is not without danger, especially when, as in the reception of *My Son the Fanatic*, it is mistaken for reality. But *The Passion* seemingly challenges the certainties of Schrader and others who are sceptical of the abilities of popular cinema to act as a vehicle for the spiritual. Stylistically, the film combines elements of the stasis of films like *La Passion de Jeanne d'Arc* with the excesses present in *The Ten Commandments* or *The Wicker Man*.

Visually quite different productions can, then, be sites of religious meaning; a recognition that forces attention back to the importance of the cultural contexts of production and reception. Whereas films like *The Wicker Man*, *My Son the Fanatic* and *Keeping the Faith* are less interested in the religious experience of the characters depicted, or of the audiences who watch them, exegesis has revealed their complex implication in the social and political dimensions of religious belief and practice. Religious adherents, many of whom regard their traditions as set apart, *sui generis*, might object to such cinematic treatments that may seemingly reduce religions, stripping them of their aura, but for practitioners of religious studies religion cannot be separated from culture. There is no culture-free mode of religious experience or expression (which is *not* to say that religion is the same as culture).

In a manner that goes beyond the activity of much contemporary work on religion and film, some early theorists were interested in relating the ontological status of the cinematic image (as that which displays or makes present what is an absent reality) to viewer activity as akin to, but not identical with, that entailed in religious experience.

For Jean Epstein (introduced in Chapters II and IV) cinema was distinguished from the other arts by virtue of its capacity on occasion to prompt intense affectivity, something he termed *photogénie*. As an intensely experienced moment, when one is overwhelmed by the screen image, *photogénie* is personal, subjective and essentially indescribable. Epstein's description at times comes close to classic articulations of the nature of religious experience. As such it is unsupportable theoretically,[10] but it retains value insofar as it is an invocation of the power of screen images and of the significance of the viewer's role. From this perspective, we do not just see objects on the screen, we see in them and through them:

> the memories and emotions, the projects or the regrets which we have attached to these things for a more or less lengthy time, sometimes for forever ... this is the cinematic mystery: an object ... reveals anew its moral character, its human and living expression when reproduced cinematically.[11]

171

What memories, emotions, projects and regrets are at play in *The Passion's* success? What was it about the film that resonated for audiences? Ironically, the furore that dogged the film from pre-production onwards may be a factor here. In the early twenty-first century many (American) Christians feel themselves to be embattled, under threat internationally and at home, from ideologically motivated terrorists and the liberal left. In such a context, *The Passion's* Jesus, a strong heroic figure who endures extreme suffering but ultimately emerges triumphant, promises much. (I have elsewhere suggested that *The Passion's* resurrection evokes *The Terminator* films.[12]) The campaigns to have the film modified, or boycotted, served to establish its credentials for some Christian audiences, unhappy with historical criticism's inroads into gospel faith and with liberal censuring of the conviction to preach the good news to the nations, and to establish a more securely defined role for Christian values in civic life. *The Passion of The Christ* became at once a marker of Christian identity, a medium through which audiences could proclaim and mark their affiliation.[13]

The film became a piece of event cinema, in which the decision to go to or to stay away from the movie theatre became almost as important as what was on the screen itself.

At the beginning of this book I challenged the assumption that cinema should be seen as an agent of secularisation, and questioned the extent to which academic practitioners have been able to achieve their oft-touted goal of 'dialogue' between the realms of religion and film. However the studies in subsequent chapters, and the fates and fortunes of *The Passion of The Christ*, suggest that a more radical revision of approaches is required. The dialogue metaphor, like the elision of mediatisation into secularisation, implies that 'religion' and 'film' are discrete entities – a position that is hard to sustain on closer analysis. As illustrated in Chapter IV, it is easy both to demonstrate and to dismiss the idea that religion and film may hold in common a number of functions. Leaving aside any ready correspondences it is possible to query the religion/film distinction, not on the basis of functionalism but rather on the basis of religious studies' growing interest, under the influence of cultural studies, in the articulation of what many religious adherents have known all along; namely that 'religion' is not a 'thing' but a mode of being.

The determining factor in what makes a religious film does not, then, rest with narrative or stylistic elements of the film text itself. Rather, 'religious film' is better understood as a process, a function of a dynamic exchange between screen images and sound, and viewer activity and perception. Just as identity is constituted with, and not outside, representation, so film can at times be not simply a descriptor of, or a vehicle for, religious experience, but religion itself.

Notes

I Preface

1 Carol Summerfield and Penny Babb (eds), *Social Trends*, 34, London: Stationery Office, 2004, p.201.

2 Kenneth Lloyd Billingsley, *The Seductive Image: A Christian Critique of the World of Film*, Eugene: Wipf and Stock, 2000.

3 Jürgen Habermas, *The Structural Transformation of the Public Sphere. An Inquiry into a Category of Bourgeois Society*, trans. Thomas Burger, Cambridge: Polity Press, 1992, pp.11–12.

4 Theodor Adorno and Max Horkheimer, *The Dialectic of Enlightenment*, London and New York: Verso, 1979.

5 Ali Jaafar, 'Babylon's turning', *Sight and Sound*, 16/1, 2006, p.5.

6 Gönül Dönmez-Colin, *Women, Islam and Cinema*, London: Reaktion Books, 2004, pp.96–102. As Lloyd Ridgeon points out, in his speeches on return to Iran from exile in 1979 and in his 1989 will, Ayatollah Khomeini did not oppose the cinema per se, but rather its misuse in the service of anti-Islamic values. See Lloyd Ridgeon, *Makhmalbaf's Broken Mirror: The Social-Political Significance of Modern Iranian Cinema* (Durham Middle East Papers No. 64), Durham: University of Durham Centre for Middle Eastern and Islamic Studies, 2000, pp.5–6.

7 Rudolf Otto, *The Idea of the Holy: An Inquiry into the Non-Rational Factor in the Idea of the Divine and its Relation to the Rational*, trans. John W. Harvey, Oxford: Oxford University Press, 1926, p.12.

8   Paul Schrader, *Transcendental Style in Film: Ozu, Bresson, Dreyer*, Berkeley: University of California Press, 1972, p.8.

9   Brian Bocking, 'RAP, RFL, and ROL language and religion in higher education', in Peter Masefield and Donald Wiebe (eds), *Aspects of Religion. Essays in Honour of Ninian Smart*, New York: Peter Lang, 1994, p.131.

10 Ninian Smart, *The Science of Religion and the Sociology of Knowledge*, Princeton: Princeton University Press, 1972, pp.18–19.

11   Although some of the works discussed in this book are assumed by their audiences to possess a documentary quality, I have chosen to focus on fictional narrative features, since this is the type of film produced and consumed most widely. There are, of course, many documentaries relevant to the study of religions. Notable examples include *Tibet: A Buddhist Trilogy* (Graham Coleman, 1978), which observes exiled Tibetan monks in north India, and Sandi Simcha DuBowski's illustration of the issues facing gay and lesbian *haredi* ('ultra-Orthodox') Jews, *Trembling Before G-d* (2001).

II   Some Trends in Religious Film Analysis

1   See also Ninian Smart, *The Science of Religion and The Sociology of Knowledge*, Princeton: Princeton University Press, 1973, p.7.

2   Joel W. Martin and Conrad E. Ostwalt (eds), *Screening the Sacred: Religion, Myth and Ideology in the Popular American Film*, Boulder: Westview, 1995; Clive Marsh and Gaye Ortiz (eds), *Explorations in Theology and Film: Movies and Meaning*, Oxford: Blackwell, 1997; Eric Christianson, Peter Francis and William R. Telford (eds), *Cinéma Divinité: Religion, Theology and the Bible in Film*, London: SCM, 2005.

3   Darlene M. Juschka, 'The construction of pedagogical spaces: religious studies in the university', *Studies in Religion/Sciences Religieuses*, 28/1, 1999, p.95.

4   Martin and Ostwalt: *Screening the Sacred*, p.153; Bernard Brandon Scott, *Hollywood Dreams and Biblical Stories*, Minneapolis: Fortress, 1994, p.ix; Peter W. Williams, 'Review essay: religion goes to the movies', *Religion and American Culture*, 10/2, 2000, p.225; Judith Weisenfeld, 'Teaching religion and American film', *Spotlight on Teaching*, 18/3, 2003, p.v.

5   William R. Telford, 'Religion, the Bible, and theology in recent films (1993–1999)', *Epworth Review*, 27/4, 2000, p.31.

6   Christopher Deacy, *Screen Christologies: Redemption and the Meaning of Film*, Cardiff: University of Wales Press, 2001, especially pp.1–10; John C. Lyden, *Film as Religion: Myths, Morals, and Rituals*, New York: New York University Press, 2003, especially p.3.

7   Robert K. Johnston, *Reel Spirituality: Theology and Film in Dialogue*, Grand Rapids: Baker Academic, 2000, p.64. Compare Bryan P. Stone, *Faith and Film: Theological Themes at the Cinema*, St. Louis: Chalice, 2000, p.4.

8   Julie Thompson Klein, *Crossing Boundaries: Knowledge, Disciplinarities, and Interdisciplinarities*, Charlottesville: University Press of Virginia, 1996, p.39. See also Justin J. Meggitt and Melanie J. Wright, 'Interdisciplinarity in learning and teaching in religious studies', in B. Chandramohan and Stephen Fallows (eds), *Interdisciplinary Learning and Teaching. Theory and Practice in Contemporary Higher Education*, London: RoutledgeFarmer, 2006.

9   My approach to *The Ten Commandments* in Melanie J. Wright, *Moses in America. The Cultural Uses of Biblical Narrative*. New York: Oxford University Press, 2002, pp.89–127 is clearly inadequate in its treatment of aesthetics.

10 See Chapter IV.

11 Albert J. Bergesen and Andrew M. Greeley (eds), *God in the Movies*, New Brunswick: Transaction, 2000, p.1.

12 Paul Coates, *Cinema, Religion and the Romantic Legacy: Through a Glass Darkly*, Aldershot: Ashgate, 2003.

13 Social class is relevant here. As argued by Pierre Bourdieu, the valuing of subtlety over spectacle is a learned ability reflecting middle- and upper-class accumulation (through particular types of education) of 'cultural capital'. The films we prefer are as much (or more) the result of social background as of individual preference. For a recent application of Bourdieu's ideas to the cinema see David M. Lubin, *Titanic*, London: BFI, 1999.

14 Ronald Holloway, *The Religious Dimension in Cinema: With Particular Reference to the Films of Carl Theodor Dreyer, Ingmar Bergman and Robert Bresson*, Hamburg: University of Hamburg Press, 1972, pp.93–4. See also Wright: *Moses in America*, pp.122–3.

15 John R. May (ed.), *Image and Likeness: Religious Visions in American Film Classics*, Mahwah: Paulist, 1992, pp.1, 6; Coates: *Cinema, Religion and the Romantic Legacy*, p.8.

16 Robert Jewett, *St Paul at the Movies: The Apostle's Dialogue with American Culture*, Louisville: Westminster/John Knox, 1993, p.5.

17 Scott: *Hollywood Dreams*, p.15; Margaret R. Miles, *Seeing and Believing: Religion and Values in the Movies*, Boston: Beacon, 1998, p.x; Stone: *Faith and Film*, p.12.

18 Janet Staiger, *Interpreting Films: Studies in the Historical Reception of American Cinema*, Princeton: Princeton University Press, 1992; Barbara Klinger, *Melodrama and Meaning: History, Culture and the Films of Douglas Sirk*, Bloomington: Indiana University Press, 1994; Annette Kuhn, *Everyday Magic: Cinema and Cultural Memory*, London: I.B.Tauris, 2002.

19 Telford: 'Religion, the Bible and theology in recent films 1993–1999', pp.31–40; Telford: 'Religion, theology and the Bible in recent films (1993–2004)', pp.347–52.

20 For example, Mara E. Donaldson, 'Love and duty in *Casablanca*', in May (ed.): *Image and Likeness*, pp.119–25; Peter Malone, '*Edward Scissorhands*: Christology from a surburban fairy-tale', in Marsh and Ortiz: *Explorations in Theology and Film*, pp.73–86.

21 George Aichele and Richard Walsh (eds), *Screening Scripture: Intertextual Connections between Scripture and Film*, Harrisburg: Trinity Press International, 2002.

22 Robert K. Jewett, *Saint Paul Returns to the Movies: Triumph Over Shame*, Grand Rapids: Eerdmans, 1999, pp.3–20. On Malina see Justin J. Meggitt, '*The Social World of Jesus and the Gospels*, by Bruce Malina', *Journal of Theological Studies*, 49/1, 1998, pp.215–19.

23 Johnston: *Reel Spirituality*, p.99 [my italics].

24 Maria Consuelo Maisto, 'Cinematic communion? *Babette's Feast*, transcendental style, and interdisciplinarity', in S. Brent Plate and David Jasper (eds), *Imag(in)ing Otherness: Filmic Visions of Living Together*, Atlanta: Scholars, 1999, p.86.

25 Tazim R. Kassam, 'Editorial', in *Spotlight on Teaching*, 18/3, 2003, p.i; Ivan Strenski, 'Material culture and the varieties of religious imagination', *Spotlight on Teaching*, 18/3, 2003, p.iii.

26 See Brian McFarlane, *Novel to Film: An Introduction to the Theory of Adaptation*, Oxford: Clarendon, 1992, especially pp.26–7, also '"It wasn't like that in the book"', *Literature/Film Quarterly*, 28/3, 2000, pp.163–9 and, for comparison, Jakob Lothe, *Narrative in Fiction and Film: An Introduction*, Oxford: Oxford University Press, 2000.

27 David Brown, 'Films, movies, meanings', in Marsh and Ortiz: *Explorations in Theology and Film*, pp.9—19.

28 Joel W. Martin, 'Introduction: seeing the sacred on screen', in Martin and Ostwalt: *Screening the Sacred*, p.2.

29 John Drury (ed.), *Critics of the Bible 1724—1873*, Cambridge: Cambridge University Press, 1989, p.1.

30 Thompson Klein: *Crossing Boundaries*, pp.212—16.

31 Toby Miller, 'Cinema studies doesn't matter, or I know what you did last semester', in Matthew Tinkcomm and Amy Villarejo (eds), *Keyframes: Popular Cinema and Cultural Studies*, London: Routledge, 2001, pp.303, 309. Miller also discusses the need for film to escape the thrall of literary criticism in his earlier '(How) Does film theory work?', *Continuum (Journal of Media and Cultural Studies)*, 6/1, 1992, pp.186—212. From a quite different perspective, Noël Carroll depicts a crisis in film studies in 'Prospects for film theory: a personal assessment', in David Bordwell and Noël Carroll (eds), *Post-Theory: Reconstructing Film Studies*, Madison: University of Wisconsin Press, 1996, pp.37—70.

32 Unattributed, 'The passion of the Christians', *The Economist*, 2 October 2004, p.50.

33 Peter J. Boyer, 'The Jesus war', *The New Yorker*, 15 September 2003, pp.58—71.

34 Robert Stam, *Film Theory: An Introduction*, Oxford: Blackwell, 2000, p.225. See also Graeme Turner, 'Cultural studies and film', in John Hill and Pamela Church Gibson (eds), *Film Studies: Critical Approaches*, Oxford: Oxford University Press, 2000, pp.193—9.

35 Tinkcomm and Villarejo (eds): *Keyframes*, p.13.

36 Stam: *Film Theory*, p.226.

37 Meaghan Morris, 'Brasschaat-Bombay: a way of inhabiting a culture', in Paul Willemen, *Looks and Frictions: Essays in Cultural Studies and Film Theory*, London: BFI, 1994, pp.20—1.

38 See further Dominic Strinati, *An Introduction to Theories of Popular Culture*, London: Routledge, 1995, pp.255—60.

39 See Richard Johnson, 'What is cultural studies anyway?', *Social Text*, No. 16, 1986, p.74, on open, multi-layered readings. In its crucial 1970s phase, psychoanalytic criticism analysed films for repressed contents, and evidence of the workings of unconscious desires. More recent developments have taken on board feminist and post-colonialist critiques

of the cultural specificity of Freud's work, but use psychoanalytic theories of the uncanny and bodily horror to interpret film. Structuralist film criticism, associated primarily with the influential film journal *Screen* and the work of Christian Metz, and drawing on Claude Levi-Strauss's writings on myth, which are also influential in religious studies, understands film as a language – a mode of communication that encodes or imposes a narrative logic upon its raw material in accordance with a set of identifiable conventions.

40 Malory Nye, *Religion: The Basics*, London: Routledge, 2003, p.21.

41 Vanessa Ochs, 'What makes a Jewish home Jewish?', *CrossCurrents*, 49/4, 2000, at *www.crosscurrents.org/ochsv.htm* (current on 1 November 2001). For a classic articulation see also Colleen McDannell, *Material Christianity: Religion and Popular Culture in America*, New Haven: Yale University Press, 1995.

42 Lawrence Grossberg, 'Is there a fan in the house? The affective sensibility of fandom', in Lisa Lewis (ed.), *The Adoring Audience: Fan Culture and Popular Media*, London: Routledge, 1992, pp.52–3. See also James Procter, *Stuart Hall*, London: Routledge, 2004, pp.57–72 (discussion of Hall's seminal essay on 'encoding' and 'decoding').

43 Miles: *Seeing and Believing*, p.xiii. Lyden, in *Film as Religion*, also criticises Miles's tendency to assume rather than study audience reactions (pp.28–9) but articulates a similar position (pp.246–7).

44 Victor Burgin, *The Remembered Film*, London: Reaktion, 2004, p.110.

45 An earlier, truncated version of Chapter III appeared as, 'Shot, burned, restored: *La Passion de Jeanne d'Arc*', in Christianson, Telford and Francis: *Cinéma Divinité*, pp.63–79

46 Richard Dyer, 'Introduction to film studies', in Hill and Gibson (eds): *Film Studies*, p.7; Williams: 'Review essay', p.237.

III The Passion of Joan of Arc
(Carl Theodor Dreyer, 1928)

1 Michel Winock, 'Jeanne d'Arc et les juifs', *H-Histoire*, 3, November 1979, p.227.

2 Raymond Carney, 'Learning from Dreyer – reflections on the lessons his work teaches', programme notes for *Close-Ups: Contemporary Art and Carl Theodor Dreyer*, curated by Lene Crone and Lars Movin

(Contemporary Art Center, Copenhagen, in collaboration with NIFCA), 6 November 1999–9 January 2000, p.82.

3   David Bordwell, *Filmguide to La Passion de Jeanne d'Arc*, Bloomington: Indiana University Press, 1973, p.9.

4   Mark Le Fanu, 'Bewitched', *Sight and Sound*, 13/7, 2003, p.30. Thus Mary Lea Bandy and Antonio Monda note that when choosing films for a recent faith and film series at MOMA in New York, 'some directors seemed natural, even inevitable choices, such as Carl Theodor Dreyer'. (*The Hidden God. Film and Faith*, New York: Museum of Modern Art, 2003, p.11.)

5   Tom Milne, 'Darkness and light: Carl Theodor Dreyer', *Sight and Sound*, 34/4, 1965, p.167.

6   Paolo Cherchi Usai, *Burning Passions: An Introduction to the Study of Silent Cinema*, London: BFI, 1994, p.20.

7   Although tortuous, *Jeanne*'s history is not unique. For instance, in 1989 *The Dybbuk* [Der Dibek] (Michal Waszynski, 1937), a film widely regarded as the high point in Yiddish cinema, was restored using material from five truncated versions.

8   Mark Nash, 'Jeanne complete: a Dreyer discovery', *Sight and Sound*, 54/3, 1985, pp.157–8.

9   *New York Times*, 31 March 1929, s.8, 6.

10 Gilles Deleuze, *Cinema I: The Movement-Image*, trans. Hugh Tomlinson and Barbara Habberjam, London: Athlone, 1986, p.106.

11 Nadia Margolis, 'Trial by passion: philology, film and ideology in the portrayal of Joan of Arc (1900–1930)', *Journal of Medieval and Early Modern Studies*, 27/3, Fall 1997, pp.453–66.

12 Brian McFarlane, *Novel to Film: An Introduction to the Theory of Adaptation*, Oxford: Clarendon, 1992, p.8.

13 See also Robert A. Rosenstone, *Visions of the Past. The Challenge of Film to Our Idea of History*. Cambridge, MA: Harvard University Press, 1995, pp.19–44.

14 David Bordwell, *The Films of Carl Theodor Dreyer*. Berkeley: University Of California Press, 1981, p.84.

15 Quoted in Raymond Carney, *Speaking the Language of Desire: The Films of Carl Dreyer*, Cambridge: Cambridge University Press, 1989, p.68 [my italics].

16 Quote from a radio interview given by Dreyer in 1950, in Donald Skoller (ed.), *Dreyer in Double Reflection. Translation of Carl Th. Dreyer's Writings About the Film (Om Filmen)*, New York: Dutton, 1973, p.145.

17 Michelle Gellrich, *Tragedy and Theory: The Problem of Conflict Since Aristotle*, Princeton: Princeton University Press, 1988, pp.233–5.

18 Paul Schrader, *Transcendental Style in Film: Ozu, Bresson, Dreyer*, Berkeley: University of California Press, 1972, p.125.

19 Marina Warner, *Joan of Arc: The Image of Female Heroism*, London: Vintage, 1991, p.21.

20 Warner: *Joan of Arc*, p.141.

21 Warner: *Joan of Arc*, pp.96–7, 111.

22 Warner: *Joan of Arc*, p.106.

23 For example, Bryan P. Stone, *Faith and Film: Theological Themes at the Cinema*, St. Louis: Chalice, p.94.

24 Bordwell: 'Carl Theodor Dreyer', p.65.

25 Carney: *Speaking the Language of Desire*, p.50.

26 Lloyd Baugh, *Imaging the Divine: Jesus and Christ-Figures in Film*, Franklin: Sheed and Ward, 2000, p.213.

27 Jean Fayard in review for *Candide*, 9 August 1928, quoted in Charles O'Brien, 'Rethinking national cinema: Dreyer's *La Passion de Jeanne d'Arc* and the academic aesthetic', *Cinema Journal*, 35/4, 1996, p.20.

28 Quoted in Mark Nash, *Dreyer*, London: BFI, 1977, p.53.

29 Deleuze: *Cinema 1*, p.103.

30 Deleuze: *Cinema 1*, p.106.

31 Andrew Sarris, 'The Scandinavian presence in the cinema', *Scandinavian Review*, 70/3, 1982, p.79.

32 Expressionism used visual style to express internal states of consciousness.

33 Casper Tyberg, 'Dreyer and the national film in Denmark', *Film History*, 13/1, 2001, p.32.

34 Statement issued by Dreyer in 1929, in Skoller (ed.): *Dreyer in Double Reflection*, p.50

35 Dreyer's films are stylistically diverse. The close-ups and fast cutting in *Jeanne* contrast markedly with the long takes in *The Word*.

36 Winock: 'Jeanne d'Arc et les juifs', p.228.

37 Quoted in Martha Hanna, 'Iconology and ideology: images of Joan of Arc in the idiom of the *action française*, 1908–1931', *French Historical Studies*, 14/2, 1985, p.227.

38 Hanna: 'Iconology and ideology', p.219.

39 Warner: *Joan of Arc*, p.272.

40 Schrader: *Transcendental Style*, pp.125–6.

41 Kevin Jackson (ed.), *Schrader on Schrader*, London: Faber and Faber, 1990, pp.xi, 28–9.

42 Even Adorno, wary of the consequences of film for critical consciousness, did not regard audiences as passive dupes: 'The triumph ... of the culture industry is that consumers feel compelled to buy and use its products *even though they see through them*.' (Theodor Adorno and Max Horkheimer, *The Dialectic of Enlightenment*, trans. John Cumming, London and New York: Verso, 1979, p.167 [my italics].

43 Eric Smoodin, '"Compulsory" viewing for every citizen: *Mr. Smith* and the rhetoric of reception', in Matthew Tinkcomm and Amy Villarejo (eds), *Keyframes: Popular Cinema and Cultural Studies*, London: Routledge, p.345.

44 Mordaunt Hall, 'Poignant French film – Maria Falconetti gives unequaled performance as Jeanne d'Arc', *New York Times*, 31 March 1929, s.8, 7.

45 Nash: *Dreyer*, p.54.

46 Quoted in Bordwell: *Carl Theodor Dreyer*, p.216.

47 O'Brien: 'Rethinking national cinema', p.5.

48 Hall: 'Poignant French film', p.7.

49 See unattributed articles, 'St. Joan', *The Times*, 27 April 1929, p.10, 'Joan of Arc. Celebrations in France', *The Times*, 27 April 1929, pp.13–14, and 'Joan of Arc. Celebrations at Chinon', *The Times*, 29 April 1929, p.14.

50 'A French Film', *The Times*, 12 November 1930, p.12.

51 Nash: *Dreyer*, p.19.

52 Francis M. Malpezzi and William M. Clements, 'La Passion de Jeanne d'Arc' ('The Passion of Joan of Arc'), in Frank N. Magill (ed.), *Magill's*

Survey of Cinema: Silent Films, Vol. 2, Epping: Bowker, 1982, pp.854–7.

53 Baugh: *Imaging the Divine*; Carney: *Speaking the Language of Desire*.

54 On Godard and Kaufman, see Robin Blaetz, *Visions of the Maid: Joan of Arc in American Film and Culture*, Charlottesville and London: University Press of Virginia, 2001, p.179.

55 Review for *La Gaceta literaria hispanoamericana*, reproduced in Francisco Aranda, *Luis Buñuel: A Critical Biography*, trans. David Robinson, London: Secker and Warburg, 1975, p.258. Buñuel was then working as assistant to Jean Epstein, whose views on religion and cinema are discussed in Chapter IV.

IV   The Ten Commandments
(Cecil B. DeMille, 1956)

1 Unattributed review of, '*The Ten Commandments*', *Time*, 12 November 1956, p.124.

2 M.G. Wood, *America in the Movies or, 'Santa Maria, It Had Slipped My Mind'*, London: Secker and Warburg, 1975, p.177.

3 See recently, Conrad E. Ostwalt, *Secular Steeples: Popular Culture and the Religious Imagination*, Harrisburg: Trinity Press International, 2003, p.161.

4 Patrick Sherry, *Images of Redemption: Art, Literature and Salvation*, London: T. and T. Clark, 2003, p.13; Thomas Schatz, 'Paramount Pictures', in Pam Cook and Mieke Bernink (eds), *The Cinema Book*, London: BFI, 1999, p.15. In a different vein, Adele Reinhartz describes *Commandments'* appeal for her children, who were enthralled by a film that 'gave life to a story they had heard told and retold since birth'. But her study locates the age of the epic in the past, and focuses on the use of the Bible in films such as *The Truman Show* (Peter Weir, 1998) or *Magnolia* (Paul Thomas Anderson, 1999) (*Scripture on the Silver Screen*, Louisville: Westminster John Knox, 2003, p.1).

5 On classic Hollywood cinema see Annette Kuhn, 'Classic Hollywood Narrative', in Cook and Bernink (eds): *The Cinema Book*, pp.39–41; William H. Phillips, *Film: An Introduction*, Boston: Bedford/St. Martin's, 1999, pp.235–6; Dominic Strinati, *An Introduction to Studying Popular Culture*, London: Routledge, 2000, pp.25–52 and David Bordwell, Janet Staiger and Kristin Thompson, *The Classical Hollywood Cinema: Film*

Style and Mode of Production to 1960, New York: Columbia University Press, 1985.

In the mid-twentieth century, the five majors (Warner Bros., RKO, 20th Century-Fox, Paramount and MGM) dominated international markets. They achieved this through vertical integration – ownership of film theatres and distribution companies, as well as of the means to produce films.

6 Bruce Babington and Peter W. Evans, *Biblical Epics: Sacred Narrative and the Hollywood Cinema*, Manchester: Manchester University Press, 1993, p.3.

7 Frank Dyer, 'The moral development of the silent drama', *Edison Kinematogram*, 15 April 1910, p.11. More generally, see William Urrichio and Roberta E. Pearson, *Reframing Culture: The Case of the Vitagraph Quality Films*. Princeton: Princeton University Press, 1993.

8 On the postwar investigation of Hollywood see Robert Sklar, *Movie-Made America: A Cultural History of American Movies*, London: Chappell, 1975, pp.249–68.

9 Michel Mourlet, quoted in Erica Sheen, '"The Light of God's Law": violence and metaphysics in the '50s widescreen biblical epic', in *Biblical Interpretation*, 6, 1998, p.311.

10 See Melanie J. Wright, *Moses in America. The Cultural Uses of Biblical Narrative*, New York: Oxford University Press, 2002, p.89.

11 The quotation is from a 1932 work by Q.D. Leavis, the attitude not uniquely hers. Dominic Strinati, *An Introduction to Theories of Popular Culture*, London: Routledge, 1995, pp.10–21 gives an overview on mass culture.

12 Quoted in Robert Stam, *Film Theory: An Introduction*, Oxford: Blackwell, 2000, p.34–6, 85.

13 Stam: *Film Theory*, p.88.

14 Charles Higham, *Cecil B. DeMille*, London: W.H. Allen, 1974, p.x.

15 For an overview of the relevant topics, see John Barton and John Muddiman (eds), *The Oxford Bible Commentary*, Oxford: Oxford University Press, 2001, pp.1–2 (Biblical criticism), 6–7 (authorship of the Hebrew Bible) and 8–9 (Hebrew Bible genres).

16 Henry S. Noerdlinger offers a somewhat tenuous account of the reasoning behind this innovation in *Moses and Egypt: The Documentation to the*

Motion Picture The Ten Commandments, Los Angeles: University of Southern California Press, 1956, p.61.

17 Jeffery A. Smith, 'Hollywood theology: the commodification of religion in twentieth-century films', *Religion and American Culture*, 11/2, 2001, p.207.

18 According to Noerdlinger, banishment was thought to be more in keeping with Moses' heroic character than the Bible's suggestion that he ran away: *Moses and Egypt*, p.22.

19 Ilana Pardes, 'Moses goes down to Hollywood: miracles and special effects', *Semeia*, 74, 1996, p.23. As demonstrated by the next section of the chapter, the hermeneutic is not an exclusive one, and complements, rather than overturns, Babington and Evans' claim about Wood's interpretation of the film's final imagery (*Biblical Epics: Sacred Narrative in the Hollywood Cinema*, Manchester: Manchester University Press, p.187).

20 Quoted in Paul Swann, *The Hollywood Feature Film in Postwar Britain*, London: Croom Helm, 1987, p.55.

21 Wright: *Moses in America*, pp.104–9.

22 Strinati: *Studying Popular Culture*, p.28.

23 On biblical metaphors and American identity see Wright: *Moses in America*, pp.9–12.

24 Babington and Evans: *Biblical Epics*, pp.11–12; Pardes: 'Moses Goes Down to Hollywood', p.19; Wood: *America in the Movies*, p.187.

25 See briefly Michael Haralambos and Michael Holborn, *Sociology: Themes and Perspectives*, fourth edition, London: Collins Educational, 1995, pp.450–2.

26 See Alan Nadel, 'God's Law and the wide screen: *The Ten Commandments* as Cold War epic', *Proceedings of the Modern Language Association of America*, 108, pp.427. Further discussion of *Commandments* as an anti-Communist film is offered in Caroline T. Schroeder, 'Ancient Egyptian rites on the silver screen: modern anxieties about race, ethnicity and religion', *Journal of Religion and Film*, 7/2, 2003, available at *www.un omaha.edu/~wwwjrf/Vol7No2/ancientegypt.htm* (current on 22 October 2003).

27 Wright: *Moses in America*, pp.109–10.

28 Timothy K. Beal, 'Behold thou the behemoth: imaging the unimaginable in monster movies', in S. Brent Plate and David Jasper (eds), *Imag(in)ing*

Otherness: Filmic Visions of Living Together, Atlanta: Scholars, 1999, p.198. Similar assessment is offered in Ina Rae Hard (ed.), *Exhibition: The Film Reader*, London: Routledge, 2002, p.10.

29 Vijay Mishra, *Bollywood Cinema: Temples of Desire*, London: Routledge, 2002, p.1.

30 Alex Wright, *Why Bother With Theology?*, London: Darton, Longman and Todd, 2002, p.94.

31 On trailers and teasers see David Bordwell, *The McGraw-Hill Film Viewer's Guide*, New York: McGraw-Hill, 2001, pp.5–6.

32 On this kind of strategy see Barbara Klinger, 'Digressions at the cinema: reception and mass culture', *Cinema Journal*, 28/4, 1989, p.10.

33 The most significant example of usage is the borrowing from Josephus *Antiquities* (Book 2, sections 210–23) of the idea that Moses' birth is a divine response to the cries of slaves in bondage. (Wright: *Moses in America*, pp.96–9.)

34 As described in Chapter VII, *Keeping the Faith* deliberately references classic Hollywood style; examples of films to do this in the 1970s and 80s include *Star Wars* (George Lucas, 1977) which blended themes from fantasy, war and western films, and Steven Spielberg's *Raiders of the Lost Ark* (1981).

35 Robert Evett, 'There was a young fellow from Goshen', *The New Republic*, 135/24, 1956, p.20.

36 On the specifics of film reviewing in the 1950s see Barbara Klinger, *Melodrama and Meaning: History, Culture and the Films of Douglas Sirk*, Bloomington: Indiana University Press, 1994, especially pp.69–70.

37 Unattributed review of *The Ten Commandments* in *Newsweek*, 5 November 1956, quoted in Gene Ringgold and De W. Bodeen, *The Films of Cecil B. DeMille*, New York: Citadel, 1969, p.41.

38 Bosley Crowther, '*The Ten Commandments*' [review] in George Amberg (ed.), *The New York Times Film Reviews: A One Volume Selection 1913–1970*, New York: Arno, 1971, p. 307.

39 Evett: 'There was a young fellow from Goshen', p.20.

40 Unattributed: '*The Ten Commandments*' [review], *Time*, p.124.

41 Peter Baker, '*The Ten Commandments*' [review], *Films and Filming*, 4/4, 1958, p.24.

42 Robert Hatch, 'Theatre and films', *Nation*, 8 December 1956, p.506.

43 Unattributed: '*The Ten Commandments*' [review], *Time*, p.124

44 Laurence Kitchin, '*The Ten Commandments*' [review], *Sight and Sound*, 27, 1957, p.149.

45 Unattributed: '*The Ten Commandments*' [review], *Time*, p.124.

46 Kitchin: '*The Ten Commandments*', p.149.

47 Evett: 'There was a young fellow from Goshen', p.20.

48 T.S. Driver, 'Hollywood in the wilderness: a review article', *The Christian Century*, 73/48, 1956, p.1390.

49 Driver: 'Hollywood in the wilderness', p.1390.

50 Driver: 'Hollywood in the wilderness', p.1391.

51 Comments by Kennedy and Young in G. Kennedy, H.L. Clark, D.M. Stowe, L.C. Moorehead, and W. Lindsay Young, 'Through different eyes', *The Christian Century*, 74/1, 1957, p.20–1.

52 Kennedy *et al*: 'Through different eyes', p.21.

53 David Riesmand and Evelyn T. Riesman, 'Movies and audiences', in *American* Quarterly, 4/3, 1952, pp.195–202 is an early landmark article on reception, dating from the same era as *Commandments*.

54 See Peter Malone, Roberto Pazos and Ferdinand Poswick, '*The Prince of Egypt*', *Cine and Media*, 1, 1999, pp.5–8; Simon Louvish, 'The Bible from God to Dreamworks', in *Sight and Sound*, 9/1, 1999, pp.22–5, which identifies America as 'tinseltown's Promised Land', and Jennifer Rohrer-Walsh, 'Coming-of-age in *The Prince of Egypt*', in George Aichele and Richard Walsh (eds), *Screening Scripture: Intertextual Connections Between Scripture and Film*, Harrisburg: Trinity Press International, 2002, pp.77–99.

55 R.M. Hodgens, '*The Ten Commandments*', *Film Quarterly*, 20/1, 1966, p.59.

56 Pardes: 'Moses goes down', pp.26–7.

57 Sheen: '"The Light of God's Law"', p.310.

58 A point also noted by Eric Christianson, 'Movie Moses: A Man for All Seasons', unpublished paper, Theology and Film weekend, St. Deiniol's, Hawarden, April 2000.

59 Klinger: *Melodrama and Meaning*, p.159.

V   The Wicker Man
   (Robin Hardy, 1973)

1   Christopher Lee, in David Bartholomew, '*The Wicker Man*', *Cinefantastique*, 6/3, 1977, p.34.

2   David Bruce, *Scotland the Movie*, Edinburgh: Polygon, 1996, p.244.

3   Thomas Schatz, 'Paramount Pictures', in Pam Cook and Mieke Bernink (eds), *The Cinema Book*, second edition, London: BFI, p.13.

4   Allan Brown, *Inside The Wicker Man: The Morbid Ingenuities*, London: Sidgwick and Jackson, 2000, pp.98–101, 128–9.

5   Stuart Byron, 'Something Wicker This Way Comes', in *Film Comment*, 13/6, 1977, pp.29–31.

6   Brown: *Inside The Wicker Man*, p.179.

7   Nuada is the name of several (perhaps) divine figures in early Irish tradition (see James MacKillop, *Dictionary of Celtic Mythology*, Oxford: Oxford University Press, 1998, p.307).

8   Robin Hardy, DVD commentary moderated by Mark Kermode, *The Wicker Man Director's Cut*, Canal Image UK, 2002. In an attempt to rationalise these inconsistencies, in the novel, Howie becomes an Episcopalian with a Presbyterian girlfriend (Robin Hardy and Anthony Shaffer, *The Wicker Man*, Feltham: Hamlyn, 1980, p.14).

9   Tanya Krzywinska, *A Skin For Dancing In: Possession, Witchcraft and Voodoo in Film*, Trowbridge: Flicks, 2000, p.80

10 Hardy and Shaffer: *The Wicker Man*, frontispiece.

11 Brown: *Inside The Wicker Man*, p.137.

12 Krzywinska: *A Skin For Dancing In*, p.83; Hardy and Shaffer: *The Wicker Man*, p.210.

13 Bartholomew: '*The Wicker Man*', p.9. Compare Crowder in Olga Wojtas, 'A burning passion that's close to worship', *Times Higher Education Supplement*, 11 July 2003, pp.20–1.

14 Jacqueline Simpson and Steve Roud, *A Dictionary of English Folklore*, Oxford: Oxford University Press, 2000, pp.235–6.

15 Text from the 32nd stanza of 'Song of Myself', in Donald Hall (ed.), *A Choice of Whitman's Verse*, London: Faber and Faber, 1968, p.53.

16 James George Frazer, *The Golden Bough. A Study in Magic and Religion. Part VI. The Scapegoat*, third edition, London: Macmillan, 1913, p.50.

17 James George Frazer, *The Golden Bough. A Study in Magic and Religion. Part 1 The Magic Art and the Evolution of Kings*, Vol. 1, third edition, London: Macmillan, 1911, p.152.

18 Frazer: *The Golden Bough. Part I*, Vol. 1, pp.182–6; Vol. 2, p.31.

19 Frazer: *The Golden Bough. Part I*, Vol. 1, p.149.

20 J.H. Edwards (trans.), *Caesar. The Gallic War* [Loeb Classical Library], London: Heinemann, VI, 1922, p.16; discussed in James George Frazer, *The Golden Bough. Part VII. Balder the Beautiful. The Fire Festivals of Europe and the Doctrine of the External Soul*, Vol. 1, London: Macmillan, 1913, pp.31–3.

21 Frazer: *The Golden Bough. Part VII*, Vol. 1, p.146; Vol. 2, pp.59, 66–8.

22 For descriptions see Simpson and Roud: *English Folklore*, pp.230, 231, 271.

23 Frazer: *The Golden Bough. Part VII*, Vol. 1, p.43.

24 Frazer: *The Golden Bough. Part VI*, p.v. Frazer's biography is outlined in Robert Ackerman, 'Frazer, James G.', in Mircea Eliade (ed.), *The Encyclopedia of Religion*, Vol. 5, London: Macmillan, 1987, pp.414–16 and Simpson and Roud: *Dictionary of English Folklore*, pp.134–5.

25 Shaffer in Bartholomew: '*The Wicker Man*', p.16.

26 See further Duncan Petrie, *Screening Scotland*, London: BFI, 2000, pp.1, 32.

27 Cairns Craig, 'Myths against history: tartanry and kailyardism in nineteenth century Scottish literature', in Colin McArthur (ed.), *Scotch Reels: Scotland in Cinema and Television*, London: BFI, 1982.

28 Petrie: *Screening Scotland*, p.32.

29 This is also a stock device in horror films, which are frequently characterised as based on 'true stories' or 'real events'. See for example William Friedkin's archetypal 1973 film *The Exorcist*, and recently, *The Exorcism of Emily Rose* (Scot Derricksen, 2005).

30 Quoted in Bartholomew: '*The Wicker Man*', p.12.

31 Bruce: *Scotland the Movie*, p.244.

32 Philip Kemp, *Lethal Innocence: The Cinema of Alexander Mackendrick*, London: Methuen, 1991, pp.39–40.

33 Bruce: *Scotland the Movie*, p.244.

34 On star subtexts generally see Richard Dyer, *Only Entertainment*, London: Routledge, 1992, pp.65–98. One of Britain's leading film writers, Dyer was a graduate student at Birmingham University's Centre for Contemporary Cultural Studies (1964–2002), the institution which did more than any other to define cultural studies as an independent subject in the UK.

35 Lee's neologism, quoted in Brown: *Inside the Wicker Man*, p.14.

36 Reproduced in Brown: *Inside The Wicker Man*, unnumbered page.

37 Jack Babuscio, 'Camp and the gay sensibility', in Richard Dyer (ed.), *Gays and Film*, revised edition, New York: Zoetrope, 1984, pp.40–57.

38 Shaffer in Brown: *Inside the Wicker Man*, p.24.

39 See Jonathan Rigby, *English Gothic: A Century of Horror Cinema*, second edition, London: Reynolds and Hearn, 2002, p.211.

40 British horror films were distinctively concerned with visual display. Hammer's initial move into the genre was intended to exploit the shock potential of the first *colour* images of Dracula and Frankenstein's monster. (Annette Kuhn, 'The British film industry', in Cook and Bernink (eds): *The Cinema Book*, p.87).

41 Ivan Butler, *Horror in the Cinema*, London: A. Zwemmer, 1970, pp.15–16.

42 Paul Wells, *The Horror Genre: From Beelzebub to Blair Witch*, London: Wallflower, 2000, p.21.

43 Steve Chibnall and Julian Petley, *British Horror Cinema*, London: Routledge, 2002, pp.92–3.

44 Quoted in Bartholomew: 'The Wicker Man', p.46.

45 Margaret Hinxman, 'The Wicker Man' [review], *Sunday Telegraph* 16 December 1973.

46 Unattributed, 'The Wicker Man' [review], *Financial Times* 14 December 1973; David McGillivray, 'The Wicker Man [review], *Monthly Film Bulletin*, January 1974.

47 Dilys Powell, 'The Wicker Man' [review], *Sunday Times*, 16 December 1973.

48 Patrick Gibbs, '*The Wicker Man*' [review], *Daily Telegraph* 28 December 1973.

49 Alexander Stuart, '*The Wicker Man*' [review], *Films and Filming*, 20/7, 1974, p.47.

50 Unattributed, 'British Film. The *Classic Television* top one hundred', in *Classic Television*, 5, 1998, pp.10–25

51 Stephen Appelbaum, '*The Wicker Man*', *Film Review*, Special No. 16, 1996, pp.19–24; Wojtas: 'A burning passion', pp.20–1.

52 Harvey Fenton, '*The Wicker Man*', *Flesh and Blood*, 3, 1994, p.43.

53 Chris Pizzello, '*The Wicker Man*' [DVD review], *American Cinematographer*, 83/2, 2002, p.16.

54 See, for example, Jacqueline Bobo's study, '*The Color Purple*: black women as cultural readers', in E.Dierdre Pribram (ed.), *Female Spectators: Looking at Film and Television*, London: Verso, 1988, pp.272–87. Bobo's interviews revealed that African American women were experienced at interpreting Hollywood films in ways that ran counter to those intended by their producers. In the case of *The Color Purple*, the women filtered out negative stereotypes (criticised by the film's reviewers) to discover a progressive message of empowerment.

55 Henry Jenkins, *Textual Poachers: Television Fans and Participatory Culture*, New York and London: Routledge, 1992, p.3.

56 Umberto Eco: *Travels in Hyperreality*, pp.197–8, quoted in Jenkins: *Textual Poachers*, p.50.

57 Jenkins: *Textual Poachers*, p.86.

58 Nevada's burning man festival did not originate as a tribute to Hardy's film but, as Alex Wright notes, in the cathartic burning of a human effigy by founder Larry Harvey (*Why Bother With Theology?*, London: Darton, Longman and Todd, 2002, p.44.)

59 The analysis of *The Wicker Man*'s Internet presence in this section is informed by Jenkins' book, and by Steven Cohan, 'Judy on the net: Judy Garland and "the gay thing" revisited', in Matthew Tinkcomm and Amy Villarejo (eds), *Keyframes: Popular Cinema and Cultural Studies*, London: Routledge, 2001, pp.119–36.

60 See 'Nuada, The Wicker Man Journal', available at *www.nuada98.fsnet. co.uk/nuada%203/index.html*, 'The Wicker Man – Settling the Score', available at *www.garycarpenter.net/archive/wicker.htm*, 'The Wickerman

Trail' *www.sw-scotland-screen.com/wickerman_trail/index.html* (all current on 27 December 2005).

61 See *http://movies.groups.yahoo.com/group/wickerman/*. This is a members-only discussion group, for which reason I have not named the contributors whose views are described in the text that follows.

62 For a useful development of these ideas see Marc Jancovich, 'Cult fictions: cult movies, subcultural capital and the production of cultural distinctions', *Cultural Studies*, 16/2, 2002, pp.306–22. Like Ashurst and Jenkins, Jancovich's scholarship confesses his own fannish enthusiasm for cinema and popular culture.

VI My Son the Fanatic
(Udayan Prasad, 1997)

1 Hanif Kureishi, quoted in Ruvani Ranasinha, *Hanif Kureishi*, Tavistock: Northcote House, 2002, p.81.

2 Rachel Malik, '*My Son the Fanatic*' [review], *Sight and Sound*, 8/5, 1998, p.54.

3 Jigna Desai, *Beyond Bollywood: The Cultural Politics of South Asian Diasporic Film*, London: Routledge, 2004, pp.50–1.

4 James Procter, *Stuart Hall*, London: Routledge, 2004, p.130.

5 Stuart Hall, 'Cultural identity and diaspora', in Jonathan Rutherford (ed.), *Identity: Community, Difference, Culture*, London: Lawrence and Wishart, 1990, pp.222, 225.

6 Cary Rajinder Sawnhey, 'Indian cinema and the Asian diaspora', in Wendy Earle (ed.), *Bollywood and Beyond: A Guide to Teaching Indian Cinema*, London: BFI, 2002, Unit 8, pp.1–2.

7 See 'My Son the Fanatic', in Hanif Kureishi, *Love in a Blue Time*, New York: Simon and Schuster, 1997, pp.119–31 for the short story which preceded the film.

8 Stuart Hall, 'New ethnicities', in David Morley and Kwan-Hsing Chen (eds), *Stuart Hall: Critical Dialogues in Cultural Studies*, London: Routledge, 1996, p.449 (essay first published in 1988).

9 Kobena Mercer, *Welcome to the Jungle: New Positions in Black Cultural Studies*, London: Routledge, 1994, p.92.

10 *Bend it Like Beckham* (Gurinder Chadha, 2002) was the first British Asian

film to break though commercially in North America. Art prefigures reality in the film's final scenes, which see the main characters, Jess and Jules (played by Parminder Nagra and Keira Knightley) leave England to pursue their (football) careers in the USA. Both actresses made similar journeys in the wake of the film's international success.

11 *East is East* (Damien O'Donnell, 1999) captures this well, depicting a family excursion to see an Indian film. On Asian audiences in the UK, see Sawnhey: 'Indian cinema', pp.2–6.

12 See cinematographer Alan Almond's account of this in Eric Rudolph, 'A house under siege', *American Cinematographer*, 80/7, 1999, pp.18–26.

13 According to Kureishi, 'Every self confessed fundamentalist I have met was antisemitic' ('Sex and Secularity', *Filmmaker*, 10/4, 2002, p.28).

14 Leonard Quart, *'My Son the Fanatic'* [review], *Cineaste*, 24/4, 1999, p.43.

15 Kureishi: 'Sex and Secularity', p.26. It is relevant to note here that the article appeared shortly after the terror attacks on the USA on 11 September 2001.

16 Ranasinha: *Hanif Kureishi*, p.19 discusses this further.

17 As Bart Moore-Gilbert describes, Martin Scorsese's *Taxi Driver* (1976) is an important intertext for *My Son*. Parvez and Travis Bickle share the same profession and are isolated from their colleagues. They both fall in love with prostitutes whom they see having sex with a client in the rear of the cab (*Hanif Kureishi*, Manchester: Manchester University Press, 2001, pp.169–71).

18 In a British context, *Kafir*, which has a long history of use as a derogatory label for black South Africans, has strong colonial overtones.

19 Kureishi: 'Sex and Secularity', p.28.

20 'A condition, episode, person or groups or persons emerges to become defined as a threat to societal values and interests; its nature is presented in a stylised and stereotypical fashion by the mass media; the moral barricades are manned by editors, bishops, politicians and other right-thinking people; socially accredited experts pronounce their diagnoses and solutions; ways of coping are evolved or (more often) resorted to; the condition then disappears, submerges or deteriorates and becomes more visible.' Stanley Cohen, *Folk Devils and Moral Panics: The Creation of the Mods and Rockers*, second edition, Oxford: Martin Robertson, 1980, p.9.

21 See note 1.

22 See Yvonne Tasker, *Working Girls: Gender and Sexuality in Popular Cinema*, London: Routledge, 1998, especially p.3.

23 See also Ranasinha: *Hanif Kureishi*, p.97.

24 Hanif Kureishi, *Collected Screenplays 1*, London: Faber and Faber 2002, pp.346–7, 371.

25 Office of National Statistics, April 2001 census.

26 Robert J. C. Young, *Postcolonialism. A Very Short Introduction*, Oxford: Oxford University Press, 2003, p.24. On the Honeyford and Salman Rushdie Affairs see briefly Philip Lewis, *Islamic Britain: Religion, Politics and Identity Among British Muslims*, London: I.B.Tauris, 2002, especially pp.143–72.

27 Hanif Kureishi, 'Bradford', reproduced in Susanne Schmid, 'Exploring multiculturalism. Bradford jews and Bradford Pakistanis', *Journal for the Study of British Cultures*, 4/1–2, 1997, p.169.

28 Kureishi: 'Bradford', quoted in Schmid: 'Exploring multiculturalism', pp.169, 173.

29 There are points of contact here with *The Full Monty*, in which ex-steelworker Dave has been forced to take a poorly paid job in Sheffield's Meadowhall shopping mall. Schitz' nationality also has resonances in the Bradford context. The textile boom in the town was partly created by German-Jewish merchants who came to the town in the late nineteenth century, and the commercial area where they built their warehouses was dubbed 'Little Germany'. See Schmid: 'Exploring multiculturalism', pp.163–4.

30 Jigna Desai's otherwise insightful analysis struggles to locate the film, describing Parvez as someone who 'drives a taxi away from the metropolitan London' (*Beyond Bollywood*, p.67).

31 MEP Geoffrey Bloom, quoted in Sarah Left and Simon Jeffrey, 'UKIP MEP foiled by female fury', *The Guardian*, 22 July 2004.

32 For Kaleem Aftab the differing reception of *East is East* by Asian and non-Asian Britons is a salient reminder that the rise of Bollywood and British Asian cinema may be as much about the erection and maintenance of cultural boundaries as it is about their transcendence. See 'Brown: the new black! Bollywood in Britain', *Critical Quarterly*, 44/3, 2002, pp.88–98.

33 See Christine Geraghty, *My Beautiful Laundrette*, London: I.B.Tauris, 2005, p.78.

34 David Parkinson, '*My Son the Fanatic*' [review], *Empire*, 108, 1998, p.52; Sheila Johnston, '*My Son the Fanatic*' [review], *Screen International*, 1107, 9 May 1997, p.23.

35 Kureishi: 'Sex and Secularity', p.26.

36 'My Son the Fanatic' by Matt Seaton, *The Guardian*, 2 January 2002, available online at *www.guardian.co.uk/ukresponse/story/0,11017,626641,00.html* (current on 8 January 2006).

37 Dohra Ahmad, '"This fundo stuff is really something new": fundamentalism and hybridity in *The Moor's Last Sigh*', *Yale Journal of Criticism*, 18/1, 2005, p.1.

38 June Thomas, 'The first 7/7 movie', in *Slate*. Available online at *http://slate.msn.com/id/2122935* (current on 14 September 2005).

39 Ranasinha: *Hanif Kureishi*, p.101.

40 Quoted in Susie Thomas, *Hanif Kureishi. A Reader's Guide to Essential Criticism*, London: Palgrave, 2005, p.129.

41 'Bradford rocked by riots', unattributed article, *This is Bradford.co.uk*, online at : *www.thisisbradford.co.uk/bradford__district/100_years/1995.html*.

42 Gillian Rose, 'Beginnings of the day: fascism and representation', in Bryan Cheyette and Laura Marcus (eds), *Modernity, Culture and 'the Jew'*, Cambridge: Polity Press, 1998.

43 The problems with realism as the mode of addressing religion in the cinema are discussed further in this book's conclusions.

VII Keeping the Faith
(Edward Norton, 2000)

1 Nora Ephron, 'Why Not Him?', *Interview*, 30/4, 2000, p.120.

2 Anwar Brett, '*Keeping the Faith*' [review], *Film Review*, 598, 2000, p.33.

3 *Keeping the Faith* is the first film to officially credit Norton. However director Tony Kaye claims that *American History X* (1998), in which Norton plays a reformed white supremacist, was edited beyond recognition by the actor and the studio.

4   Conservative Judaism offers a middle path between Orthodoxy and Reform. It emphasises the notion of *kelal Yisroel* ('Catholic Israel' or the community of Israel) as both the locus of authority and an aspiration guiding Jewish religious practice. In the mid-twentieth century it was the numerically dominant movement within American Judaism. See further Melanie J. Wright, *Understanding Judaism*, Cambridge: Orchard Academic, 2003, pp.54–8.

5   Ian Freer, '*Keeping the Faith*' [review], *Empire*, 136, 2000, p.45; Emmanuel Levy, 'Slick show of "faith"', *Variety*, 3–9 April, 2000, p.32.

6   Charles Affron, *Cinema and Sentiment*, Chicago: University of Chicago Press, 1982, p.4.

7   Elfman brings a strong subtext to the film for American viewers. Between 1997 and 2002 she starred in *Dharma and Greg*, a television comedy about a couple with differing personalities and spiritualities. She is also a prominent Scientologist.

8   See Geoff King, *New Hollywood. An Introduction*, London: I.B.Tauris, 2002 and, for a brief survey, Noel King, 'New Hollywood', in Pam Cook and Mieke Bernink (eds), *The Cinema Book*, second edition, London: BFI, 1999, pp.98–106.

9   Noël Carroll, 'The future of allusion: Hollywood in the seventies (and beyond)', in *October*, 20, spring 1982, p.74.

10 Wright: *Understanding Judaism*, p.115.

11 The two men's innovations also reflect trends towards new forms of worship within Progressive Judaism and some Christian churches. Moreover, according to the DVD audio commentary, Brian's 'Faith as a Hunch' sermon was first preached in Santa Monica by Father John Collins of St. Paul's Cathedral, New York.

12 'Day of Atonement' – the high point of the Jewish calendar (Wright: *Understanding Judaism*, pp.86–9) and for Jake the day on which his fitness for the role for Senior Rabbi will be decided.

13 United States Conference of Catholic Bishops, 'Film and broadcasting. *Keeping the Faith*' [review], available at *www.usccb.org/movies/k/keeping thefaith2000.htm* (current on 1 February 2006). Donna Bowman, '*Keeping the Faith*' [review], in *Journal of Religion and Film*, 4/2, 2000, available at *www.unomaha.edu/jrf/Faith.htm* (current on 1 February 2006).

14 Joseph Greenblum, 'Does Hollywood still glorify Jewish intermarriage? The case of *The Jazz Singer*', *American Jewish History*, 83/1, 1995, p.461.

15 Wright: *Understanding Judaism*, p.199.

16 See Patricia White, 'Feminism and film', in John Hill and Pamel Church Gibson (eds), *Film Studies: Critical Approaches*, Oxford: Oxford University Press, pp.119–23.

17 Janice Radway, *Reading the Romance: Women, Patriarchy, and Popular Literature*, Chapel Hill: University of North Carolina Press, 1984, p.80.

18 Norton quoted in Nora Ephron, 'Why not him?', in *Interview*, 30/4, 2000, p.122.

19 Eva Kosofsky Sedgwick, *Between Men: English Literature and Male Homosocial Desire*, New York: Columbia University Press, 1985, p.3.

20 Sedgwick, *Between Men*, p.23.

VIII Lagaan
(Ashutosh Gowariker, 2001)

1 Diana L. Eck, *Darśan. Seeing the Divine Image in India*, third edition, New York: Columbia University Press, 1998, p.11.

2 Jyotika Virdi, *The Cinematic ImagiNation: Indian Popular Films as Social History*, New Brunswick: Rutgers University Press, 2003, p.205.

3 Hindi, a largely northern Indian language, was designated a national language after independence (English is the other), but Indians speak many different languages and dialects. As a popular art form nevertheless implicated in the circulation of Hindi, Bollywood cinema occupies an ambiguous position in Indian language politics. (See Virdi: *The Cinematic ImagiNation*, pp.17–21).

4 Paul Willemen, *Looks and Frictions: Essays in Cultural Studies in Film Theory*, London: BFI, 1994, p.211.

5 There are many regional cinemas in India, but as the largest, the Bombay/ Mumbai-based industry is the closest to an all-India cinema and serves as a model for the others.

6 Vijay Mishra, *Bollywood Cinema: Temples of Desire*, London: Routledge, 2002, p.13.

7 On the refusal of conventional realism see Ashis Nandy, 'Notes towards an agenda for the next generation of film theorists in India', *South Asian Popular Culture*, 1/1, 2003, p.80.

8 J. Geetha, 'Bollywood Ending', *Sight and Sound*, 13/6, 2003, p.31.

9   William O. Beeman, 'The use of music in popular film: east and west', *India International Film Quarterly*, 8/1, 1980, p.83; Rosie Thomas, 'Indian cinema: pleasures and popularity', *Screen*, 26/3–4, 1985, p.130. *Dharma* refers to norms of behaviour (some universal, some caste-specific) transmitted by example and in stories and myths.

10 Thomas suggests that in castigating popular Hindi film, Western critics take their cue from Indian upper–middle class preferences for art film ('Indian cinema', p.117). Kishore Valicha, *The Moving Image: A Study of Indian Cinema*, Bombay: Orient Longman, 1988, pp.26–7 acknowledges and participates in the discourse separating Hindi film from 'serious' cinema. See also Mishra: *Bollywood Cinema*, p.xviii, and Nandy: 'Notes towards an agenda', pp.79–84.

11 For example, K. Moti Gokulsing and Wimal Dissanayake, *Indian Popular Cinema: A Narrative of Cultural Change*, London: Trentham, 1998, pp.17–22. Contemporary influences on Bollywood include Hollywood and MTV.

12 Rachel Dwyer and Divia Patel, *Cinema India: The Visual Culture of Hindi Film*, London: Reaktion, 2002, pp.13–15.

13 See Mishra: *Bollywood Cinema*, pp.13–14; Gokulsing and Dissanayake: *Indian Popular Cinema*, p.102.

14 Satyajit Bhatkal, *The Spirit of Lagaan*, Mumbai: Popular Prakashan, 2002, pp.43; 51.

15 See *www.indiacensus.net*. In 2001, India's population was 1,027,015,247.

16 Quoted in Gokulsing and Dissanayake: *Indian Popular Cinema*, p.7.

17 The order (status group) traditionally associated with the performance of ritual, and the study and teaching of sacred texts.

18 Gokulsing and Dissanayake: *Indian Popular Cinema*, pp.17–18.

19 Barbara D. Metcalf and Thomas R. Metcalf, *A Concise History of India*, Cambridge: Cambridge University Press, 2002, pp.270–1.

20 Veena Das, 'The mythological film and its framework of meaning: an analysis of *Jai Santoshi Ma*', *India International Centre Quarterly*, 8/1, 1980, pp.43–56

21 Julius Lipner, *Hindus: Their Religious Beliefs and Practices*, London: Routledge, 1988, pp.124–35.

22 Mishra: *Bollywood Cinema*, p.4.

23 Quoted in Nasreen Munni Kabir, *Bollywood: The Indian Cinema Story*, London: Channel 4 Books, 2001, p.26

24 Compare the depiction of Hindu and Muslim in *Bombay* (Mani Ratman, 1995). See Ravi. S. Vasudevan, '*Bombay* and its public', in Rachel Dwyer and Christopher Pinney (eds), *Pleasure and the Nation: The History, Politics, and Consumption of Public Culture in India*, Oxford: Oxford University Press, 2001, pp.186–211.

25 See Eck: *Darśan*, pp.1–6; Robert Jackson and Dermot Killingley, *Approaches to Hinduism*, London: John Murray, 1988, pp.106–7.

26 It is important to note here, however, that deities like Brahma and Vishnu are comparatively rarely represented. For this point I am indebted to Srijana Das of Clare Hall, Cambridge University.

27 See Mishra: *Temples of Desire*, pp.48–9. On Ramachandran, see Ashish Rajadhyaksha, 'Indian cinema: origins to independence', in Geoffrey Nowell-Smith (ed.), *The Oxford History of World Cinema*, Oxford: Oxford University Press, 1996, pp.406–7.

28 Given the influence of Romanticism on Indian elite imaginations, Coates's lack of discussion of Indian cinema is, perhaps, regrettable. See Melanie J. Wright, '*Cinema and the Romantic Legacy: Through a Glass Darkly*, by Paul Coates' [review], *Reviews in Religion and Theology*, 11/1, 2004, pp. 113–16.

29 Ira Bhaskar, 'Postmodernism and neo-orientalism: Peter Brook's *Mahabharata* – producing India through a body of multicultural images', in S. Brent Plate and David Jasper (eds) *Imag(in)ing Otherness: Filmic Visions of Living Together*, Atlanta: Scholars, 1999, p.141.

30 Metcalf and Metcalf: *A Concise History of India*, pp.254–5, 261, 268–73.

31 On caste, see Susan Bayly, *Caste, Society and Politics in India From the Eighteenth Century to the Modern Age*, Cambridge: Cambridge University Press, 2001.

32 Mishra: *Bollywood Cinema*, p.30.

33 Whilst sharing Nandy's ('Notes towards an agenda', pp.79–84) impatience with critics who expect Indian film-makers to compensate for society's failure to deliver equality, and acknowledging that Hindi film tends in general towards stereotyping, I do not think that these factors alone invalidate examination of how the various types are presented.

34 Indu Banga, 'The Sikhs under colonial rule', in J.S. Grewal and Indu Banga (eds), *The Khalsa Over Three Hundred Years*, New Delhi: Tulika, 1999, pp.113, 116; Metcalf and Metcalf: *A Concise History of India*, pp.104–5.

35 Bhatkal: *Spirit of Lagaan*, p.8; comments by Aamir Khan in Asif Kapadia, 'Aamir Khan: questions from the floor' [transcript of a question-and-answer session at the National Film Theatre, London, Sunday, 27 October 2002], online at *http://film.guardian.co.uk/interview/interviewpages/0,6737,829913,00.html* (current on 6 November 2003).

36 Quoted in Rajadhyaksha: 'Indian cinema: origins to independence', p.402.

37 Metcalf and Metcalf: *A Concise History of India*, p.152.

38 See further Sumita S. Chakravarty, *National Identity in Indian Popular Cinema 1947–1987*, Austin: University of Texas Press, 1993; Prem Chowdhry, *Colonial India and the Making of Empire Cinema: Image, Ideology and Identity*, Manchester: Manchester University Press, 2000, pp.1–2.

39 Quoted in Metcalf and Metcalf: *A Concise History of India*, p.277.

40 Amin Hajee, actor in *Lagaan* (Bagha, the mute) quoted in Chris England, *Balham to Bollywood*, London: Hodder and Stoughton, 2002, p.73.

41 In this respect, *Lagaan*'s narrative strategy challenges Paul Coates's declaration that 'Indian films are those either of believers or of non-believers' (*Cinema, Religion and the Romantic Legacy: Through a Glass Darkly*, Aldershot: Ashgate, 2003, p.9).

42 Derek Elley, '*Lagaan: Once Upon a Time in India*' [review], *Variety*, 30 July 2001, p.18.

43 Bhatkal: *Spirit of Lagaan*, pp.13–15.

44 Ziya Us Salam, 'Cinema: *Lagaan*' [review], *The Hindu*, 22 June 2001, online at *www.hinduonnet.com/thehindu/2001/06/22/stories/09220227.htm* (current on 3 September 2003).

45 Rachel Dwyer, 'Shooting stars: the Indian film magazine, *Stardust*', in Rachel Dwyer and Christopher Pinney (eds), *Pleasure and the Nation: The History, Politics and Consumption of Popular Culture in India*, Oxford: Oxford University Press, 2001, p.261. *Filmfare* and other journals also appear in Hindi editions, as does the popular *Mayipuri* (with thanks to Srijana Das).

46 Shubha, '"I Was Passionately Involved": Gracy on Aamir and *Lagaan*', in *Cinéblitz International*, 13/3, 2001, pp.30–2.

47 Purnima Lamchhane, 'Aamir's Crazy Obsession', in *Cinéblitz International*, 12/1, 2000, pp.66–8.

48 See Asif Kapadia: 'Aamir Khan: questions from the floor'.

49 Comments by Aamir Khan in Asif Kapadia: 'Aamir Khan: questions from the floor'.

50 Rachel Dwyer, '*Lagaan*' [review], *Sight and Sound*, 11/10, 2001, pp.51–2 and Geoffrey Macnab, Lucy Neville and Ben Walters, '*Lagaan*' [DVD review], *Sight and Sound*, 12/7, 2002, p.60.

51 Roger Ebert, '*Lagaan: Once Upon a Time in India*' [review], *Chicago SunTimes*, 7 June 2002, online at *http://rogerebert.suntimes.com/apps/ pbcs.dll/article?AID=/20020607/REVIEWS/206070305/1023* (current on 8 January 2006); Ed Halter, 'Moulin Raj. *Lagaan: Once Upon a Time in India*' [review], *The Village Voice*, 6 May 2002, online at *www.villagevoice.com /film/0219,halter,34560,20.html* (current on 8 January 2006).

52 Derek Malcolm, 'Epic changes Bollywood for better: *Lagaan: Once Upon a Time in India*', *Screen International*, No. 1321, 24 August 2001, p.34; Anderson Tepper, 'Hooray for Bollywood!', *Vanity Fair*, No. 502, 2002, p.38. On *Lagaan* as entrée to Indian cinema, note, however, the scepticism of Kaleem Aftab in 'Brown: the new black! Bollywood in Britain', *Critical Quarterly*, 44/3, 2002, pp.88–98.

53 Ajit Duara, 'Hollywood magic in India', *The Hindu*, 3 March 2002, online at *www.hinduonnet.com/thehindu/mag/2002/03/03stories/20020 30300380200.htm* (current on 3 September 2003).

54 Shiva Kiran, 'Why *Lagaan* Does Not Need an Oscar', *The Hindu*, 28 March 2002, online at *www.hinduonnet.com/thehindu/mp/2002/03/28/ stories/2002032800260400.htm* (current on 3 September 2003).

55 Gowri Ramnarayan, 'It was *Lagaan* All the Way', *The Hindu*, 2 August 2002, online at *www.hinduonnet.com/thehindu/mp/2002/08/02/stories/ 2002080200030100.htm* (current on 3 September 2003).

IX Conclusions

1 *The Passion of The Christ. Production Notes*, Icon Productions, 2004, p.6.

2 See Eugene Fisher, 'Nostra Aetate', in Edward Kessler and Neil Wenborn (eds), *A Dictionary of Jewish-Christian Relations*, Cambridge: Cambridge University Press, 2006, pp.320–1.

3 See 'All-Time USA Box Office', The Internet Movie Database, online at *http://us.imdb.com/boxoffice/alltimegross* (current on 15 January 2006).

4   Anne Catherine Emmerich, *The Dolorous Passion of Our Lord, Jesus Christ*, El Sobrante: North Bay Books, 2004. Unsurprisingly, this book is now marketed as the work that inspired Gibson's film.

5   See earlier, Chapter II and also Melanie J. Wright, 'Cinema and Film', in Kessler and Wenborn (eds): *Dictionary*, p.98.

6   Mark Kermode, *The Passion of The Christ* [review], *Sight and Sound*, 14/4, 2004, pp.62–3 offers the best succinct account of Gibson's production as a horror film.

7   'Stations of the Cross' refers both to the pictures depicting aspects of Christ's passion and to the particular devotions associated with these images in Catholic tradition. The rosary is a repetitive prayer form, in which worshippers meditate on aspects of the life, death and resurrection of Jesus.

8   On this latter point see Nick James, 'Hell in Jerusalem', *Sight and Sound*, 14/4, 2004, p.17.

9   Paul Schrader, *Transcendental Style in Film: Ozu, Bresson, Dreyer*, Berkley: University of California Press, 1972; Paul Coates, *Cinema, Religion, and the Romantic Legacy: Through a Glass Darkly*, Aldershot: Ashgate, 2003, p.187.

10 See Bordwell in Paul Willemen, *Looks and Frictions: Essays in Cultural Studies and Film Theory*, London: BFI, 1994, p.125.

11 Jean Epstein, 'For a new avant-garde', in P. Adams Sitney (ed.), *The Avant-Garde Film: A Reader of Theory and Criticism*, New York: New York University Press, 1978, p.29.

12 Tom Aitken, Eric Christianson, Peter Francis, Jeffrey F. Keuss, Robert Pope, William R. Telford and Melanie J. Wright, 'Table talk: reflections on *The Passion of The Christ*', in Eric Christianson, Peter Francis and William R. Telford (eds), *Cinéma Divinité: Religion, Theology and the Bible in Film*, London, SCM, 2005, p.321.

13 More generally on religion and media see Jeremy Stolow, 'Religion and/as media', *Theory, Culture and Society*, 22/4, 2005, p.125.

Bibliography

Ackeran, Robert, 'Frazer, James G', in Mircea Eliade (ed.), *The Encyclopedia of Religion*, Vol. 5, London and New York: Macmillan, 1987, pp.414–16.

Adorno, Theodor in J.M. Bernstein (ed.), *The Culture Industry. Selected Essays on Mass Culture*, London: Routledge, 1991.

——and Max Horkheimer, *The Dialactic of Enlightenment*, trans. John Cumming, London and New York: Verso, 1979.

Affron, Charles, *Cinema and Sentiment*, Chicago: University of Chicago Press, 1982.

Aftab, Kaleem, 'Brown: the new black! Bollywood in Britain', *Critical Quarterly*, 4/3, 2002, pp.88–98.

Ahmad, Dohra, '"This fundo stuff is really something new": fundamentalism and hybridity in *The Moor's Last Sigh*', *Yale Journal of Criticism*, 18/1, 2005.

Aichele, George and Richard Walsh (eds), *Screening Scripture: Intertextual Connections Between Scripture and Film*, Harrisburg: Trinity Press International, 2002.

Aitken, Tom, Eric Christianson, Peter Francis, Jeffrey F. Keuss, Robert Pope, William R. Telford and Melanie J. Wright, 'Table talk: reflections on *The Passion of The Christ*', in Christianson, Francis and Telford (eds): *Cinéma Divinité*, pp.311–30.

Altmam, Charles F., 'Towards a historiography of American film', *Cinema Journal*, 16/2, 1977, pp.1–25.

Amberg, George (ed.), *The New York Times Film Reviews: A One Volume Selection 1913–1970*, New York: Arno, 1971.

Appiah, Kwame Anthony, 'Identity crisis', *New York Times*, 17 September 1995, p.42.

Applebaum, Steven, '*The Wicker Man*', *Film Review*, Special No. 16, 1996, pp.19–24.

Aranda, Francisco, *Luis Buñuel: A Critical Biography*, trans. David Robinson, London: Secker and Warburg, 1975.

Babington, Bruce and Peter W. Evans, *Affairs to Remember: The Hollywood Comedy of the Sexes*, Manchester: Manchester University Press, 1989.

—— *Biblical Epics: Sacred Narrative in the Hollywood Cinema*. Manchester: Manchester University Press, 1993.

Babuscio, Jack, 'Camp and the gay sensibility', in Dyer (ed.): *Gays and Film*, pp.40–57.

Baker, Peter, '*The Ten Commandments*' [review], *Films and Filming*, 4/4, 1958, pp.23–4.

Balasubramaniam, Rajes, 'Myth, women and Indian cinema', unpublished pamphlet, London, 1988.

Bandy, Mary Lea and Antonio Monda (eds), *The Hidden God. Film and Faith*, New York: Museum of Modern Art, 2003.

Banga, Indu, 'The Sikhs under colonial rule', in Grewal and Banga (eds): *Khalsa Over Three Hundred*, pp.111–20.

Bartholemew, David, '*The Wicker Man*', *Cinéfantastique*, 6/3, 1977, pp.4–18, 32–42, 46.

Barton, John and John Muddiman (eds), *The Oxford Bible Commentary*, Oxford: Oxford University Press, 2001.

Baugh, Lloyd, *Imaging the Divine: Jesus and Christ-Figures in Film*. Franklin: Sheed and Ward, 2000.

Bayly, Susan, *Caste, Society and Politics in India From the Eighteenth Century to the Modern Age*, Cambridge: Cambridge University Press, 2001.

Bazin, André in Bert Cadullo (ed.), *Bazin at Work: Major Essays and reviews from the Forties and Fifties*, London: Routledge, 1997.

—— 'Cinema and theology', in Bazin: *Bazin at Work*, pp.237–45.

Beal, Timothy K., 'Behold thou the behemoth: imaging the unimaginable in monster movies', in Plate and Jasper (eds): *Imag(in)ing Otherness*, pp.197–211.

Beeman, William O., 'The use of music in popular film: east and west', *India International Film Quarterly*, 8/1, 1980, pp.77–87.

Bergesen, Albert J. and Andrew M. Greeley, *God in the Movies*. New Brunswick: Transaction, 2000.

Bhaskar, Ira, 'Postmodernism and neo-Orientalism: Peter Brook's *Mahabharata* – producing India through a body of multicultural images', in Plate and Jasper (eds): *Imag(in)ing Otherness*, pp.133–65.

Bhatkal, Satyajit, *The Spirit of Lagaan*, Mumbai: Popular Prakashan, 2002.

Billingsley, Kenneth Lloyd, *The Seductive Image: A Christian Critique of the World of Film*, Eugene: Wipf and Stock, 2000.

Binn, John, '*Kadosh*' [review], *Film Review*, 596, 2000, p.30.

Biskind, Peter, *Down and Dirty Pictures: Miramax, Sundance and the Rise of Independent Film*, London: Bloomsbury, 2004.

Black, Gregory D., *Hollywood Censored: Morality, Codes, Catholics and the Movies*. Cambridge: Cambridge University Press, 1994.

—— *The Catholic Crusade Against the Movies, 1940–1975*, Cambridge: Cambridge University Press, 1998.

Blaetz, Robin, *Visions of the Maid: Joan of Arc in American Film and Culture*, Charlottesville: University Press of Virginia, 2001.

Bobo, Jacqueline, '*The Color Purple*: black women as cultural readers', in Pribram (ed.), *Female Spectators*, pp. 90–109.

Bocking, Brian, 'RAP, RFL, and ROL language and religion in higher education', in Masefield and Wiebe (eds): *Aspects of Religion*, pp.131–49.

Bordwell, David, *Filmguide to La Passion de Jeanne d'Arc*, Bloomington: Indiana University Press, 1973.

—— *The Films of Carl Theodor Dreyer*. Berkeley: University Of California Press, 1981.

—— 'Carl Theodor Dreyer: discoveries and rediscoveries', *Scandinavian Review*, 70/2, 1982, pp.60–70.

—— *The McGraw-Hill Film Viewer's Guide*, New York: McGraw-Hill, 2001.

—— and Noël Carroll (eds), *Post-Theory: Reconstructing Film Studies*, Madison, WI: University of Wisconsin Press, 1996.

—— Janet Staiger and Kristin Thompson, *The Classical Hollywood Cinema: Film Style and Mode of Production to 1960*, New York: Columbia University Press, 1985.

Bounds, Philip, *Cultural Studies*. Plymouth: Studymates, 1999.

Boyer, Peter J., 'The Jesus war', *The New Yorker*, 15 September 2003, pp.58–71.

Brackman, Harold, 'The attack on "Jewish Hollywood": a chapter in the history of modern American antisemitism', *Modern Judaism*, 20, 2000, pp.1–19.

Brakhage, Stan, *The Brakhage Lectures: Georges Méliès, David Wark Griffith, Carl Theodor Dreyer, Sergei Eisenstein*, Chicago: The GoodLion, 1972.

Branston, Gill, *Cinema and Cultural Modernity*, Buckingham: Open University Press, 2000.

Brett, Anwar, '*Keeping the Faith*' [review], *Film Review*, 598, 2000, p.33.

Brooker, Will, *Teach Yourself Cultural Studies*, London: Hodder Headline, 1998.

Brottman, Mikita, '*The Wicker Man*', in Bandy and Monda (eds): *The Hidden God*, pp.140–4.

Brown, Allan, *The Wicker Man: The Morbid Ingenuities*, London: Sidgwick and Jackson, 2000.

Brown, David, 'Films, movies, meanings', in Marsh and Ortiz (eds): *Explorations in Theology and Film*, pp.9–19.

Brown, Frank Burch, *Good Taste, Bad Taste, and Christian Taste: Aesthetics in Religious Life*, Oxford: Oxford University Press, 2000.

Bruce, David, *Scotland the Movie*, Edinburgh: Polygon, 1996.

Bruzzi, Stella, *Undressing Cinema: Clothing and Identity in the Movies*, London: Routledge, 1997.

Buckland, Warren, *Teach Yourself Film Studies*, London: Hodder Headline, 1998.

Burgin, Victor, *The Remembered Film*, London: Reaktion, 2004.

Butler, Alison, *Women's Cinema: The Contested Screen*, London: Wallflower, 2002.

Butler, Christopher, *Postmodernism: A Very Short Introduction*, Oxford: Oxford University Press, 2002.

Butler, Ivan, *Horror in the Cinema*, London: A. Zwemmer, 1970.

Byron, Stuart, 'Something Wicker This Way Comes', *Film Comment*, 13/6, 1977, pp.29–31.

Carney, Raymond, *Speaking the Language of Desire: The Films of Carl Dreyer*, Cambridge: Cambridge University Press, 1989.

—— 'Learning from Dreyer – reflections on the lessons his work teaches', programme notes for *Close-Ups: Contemporary Art and Carl Theodor Dreyer*, curated by Lene Crone and Lars Movin (Contemprary Art Center, Copenhagen, in collaboration with NIFCA), 9 November 1999–9 January 2000, pp.82–7.

Carroll, Noël, 'The future of allusion: Hollywood in the seventies (and beyond)', *October*, 20, spring 1982.

—— 'Prospects for film theory: a personal assessment', in Bordwell and Carroll (eds): *Post-Theory*, pp.37–70.

Cawkwell, Tim, *The Filmgoer's Guide to God*, London: Darton, Longman and Todd, 2004.

Ceretto, Luisa, '*Kadosh* (Kadosh)' [review], *Film Tutti I Film Della Stagione*, 8/45, 2000, pp.45–6.

Chakravarty, Sunita S., *National Identity in Indian Popular Cinema 1947–1987*, Austin: University of Texas Press, 1993.

Cherchi Usai, Paolo, *Burning Passions: An Introduction to the Study of Silent Cinema*, London: BFI Publishing, 1994.

Chibnall, Steve and Julian Petley, *British Horror Cinema*, London: Routledge, 2002.

Chowdhry, Prem, *Colonial India and the Making of Empire Cinema: Image, Ideology, and Identity*, Manchester: Manchester University Press, 2000.

Christianson, Eric, 'Movie Moses: a man for all seasons', unpublished paper, Theology and Film weekend, St. Deiniol's, Hawarden, April 2000.

—— 'A fistful of shekels: scrutinizing Ehud's entertaining violence (Judges 3:12–30', *Biblical Interpretation*, 11/1, 2003, pp.53–70.

—— Peter Frances and William R. Telford (eds), *Cinéma Divinité: Religion, Theology and the Bible in Film*, London, SCM Press, 2005.

Christie, Ian, 'The rules of the game', *Sight and Sound*, 12/9, 2002, pp.24–36.

Christopher, David, *British Culture: An Introduction*, Routledge: London, 1999.

Chute, David, '*Lagaan: Once Upon a Time in India*', *Film Comment*, 38/2, 2002, pp.72–3.

Clifton, N. Roy. *The Figure in Film*. London: Associated University Presses, 1983.

Coates, Paul, *Cinema, Religion and the Romantic Legacy: Through a Glass Darkly*, Aldershot: Ashgate, 2003.

Cohan, Steven, 'Judy on the net: Judy Garland and "the gay thing" revisited', in Tinkcomm and Villarejo (eds): *Keyframes*, pp.119–36.

Cohen, Sarah Blacher (ed.), *From Hester Street to Hollywood: The Jewish–American Stage and Screen*, Bloomington, IN: Bloomington University Press, 1983.

Cohen, Stanley, *Folk Devils and Moral Panics: The Creation of the Mods and Rockers*, 2nd edition, Oxford: Martin Robertson, 1980.

Cone, Annabelle, 'The politics of intimacy in Hanif Kuerishi's films and fiction', *Literature/Film Quarterly*, 32/4, 2004, pp.261–4.

Cook, Pam and Mieke Bernink (eds), *The Cinema Book*, 2nd edition, London: BFI, 1999.

Corrigan, Timothy, *A Short Guide to Writing about Film*, New York: HarperCollins, 1989.

Cowie, Peter, *Scandinavian Cinema: A Survey of the Films and Film-Makers of Denmark, Finland, Iceland, Norway and Sweden*, London: Tantivy, 1992.

Craig, Cairns, 'Myths against history: tartanry and kailyard in nineteenth century Scottish literature', in McArthur (ed.): *Scotch Reels*, pp.7–15.

Crofts, Stephen, 'Concepts of national cinema', in Hill and Gibson (eds): *World Cinema*, pp.1–10.

Crowther, Bosley, '*The Ten Commandments*' [review], in Amberg (ed.), *New York Times Reviews*, pp.306–8.

Cunneen, Joseph, *Robert Bresson: A Spiritual Style in Film*, New York: Continuum, 2003.

Curran, James and Vincent Porter (eds), *British Cinema History*, London: Weidenfeld and Nicolson, 1983.

Das, Veena. 'The mythological film and its framework of meaning: an analysis of *Jai Santoshi Ma*', *India International Centre Quarterly*, 8/1, 1980, pp.43–56.

Davies, Andrew, 'Cinema and broadcasting', in Paul Johnson (ed.), *Twentieth Century Britain: Economic, Social and Cultural Change*, London: Longman, 1994.

Davies, Jude and Carol R. Smith, *Gender, Ethnicity and Sexuality in Contemporary American Film*, Edinburgh: Keele University Press, 1997.

Davies, Philip R., 'Life of Brian research', in Exum and Moore (eds): *Biblical Studies, Cultural Studies*, pp.400–14.

Deacy, Christopher, *Screen Christologies: Redemption and the Meaning of Film*, Cardiff: University of Wales Press, 2001.

Deleuze, Gilles, *Cinema I: The Movement-Image*, trans. Hugh Tomlinson and Barbara Habberjam, London: Athlone, 1986.

DeMille, Cecil B. in D. Hayne (ed.), *The Autobiography of Cecil B. DeMille*, London: W.H. Allen, 1960.

Desai, Jigna, *Beyond Bollywood: The Cultural Politics of South Asian Diasporic Film*, London: Routledge, 2004.

Dissanayake, Wimal (ed.), *Cinema and Cultural Identity: Reflections on Films from Japan, India and China*, Lanham: University Press of America, 1988.

Donaldson, Mara E., 'Love and duty in *Casablanca*', in May (ed.): *Image and Likeness*, pp.119–25.

Dönmez-Colin, Gönül, *Women, Islam and Cinema*, London: Reaktion, 2004.

Dorsky, Nathaniel, 'Devotional cinema', in Bandy and Monda (eds): *The Hidden God*, pp.261–80.

Driver, T.S., 'Hollywood in the wilderness: a review article', *The Christian Century*, 73/48, 1956, pp.1390–1.

Drury, John (ed.), *Critics of the Bible, 1724–1873*, Cambridge: Cambridge University Press, 1989.

Duara, Ajit, 'Hollywood magic in India', *The Hindu*, 3 March 2002, online at *www.hinduonnet.com/thehindu/mag/2002/03/03/stories/2002030300380200.htm* (current on 3 September 2003).

Dwyer, Rachel, 'Shooting stars: the Indian film magazine, *Stardust*', in Dwyer and Pinney (eds): *Pleasure and the Nation*, pp.247–85.

—— '*Lagaan*' [review], *Sight and Sound*, 11/10, 2001, pp.51–2.

—— and Divia Patel (eds), *Cinema India: The Visual Culture of Hindi Film*, London: Reaktion, 2002.

Dwyer, Rachel and Christopher Pinney (eds), *Pleasure and the Nation: The History, Politics and Consumption of Popular Culture in India*, Oxford: Oxford University Press, 2001.

Dyer, Frank, 'The moral development of the silent drama', *Edison Kinematogram*, 15 April 1910, p.11.

Dyer, Richard (ed.), *Gays and Film*, revised edition, New York: Zoetrope, 1984.

—— *Only Entertainment*, London: Routledge, 1992.

—— 'Introduction to film studies', in Hill and Gibson (eds): *Film Studies*, pp.1–8.

Earle, Wendy (ed.), *Bollywood and Beyond: A Guide to Teaching Indian Cinema*, London: BFI, 2002.

Ebert, Roger, '*Lagaan: Once Upon a Time in India*' [review], *Chicago SunTimes*, 7 June 2002, online at *http://rogerebert.suntimes.com /apps/pbcs.dll/article?AID=/20020607/REIEWS/206070305/ 1023* (current on 8 January 2006).

Eck, Diana, *Darśan. Seeing the Divine Image in India*, 3rd edition, New York: Columbia University Press, 1998.

Eco, Umberto, *Travels in Hyperreality*, San Diego: Harcourt Brace Jovanovich, 1986.

Edwards, H.J., (trans.), *Caesar. The Gallic War* (Loeb Classical Library), London: William Heinemann, 1922.

Eliade, Mircea (ed.), *The Encyclopedia of Religion*, London and New York: Macmillan, 1987.

Elley, Derek, '*Lagaan: Once Upon a Time in India*', *Variety*, 30 July 2001, pp.18–19.

Emmerich, Anne Catherine, *The Dolorous Passion of Our Lord, Jesus Christ*, El Sobrante: North Bay Books, 2004.

England, Chris, *Balham to Bollywood*, London: Hodder and Stoughton, 2002.

Ephron, Nora, 'Why not him?', *Interview*, 30/4, 2000, pp.118–23.

Epstein, Jean, 'For a new avant-garde', in Sitney (ed.): *The Avant-Garde Film*, pp.26–30.

Evett, Robert, 'There was a young fellow from Goshen', *New Republic*, 135/24, 1956, p.20.

Exum, J. Cheryl and Stephen D. Moore (eds), *Biblical Studies, Cultural Studies. The Third Sheffield Colloquium*, Sheffield: Sheffield Academic, 1998.

Fainaru, Dan, '*Holy (Kadosh)*' [review], *Cinemaya*, 46, 1999, pp.26–7.

Farsoun, Samih K. and Mehrdad Mashayekhi (eds), *Iran: Political Culture in the Islamic Republic*, London: Routledge, 1992.

Fenton, Harvey, '*The Wicker Man*', *Flesh and Blood*, 3, 1994, p.43.

Field, Norman, *Silent Films to 'Talkies.' A History of the Empire Cinema, Littleport*, Littleport: Littleport Society, 1989.

Fields, Doug and Eddie James, *Videos That Teach: Teachable Movie Moments from 75 Modern Film Classics*, Grand Rapids: Zondervan, 1999.

Fisher, Eugene, 'Nostra Aetate', in Kessler and Wenborn (eds): *Dictionary of Jewish-Christian Relations*, pp.320–1.

Fiske, John, *Reading the Popular*, Boston: Unwin Hyman, 1989.

Frayling, Christopher, *Nightmare: The Birth of Horror*, London: BBC Books, 1996.

Frazer, James George, *The Golden Bough. A Study in Magic and Religion. Part I. The Magic Art and the Evolution of Kings*, 2 vols., 3rd edition, London: Macmillan, 1911.

—— *The Golden Bough. A Study in Magic and Religion. Part VI. The Scapegoat*, 3rd edition, London: Macmillan, 1913.

—— *The Golden Bough. A Study in Magic and Religion. Part VII. Balder the Beautiful: The Fire Festivals of Europe and the Doctrine of the External Soul*, 2 vols., 3rd edition, London: Macmillan, 1913.

—— *The Golden Bough. A Study in Magic and Religion*, abridged edition, London: Macmillan, 1963.

Freer, Ian, '*Keeping the Faith*' [review], *Empire*, 136, 2000, p.45.

—— 'In person: Jenna Elfman', *Empire*, 136, 2000, pp.100–1.

Friedman, Lester D. (ed.), *Unspeakable Images: Ethnicity and the American Cinema*, Chicago: University of Illinois Press, 1991.

Geetha, J., 'Bollywood ending', *Sight and Sound*, 13/6, 2003, pp.31–2.

Gellrich, Michelle, *Tragedy and Theory: The Problem of Conflict Since Aristotle*, Princeton: Princeton University Press, 1988.

Geraghty, Christine, *My Beautiful Laundrette*, London: I.B.Tauris, 2004.

Gibbs, Patrick, '*The Wicker Man*' [review], *Daily Telegraph*, 28 December 1973.

Gledhill, Christine, 'The horror film', in Cook and Bernink (eds): *The Cinema Book*, pp.194–204.

Gokulsing, K. Moti and Wimal Dissanayake, *Indian Popular Cinema – A Narrative of Cultural Change*. London: Trentham, 1998.

Greenblum, Joseph, 'Does Hollywood still glorify Jewish intermarriage? The case of the Jazz Singer', *American Jewish History*, 83/1, 1995.

Grewal, J.S. and Indu Banga (eds), *The Khalsa Over Three Hundred Years*, New Delhi: Tulika, 1999.

Grieseson, Lee, '"A kind of recreative school for the whole family": making cinema respectable, 1907–09', *Screen*, 42/1, 2001, pp.64–76.

Grossberg, Lawrence, 'Is there a fan in the house?: the affective sensibility of fandom', in Lewis (ed.): *Adoring Audience: Fan Culture*, pp.40–54.

Gunston, David. 'Carl Dreyer: film-maker of genius', *American Scandinavian Review*, 46, 1958, pp.229–37.

Gunter, Barry and Rachel Viney, *Seeing is Believing: Religion and Television in the 1990s*, London: John Libbey, 1994.

Habermas, Jürgen, *The Structural Transformation of the Public Sphere. An Inquiry into a Category of Bourgeois Society*, trans. Thomas Burger, Cambridge: Polity Press, 1992.

Hall, Donald (ed.), *A Choice of Whitman's Verse*, London: Faber and Faber, 1968.

Hall, Mordaunt, 'Poignant French film – Maria Falconetti gives unequaled performance as Jeanne d'Arc', *New York Times*, 31 March 1929, s.8, 7.

Hall, Stuart, 'New ethnicities', in Morley and Chen (eds): *Stuart Hall*, pp.441–9.

—— 'Cultural identity and diaspora', in Rutherford (ed.): *Identity*, pp.222–37.

Halter, Ed, 'Moulin Raj. *Lagaan: Once Upon a Time in India*' [review], *The Village* Voice, 6 May 2002, online at *www.villagevoice.com/film/0219,halter,34560,20.html* (current on 8 January 2006).

Hames, Peter (ed.), *The Cinema of Central Europe*, London: Wallflower, 2004.

Hanna, Martha, 'Iconology and ideology: images of Joan of Arc in the idiom of the *Action française*, 1908–1931', *French Historical Studies*, 14/2, 1985, pp.215–39.

Hanson, R.P.C., *Allegory and Event: A Study of the Sources and Significance of Origen's Interpretation of Scripture*, London: SCM, 1959.

Haralambos, Michael and Michael Holborn, *Sociology: Themes and Perspectives*, 4th edition, London: Collins Educational, 1995.

Hardy, Robin and Anthony Shaffer, *The Wicker Man*, Feltham: Hamlyn, 1980.

Hark, Ina Rae (ed.), *Exhibition: The Film Reader*, London: Routledge, 2002.

Harries, Martin, 'Forgetting Lot's wife: Artaud, spectatorship and catastrophe', *Yale Journal of Criticism*, 11/1, 1998, pp.221–38.

Hatch, Robert, 'Theatre and films', *Nation*, 8 December 1956, p.506.

Hayward, Susan, *Cinema Studies. The Key Concepts*, 2nd edition, London: Routledge, 2000.

Hebdige, Dick, *Subculture: The Meaning of Style*, London: Methuen, 1979.

Higham, Charles, *Cecil B. DeMille*, London: W.H. Allen, 1974.

Hill, John and Pamela Church Gibson (eds), *Film Studies: Critical Approaches*. Oxford: Oxford University Press, 2000.

—— —— (eds), *World Cinema: Critical Approaches*. Oxford: Oxford University Press, 2000.

Hinxman, Margaret, 'The Wicker Man' [review], *Sunday Telegraph*, 16 December 1973.

Hodgens, R.M., 'The Ten Commandments', *Film Quarterly*, 20/1, 1966, pp.59–60.

Holloway, Ronald, *The Religious Dimension in Cinema: With Particular Reference to the Films of Carl Theodor Dreyer, Ingmar Bergman and Robert Bresson*. Hamburg: University Of Hamburg Press, 1972.

Hunter, Allan, 'Sacred (Kadosh)' [review], *Screen International*, 21 May 1999, p.18.

Hutchings, Peter, *Hammer and Beyond: The British Horror Film*, Manchester: Manchester University Press, 1993.

Jaafar, Ali, 'Babylon's turning', *Sight and Sound*, 16/1, 2006, p.5.

Jackson, Kevin (ed.), *Schrader on Schrader*, London: Faber and Faber, 1990.

Jackson, Robert and Dermot Killingley, *Approaches to Hinduism*, London: John Murray, 1988.

James, Nick, 'In a harsh light', *Sight and Sound*, 10/8, 2000, pp.28–30.

—— 'Hell in Jerusalem', *Sight and Sound*, 14/4, 2004, pp.15–18.

Jancovich, Marc, 'Cult fictions: cult movies, subcultural capital and the production of cultural distinctions', *Cultural Studies*, 16/2, 2002, pp.306–22.

Jasper, David, 'On systematizing the unsystematic: a response', in Marsh and Ortiz (eds): *Explorations in Theology and Film*, pp.235–44.

Jenkins, Henry, *Textual Poachers: Television Fans and Participatory Culture*, London: Routledge, 1992.

—— 'Bombay awakes!', *Technology Review*, 2 July 2004, online at *www.technologyreview.com/InfoTech/wtr_13706,258,p1.html* (current on 5 December 2005).

Jewett, Robert, *Saint Paul at the Movies: The Apostle's Dialogue with American Culture*, Louisville: Westminster/John Knox, 1993.

—— *Saint Paul Returns to the Movies: Triumph Over Shame*, Grand Rapids: Eerdmans, 1999.

Johnson, Paul (ed.), *Twentieth Century Britain: Economic, Social and Cultural Change*, London: Longman, 1994.

Johnson, Richard, 'What is cultural studies anyway?', *Social Text*, 16, 1986, pp.38–80.

Johnston, Robert K., *Reel Spirituality: Theology and Film in Dialogue*, Grand Rapids: Baker Academic, 2000.

Johnston, Sheila, 'My Son the Fanatic' [review], *Screen International*, 1107, 9 May 1997.

Juschka, Darlene M., 'The construction of pedagogical spaces: religious studies in the university', *Studies in Religion/Sciences Religieuses*, 28/1, 1999, pp.85–97.

Kabir, Nasreen Munni, *Bollywood: The Indian Cinema Story*, London: Channel 4 Books, 2001.

Kakar, Sudhir, 'The ties that bind: family relationships in the mythology of Hindi cinema', *India International Centre Quarterly*, 8/1, 1980, pp.11–21.

Kaleta, Kenneth C., *Hanif Kureihi. Postcolonial Storyteller*, Austin: University of Texas Press, 1998.

Kapadia, Asif, 'Aamir Khan: questions from the floor' [transcript of a question-and answer-session at the National Film Theatre, London, 27 October 2002], online at *http://film.guardian.co.uk/*

interview/interviewpages/0,6737,829913,00.html (current on 6 November 2003).

Kassam, Tazim R., 'Editorial', *Spotlight on Teaching*, 18/3, 2003, p.i.

Kemp, Philip, *Lethal Innocence: The Cinema of Alexander Mackendrick*, London: Methuen, 1991, pp.39–40.

—— 'Keeping the Faith' [review], *Sight and Sound*, 10/10, 2000, pp.48–9.

Kennedy, G., H.L. Clark, D.M. Stowe, L.C. Moorehead and W. Lindsay Young, 'Through different eyes', *Christian Century*, 74/1, 1957, pp.20–1.

Kermode, Mark, *The Passion of The Christ* [review], *Sight and Sound*, 14/4, 2004, pp.62–3.

Kessler, Edward and Neil Wenborn (eds), *A Dictionary of Jewish–Christian Relations*, Cambridge: Cambridge University Press, 2006.

—— and Melanie J. Wright (eds), *Themes in Jewish–Christian Relations*, Cambridge: Orchard Academic, 2005.

King, Geoff, *New Hollywood Cinema. An Introduction*, London, I.B.Tauris, 2002.

King, Noel, 'New Hollywood', in Cook and Bernink (eds): *The Cinema Book*, pp.98–106.

Kiran, Shiva, 'Why *Lagaan* does not need an Oscar', *The Hindu*, 28 March 2002, online at *www.hinduonnet.com/thehindu/mp/2002/03/28/stories/2002032800260400.htm* (current on 3 September 2003).

Kitchin, Laurence, *'The Ten Commandments'* [review], *Sight and Sound*, 27, 1957, pp.148–9.

Klepper, Robert, '*The Ten Commandments*', *Classic Images*, 285, 1999, pp.41–2.

Klein, Julie Thompson, *Crossing Boundaries: Knowledge, Disciplinarities, and Interdisciplinarities*, Charlottesville and London: University Press of Virginia, 1996.

Klinger, Barbara, 'Digressions at the cinema: reception and mass culture', *Cinema Journal*, 28/4, 1989, pp.3–19.

—— *Melodrama and Meaning: History, Culture and the Films of Douglas Sirk*, Bloomington: Indiana University Press, 1994.

Konigsberg, Ira, '"The only I" in the world: religion, psychoanalysis, and *The Dubbuk*', in Paskin (ed.): *When Joseph Met Molly*, pp.169–99.

Kreitzer, Larry J., *The New Testament in Fiction and Film: On Reversing the Hermeneutical Flow*, Sheffield: JSOT, 1993.

—— *The Old Testament in Fiction and Film: On Reversing the Hermeneutical Flow*, Sheffield: Sheffield Academic, 1994.

Krzywinska, Tanya, *A Skin for Dancing In: Possession, Witchcraft and Voodoo in Film*, Trowbridge: Flicks, 2000.

Kuhn, Annette, 'Classic Hollywood narrative', in Cook and Bernink (eds): *The Cinema Book*, pp.39–41.

—— 'The British film industry', in Cook and Bernink (eds): *The Cinema Book*, pp.83–9.

—— *Everyday Magic – Cinema and Cultural Memory*, London: I.B.Tauris, 2002.

Kureishi, Hanif, 'My Son the Fanatic', in *Love in a Blue Time*, New York: Simon and Schuster, 1999, pp.119–31.

—— *Love in a Blue Time*, New York: Simon and Schuster, 1999.

—— 'Sex and secularity', *Filmmaker*, 10/4, 2002, pp.26–8.

—— *Collected Screenplays 1. My Beautiful Laundrette, Sammy and Rosie Get Laid, London Kills Me, My Son the Fanatic*, London: Faber and Faber, 2002.

Kurtz, Stanley N., *All the Mothers are One: Hindu India and the Cultural Reshaping of Psychoanalysis*, New York: Columbia University Press, 1992.

Lamchhane, Purnima, 'Aamir's crazy obsession', *Cinéblitz International*, 12/1, 2000, pp.66–8.

Lapsley, Robert and Michael Westlake, *Film Theory: An Introduction.* Manchester: Manchester University Press, 1998.

Le Fanu, Mark, 'Bewitched', *Sight and Sound*, 13/7, 2003, pp.30–2.

Levy, Emanuel, 'Slick show of "faith"' [review],*Variety*, 3 April 2000, pp.32, 43.

Lewis, Lisa (ed.), *The Adoring Audience: Fan Culture and Popular Media*, London: Routledge, 1992.

Lewis, Philip, *Islamic Britain: Religion, Politics and Identity Among British Muslims*, London: I.B.Tauris, 2002.

Lindvall, Terry, *The Silents of God: Selected Issues and Documents in Silent American Film and Religion 1908–1925*, London and Lanham: Scarecrow Press, 2001.

Lipner, Julius, *Hindus: Their Religious Beliefs and Practices*, London: Routledge, 1994.

Lothe, Jakob, *Narrative in Fiction and Film: An Introduction.* Oxford: Oxford University Press, 2000.

Loughlin, Gerard, 'Breezes. Religious images in the age of mechanical reproduction', *Louvain Studies*, 27, 2002, pp.265–79.

Louvish, Simon, 'The Bible from God to Dreamworks', *Sight and Sound*, 9/1 , 1999, pp.22–5.

Lubin, David M., *Titanic* (BFI Modern Classics), London: BFI, 1999.

Luhr, William, (ed.), *World Cinema Since 1945*, New York: Ungar, 1987.

Lyden, John C., *Film as Religion: Myths, Morals and Rituals*, New York: New York University Press, 2003.

McArthur, Colin, (ed.), *Scotch Reels: Scotland in Cinema and Television*, London: British Film Institute Publishing, 1982.

McDannell, Colleen, *Material Christianity: Religion and Popular Culture in America*, New Haven and London: Yale University Press, 1995.

McFarlane, Brian, *Novel to Film: An Introduction to the Theory of Adaptation.* Oxford: Clarendon, 1992.

McFarlane, Brian, '"It Wasn't Like That in the Book"', *Literature/Film Quarterly*, 28/3, 2000, pp.163–9.

McGillivray, David, '*The Wicker Man* [review], *Monthly Film Bulletin*, January 1974.

MacKillop, James, *Dictionary of Celtic Mythology*, Oxford: Oxford University Press, 1998.

MacNab, Geoffrey, Lucy Neville and Ben Walters, '*Lagaan*' [DVD review], *Sight and Sound*, 12/7, 2002.

McLeod, Hew, *Sikhism*, London: Penguin, 1997.

Magill, Frank N. (ed.), *Magill's Survey of Cinema: Silent Films*, Vol. 2, Epping: Bowker, 1982.

Maisto, Maria Consuelo, 'Cinematic communion? *Babette's Feast*, transcendental style, and interdisciplinarity', in Plate and Jasper (eds): *Imag(in)ing Otherness*, pp.83–98.

Malcolm, Derek, 'Epic changes Bollywood for better. *Lagaan: Once Upon a Time in India*', *Screen International*, 1321, 2001, p.34.

Malik, Rachel, '*My Son the Fanatic*' [review], *Sight and Sound*, 8/5, 1998, pp.53–4.

Malone, Peter, '*Edward Scissorhands*: Christology from a suburban fairy-tale', in Marsh and Ortiz (eds): *Explorations in Theology and Film*, pp.73–86.

—— Roberto Pazos and Ferdinand Poswick, '*The Prince of Egypt*', *Cine and Media*, 1, 1999, pp.5–8.

Malpezzi, Frances M. and William M. Clements, 'The Passion of Joan of Arc (La Passion de Jeanne d'Arc)', in Magill (ed.): *Magill's Survey of Cinema*, pp.854–7

Margolis, Nadia, 'Trial by passion: philology, film and ideology in the portrayal of Joan of Arc (1900–1930)', *Journal of Medieval and Early Modern Studies*, 27/3, 1997, pp.445–93.

Marsh, Clive and Gaye Ortiz (eds), *Explorations in Theology and Film: Movies and Meaning*. Oxford: Blackwell, 1997.

Martin, Joel W., 'Introduction: seeing the sacred on the screen', in Martin and Ostwalt (eds): *Screening the Sacred*, pp.1–12.

Martin, Joel W. and Conrad E. Ostwalt (eds), *Screening the Sacred: Religion, Myth, and Ideology in Popular American Film*, Boulder, CO: Westview, 1995.

Masefield, Peter and Donald Wiebe (eds), *Aspects of Religion. Essays in Honour of Ninian Smart*, New York: Peter Lang, 1994.

May, John R., *Image and Likeness: Religious Visions in American Film Classics*. Mahwah, NJ: Paulist, 1992.

Meggitt, Justin J., '*The Social World of Jesus and the Gospels*, by Bruce Malina' [review], *Journal of Theological Studies*, 49/1, 1998, pp.215–19.

——and Melanie J. Wright, 'Interdisciplinarity in learning and teaching in religious studies', in Balasubramanyam Chandramohan and Stephen Fallows (eds), *Interdisciplinary Learning and Teaching. Theory and Practice in Contemporary Higher Education*, London: RoutledgeFarmer, in press 2006.

Mercer, Kobena, *Welcome to the Jungle: New Positions in Black Cultural Studies*, London: Routledge, 1994.

—— *Black Film British Cinema*, ICA Documents 7, London: BFI, c.1988.

Metcalf, Barbara D. and Thomas R. Metcalf, *A Concise History of India*, Cambridge: Cambridge University Press, 2002.

Miles, Margaret R., *Seeing and Believing: Religion and Values in the Movies*, Boston: Beacon, 1998.

Miller, Toby, '(How) Does film theory work?', *Continuum: Journal of Media and Cultural Studies*, 6/1, 1992, pp.186–211.

—— 'Cinema studies doesn't matter; or, I know what you did last semester', in Tinkcomm and Villarejo (eds): *Keyframes*, pp.303–11.

Milne, Tom, 'Darkness and light: Carl Theodor Dreyer', *Sight and Sound*, 34/4, 1965, pp.167–72.

Mini, 'Wild fire! Aamir's *Lagaan* magic', *Cinéblitz International*, 13/4, 2001, pp.46–8, 50, 52.

Mishra, Vijay, *Bollywood Cinema: Temples of Desire*, London: Routledge, 2002.

Monaco, James, *How to Read a Film: The World of Movies, Media, Multimedia: Language, History, Theory*, 3rd edition, Oxford: Oxford University Press, 2000.

Moore, Robert L., *Religious Outsiders and the Making of Americans*. Oxford: Oxford University Press, 1986.

Moore-Gilbert, Bart, *Hanif Kureishi*, Manchester: Manchester University Press, 2001.

Moran, Joe, *Interdisciplinarity*, London: Routledge, 2002.

Morley, David, and Kuan-hsing Chen (eds), *Stuart Hall: Critical Dialogues in Cultural Studies*, London: Routledge, 1996.

—— and Kevin Robins (eds), *British Cultural Studies: Geography, Nationality, Identity*, Oxford: Oxford University Press, 2001.

Morris, Meaghan, 'Brasschaat-Bombay: a way of inhabiting a culture', in Paul Willemen, *Looks and Frictions: Essays in Cultural Studies and Film Theory*, London: BFI, 1994, pp.1–23.

Musser, Charles, 'Passions and the passion play: theatre, film and religion in America, 1880–1900', *Film History*, 5, 1993, pp.419–56.

Nadel, Alan, 'God's Law and the wide screen: *The Ten Commandments* as Cold War epic', *Proceedings of the Modern Language Association of America*, 108, pp.415–30.

Nandy, Ashis, 'Notes towards an agenda for the next generation of film theorists in India', *South Asian Popular Culture*, 1/1, 2003, pp.79–84.

Nash, Mark, *Dreyer*. London: BFI, 1977.

—— 'Joan complete: a Dreyer discovery', *Sight and Sound*, 54/3, 1985, pp.157–8.

Neale, Steve (ed.), *Genre and Contemporary Hollywood*, London: British Film Institute Publishing, 2002.

Nelson, Richard Alan, 'Mormons as silent cinema villains: propaganda and entertainment', *Historical Journal of Film, Radio and Television*, 4/1, 1984, pp.3-14.

Nesselson, Lisa, '*Sacred (Kadosh)*' [review], *Variety*, 17 May 1999, pp.53, 57.

Noerdlnger, Henry S., *Moses and Egypt: The Documentation to the Motion Picture* The Ten Commandments, Los Angeles: University of Southern California Press, 1956.

Nolan, Steve, 'The books of the films: trends in religious film-analysis', *Literature and Theology*, 12/1, 1998, pp.1–15.

Nowell-Smith, Geoffrey (ed.), *The Oxford History of World Cinema*, Oxford: Oxford University Press, 1996.

Nye, Malory, *Religion: The Basics*, London: Routledge, 2003.

O'Brien, Charles, 'Rethinking national cinema: Dreyer's *La Passion de Jeanne D'Arc* and the academic aesthetic', *Cinema Journal*, 35/4, 1996, pp.3–30.

Ochs, Vanessa, 'What makes a Jewish home Jewish?', *CrossCurrents*, 49/4, 2000, available at *www.crosscurrents.org/ochsv.htm* (current on 1 November 2001).

Ostwalt, Conrad E., 'Conclusion: religion, film and cultural analysis', in Martin and Ostwalt (eds): *Screening the Sacred*, pp.152–9.

—— *Secular Steeples: Popular Culture and the Religious Imagination*, Harrisburg: Trinity Press International, 2003.

Otto, Rudolf, *The Idea of Holy: An Inquiry into the Non-Rational Factor in the Idea of the Divine and its Relation to the Rational*, trans. John W. Harvey, Oxford: Oxford University Press, 1926.

Ouellet, B., 'Three different stories about religion in society', *Ciné et Média*, 5, 1999, pp.22–3.

Pardes, Ilana, 'Moses goes down to Hollywood: miracles and special effects', *Semeia*, 74, 1996, pp.15–31.

Parkinson, David, '*My Son the Fanatic*' [review], *Empire*, 108, 1998.

Paskin, Sylvia (ed.), *When Joseph Met Molly. A Reader on Yiddish Film*, Nottingham: Fine leaves, 1999.

Perotti, Luca, '*Tentazioni d'Amore*' ('*Keeping the Faith*') [review], *Film Tutti I Film Della Stagione*, 8/48, 2000, pp.58–9.

Peters, Patrick, '*Kadosh*' ('*Keeping the Faith*') [review], *Empire*, 135, 2000, p.59.

Petrie, Duncan, 'British cinema: the search for identity', in Nowell-Smith (ed.): *Oxford History of World Cinema*, pp.604–13.

—— *Screening Scotland*, London: BFI, 2000.

Peucker, Brigitte, *Incorporating Images: Film and the Rival Arts*. Princeton: Princeton University Press, 1995.

Phillips, William H, *Film: An Introduction*. Boston: Bedford St. Martins, 1999.

Pines, Jim and Paul Willemen (eds), *Questions of Third Cinema*, London: BFI, 1989.

Pipolo, Tony, 'The spectre of Joan of Arc: textual variations in the key prints of Carl Dreyer's film', *Film History*, 2/4, 1988, pp.301–24.

Pizzello, Chris, '*The Wicker Man*' [DVD review], *American Cinematographer*, 83/2, 2002, pp.16, 18.

Plate, S. Brent, 'Religion/literature/film: toward a religious visuality of film', *Literature and Theology*, 12/1, 1998, pp.16–38.

——and David Jasper (eds), *Imag(in)ing Otherness: Filmic Visions of Living Together*. Atlanta: Scholars, 1999.

Porter, Vincent, 'The context of creativity: Ealing Studios and Hammer films', in Curran and Porter (eds): *British Cinema History*, pp.179–207.

Powell, Dilys, '*The Wicker Man*' [review], *Sunday Times*, 16 December 1973

Prasad, M. Madhava, *Ideology of the Hindi Film: A Historical Construction*, Delhi: Oxford University Press, 1998.

Pribram, D.B. (ed.), *Female Spectators: Looking at Film and Television*, London: Verso, 1988.

Price, Roger, *A Concise History of France*. Cambridge: Cambridge University Press, 1993.

Procter, James, *Stuart Hall*, London: Routledge, 2004.

Quart, Leonard, '*My Son the Fanatic* [review]', *Cineaste*, 24/4, 1999, pp.42–3.

Qureshi, Irtiza, 'Fundamental truths', *Black Film Bulletin*, 5/2, 1997, pp.32–3.

Radway, Janice, *Reading the Romance: Women, Patriarchy, and Popular Literature*, Chapel Hill: University of North Carolina Press, 1984.

Rajadhyaksha, Ashish, 'Indian cinema: origins to independence', in Nowell-Smith (ed.): *Oxford History of World Cinema*, pp.398–409.

—— 'Indian cinema', in Hill and Gibson (eds): *World Cinema*, pp.151–6.

Ramnarayan, Gowri, 'It was *Lagaan* all the way', *The Hindu*, 2 August 2002, online at *www.hinduonnet.com/thehindu/mp/2002/08/02/stories/2002080200030100.htm* (current on 3 September 2003).

Ranasinha, Ruvani, *Hanif Kureishi*, Tavistock: Northcote House, 2002.

Ray, Robert B., *How a Film Theory Got Lost and Other Mysteries in Cultural Studies*, Bloomington: Indiana University Press, 2001.

Reinhartz, Adele, *Scripture on the Silver Screen*, Louisville: Westminster John Knox, 2003.

Ridgeon, Lloyd, *Makhmalbaf's Broken Mirror: The Social–Political Significance of Modern Iranian Cinema* (Durham Middle East Papers No. 64), Durham: University of Durham Centre for Middle Eastern and Islamic Studies.

Riesman, David and Evelyn T. Riesman, 'Movies and audiences', *American Quarterly*, 4/3, 1952, pp.195–202.

Rigby, Jonathan, *English Gothic: A Century of Horror Cinema*, 2nd edition, London: Reynolds and Hearn, 2002.

Ringgold, Gene and De W. Bodeen, *The Films of Cecil B. DeMille*, New York: Citadel, 1969.

Rohrer-Walsh, Jennifer, 'Coming-of-age in *The Prince of Egypt*', in Aichele and Walsh (eds): *Screening Scripture*, pp.77–99.

Rose, Gillian, 'Beginnings of the day: fascism and representation', in Bryan Cheyette and Laura Marcus (eds), *Modernity, Culture and 'the Jew'*, Cambridge: Polity Press, 1998.

Rosenberg, Joel, 'Jewish experience on film – an American overview', in David Singer (ed.), *Jewish Year Book 1996*, New York: American Jewish Committee, 1996, pp.1–50.

Rosenstone, Robert A., *Visions of the Past. The Challenge of Film to Our Idea of History*. Cambridge: Harvard University Press, 1995.

Rudolph, Eric, 'A house under siege', *American Cinematographer*, 80/7, 1999, pp.18–26.

Rutherford, Jonthan (ed.), *Identity: Community, Culture, Difference*, London: Lawrence and Wishart, 1990.

Sarris, Andrew, 'The Scandinavian Presence in the Cinema', *Scandinavian Review*, 70/3, 1982, pp.77–85.

Sawnhey, Cary Rajinder, 'Indian cinema and the Asian diaspora', in Earle (ed.): *Bollywood and Beyond*, Unit 8.

Schrader, Paul, *Transcendental Style in Film: Ozu, Bresson, Dreyer*. Berkeley: University of California Press, 1972.

Schroeder, Caroline T., 'Ancient Egyptian rites on the silver screen: modern anxieties about race, ethnicity and religion', *Journal of Religion and Film*, 7/2, 2003, online at *www.unomaha.edu/~wwwjrf/Vol7No2/ancientegypt.htm* (current on 22 October 2003).

Schatz, Thomas, 'Paramount Picture', in Cook and Bernink (eds): *The Cinema Book*, pp.13–16.

Schmid, Susanne, 'Exploring multiculturalism. Bradford Jews and Bradford Pakistanis', *Journal for the Study of British Cultures*, 4/1–2, 1997, pp.163–79.

Scott, Bernard Brandon, *Hollywood Dreams and Biblical Stories*. Minneapolis: Fortress, 1994.

Sedgwick, Eve Kosofsky, *Between Men: English Literature and Male Homosocial Desire*, New York: Columbia University Press, 1985.

Segal, Robert A., *Myth: A Very Short Introduction*, Oxford: Oxford University Press, 2004.

Seville, John, 'The greatest show on Earth', *Classic Images*, 220, 1993, pp.48–50.

Shaffer, Anthony, '*The Wicker Man* and Others', *Sight and Sound*, 5/8, 1995, pp.28–9.

Sharp, David, *Bigger Than Bollywood*, London: BFI National Library, 2002.

Sheen, Erica, '"The light of God's Law": violence and metaphysics in the '50s widescreen biblical epic', *Biblical Interpretation*, 6, 1998, pp.292–312.

Sherry, Patrick, *Images of Redemption: Art, Literature and Salvation*, London: T. and T. Clark, 2003.

Shubha, '"I was passionately involved...": Gracy on Aamir and *Lagaan*', *Cinéblitz International*, 13/3, 2001, pp.30–2.

Simpson, Jacqueline and Steve Roud, *A Dictionary of English Folklore*, Oxford: Oxford University Press, 2000.

Singh, Yogendra, *Culture Change in India: Identity and Globalization*, Jaipur and New Delhi: Rawat, 2000.

Sitney, P. Adams (ed.), *The Avant-Garde Film: A Reader of Theory and Criticism*, New York: New York University Press, 1978.

Skillman, Teri, 'Songs in Hindi Films: nature and function', in Dissanayake (ed.): *Cinema and Cultural Identity*, pp.149–58.

Sklar, Robert, *Movie-Made America: A Cultural History of American Movies*, London: Chappell, 1975.

Skoller, Donald (ed.), *Dreyer in Double Reflection. Translation of Carl Th. Dreyer's Writings About the Film (Om Filmen)*, New York: E.P. Dutton, 1973.

Smart, Ninian, *The Science of Religion and The Sociology of Knowledge*, Princeton: Princeton University Press, 1973.

Smelik, Anneke, 'Feminist film theory', in Cook and Bernink (eds): *The Cinema Book*, pp.353–62.

Smith, Jeffery A., 'Hollywood theology: the commodification of religion in twentieth-century films', *Religion and American Culture*, 11/2, 2001, pp.191–231.

Smoodin, Eric, '"Compulsory" viewing for every citizen: *Mr. Smith* and the rhetoric of reception', in Tinkcomm and Villarejo (eds): *Keyframes*, pp.343–58.

Sobchack, Vivian, 'The fantastic', in Nowell-Smith (ed.): *Oxford History of World Cinema*, pp.312–21.

Soila, Tytti (ed.), *The Cinema of Scandinavia*, London: Wallflower Press, 2005.

Spiegel, Alan, 'The vanishing act: a typology of the Jew in contemporary film', in Cohen (ed.): *Hester Street to Hollywood*, pp.244–67.

Staiger, Janet, *Interpreting Films: Studies in the Historical Reception of American Cinema*. Princeton: Princeton University Press, 1992.

Stam, Robert, *Film Theory: An Introduction*. Oxford: Blackwell, 2000.

Stern, Richard C., Clayton N. Jefford and Guerric Debona, *Savior on the Silver Screen*, New York: Paulist, 1999.

Stolow, Jeremy, 'Religion and/as Media', *Theory, Culture and Society*, 22/4, 2005, pp.119–45.

Stone, Bryan P., *Faith and Film: Theological Themes at the Cinema*. St. Louis: Chalice, 2000.

Strenski, Ivan, 'Material culture and the varieties of religious imagination', *Spotlight on Teaching*, 18/3, 2003, pp.iii–iv.

Strinati, Dominic, *An Introduction to Theories of Popular Culture*, London: Routledge, 1995.

—— *An Introduction to Studying Popular Culture*, London: Routledge, 2000.

Stuart, Alexander, '*The Wicker Man*' [review], *Films and Filming*, 20/7, 1974, p.47.

Summerfield, Carol and Penny Babb (eds), *Social Trends*, 34, London: Stationery Office, 2004.

Swann, Paul, *The Hollywood Feature Film in Postwar Britain*, London: Croom Helm, 1987.

Swirsky, Barbara and Marilyn P. Safir (eds), *Calling the Equality Bluff: Women in Israel*, New York and Oxford: Pergamon, 1991.

Tasker, Yvonne, *Working Girls: Gender and Sexuality in Popular Cinema*, London: Routledge, 1998.

Tatum, W. Barnes, *Jesus at the Movies: A Guide to the First Hundred Years*. Santa Rosa: Poleridge, 1997.

Telford, William R., 'Religion, the Bible and theology in recent films (1993–99)', *Epworth Review*, 27/4, 2000, pp.31–40.

—— 'Religion, theology and the Bible in recent films (1993–2004)', in Christianson *et al.* (eds): *Cinéma Divinité*, pp.347–51.

Tepper, Anderson, 'Hooray for Bollywood', *Vanity Fair*, 502, 2002, p.38.

Thomas, Deborah, *Reading Hollywood: Spaces and Meanings in American Film*, London: Wallflower, 2001.

Thomas, June, 'The first 7/7 movie', *Slate*, 18 July 2005, online at *http://slate.msn.com/id/2122935* (current on 14 September 2005).

Thomas, Rosie, 'Indian cinema: pleasures and popularity', *Screen*, 26/3–4, 1985, pp.116–31.

—— 'India,' in Luhr (ed.): *World Cinema Since 1945*, pp.301–29.

Thomas, Susie, *Hanif Kureishi. A Reader's Guide to Essential Criticism*, London: Palgrave, 2005.

Tinkcomm, Matthew and Amy Villarejo (eds), *Keyframes: Popular Cinema and Cultural Studies*. London: Routledge, 2001.

Traube, Elizabeth G., *Dreaming Identities: Class, Gender, and Generation in 1980s Hollywood Movies*, Boulder: Westview, 1992.

Tudor, Andrew, *Monsters and Mad Scientists: A Cultural History of the Horror Movie*, Oxford: Blackwell, 1989.

Tunney, Tom, 'The Ten Commandments', *Empire*, 11, 1990, pp.82–3.

Turner, Graeme, *Film as Social Practice*, 3rd edition, London: Routledge, 1999.

Turner, Graeme, 'Cultural studies and film', in Hill and Gibson (eds): *Film Studies*, pp.193–9.

Tybjerg, Casper, 'Dreyer and the national film in Denmark', *Film History*, 13/1, 2001, pp.23–36.

Unattributed, 'St. Joan', *The Times*, 27 April 1929, p.10.

—— 'Joan of Arc. Celebrations in France', *The Times*, 27 April 1929, pp.13–14.

—— 'Joan of Arc. Celebrations at Chinon', *The Times*, 29 April 1929, p.14.

—— 'A French film', *The Times*, 12 November 1930, p.12.

—— 'The Ten Commandments' [review], *Time*, 12 November 1956, p.124.

—— 'The Wicker Man' [review], *Financial Times*, 14 December 1973.

—— 'British film. The *Classic Television* top one hundred', *Classic Television*, 5, 1998, pp.10–25.

—— 'The passion of the Christians', *The Economist*, 2 October 2004, p.50.

Urrichio, William and Roberta E. Pearson, *Reframing Culture: The Case of the Vitagraph Quality Films*, Princeton: Princeton University Press, 1993.

Us Salam, Ziya, 'Cinema: *Lagaan*' [review], *The Hindu*, 22 June 2001, online at *www.hinduonnet.com/thehindu/2001/06/22/stories/09220227.htm* (current on 3 September 2003).

Valicha, Kishore, *The Moving Image – A Study of Indian Cinema*, Bombay: Orient Longman, 1988.

Vasudevan, Ravi S. (ed.), *Making Meaning in Indian Cinema*, New Delhi: Oxford University Press, 2000.

—— '*Bombay* and its public', in Dwyer and Pinney (eds): *Pleasure and the Nation*, pp.186–211.

Vaughan, Dai, 'Carl Dreyer and the Theme of Choice', *Sight and Sound*, 43/3, 1974, pp.156–62.

Vincendeau, Ginette, 'Issues in European cinema', in Hill and Gibson (eds): *World Cinema*, pp.56–64.

Virdi, Jyotika, *The Cinematic ImagiNation: Indian Popular Film as Social History*, New Brunswick: Rutgers University Press, 2003.

Walker, John (ed.), *Halliwells Film and Video Guide 2002*, London: HarperCollins, 2001.

Walsh, Richard, *Reading the Gospels in the Dark: Portrayals of Jesus in Film*, Harrisburg: Trinity Press International, 2003.

Warner, Marina, *Joan of Arc: The Image of Female Heroism*. London: Vintage, 1991.

Wegner, Beth, 'Memory as identity: the invention of the lower east side', *American Jewish History*, 85/1, 1997, pp.3–27.

Weisenfeld, Judith, 'Teaching religion and American film', *Spotlight on Teaching*, 18/3, 2003, p.v.

Wells, Paul, *The Horror Genre: From Beelzebub to Blair Witch*, London: Wallflower, 2000.

Whilte, Patricia, 'Feminism and film', in Hill and Gibson (eds): *Film Studies*, pp. 119–23.

Willemen, Paul, *Looks and Frictions: Essays in Cultural Studies and Film Theory*, London: BFI, 1994.

Williams, Peter W., 'Review essay: religion goes to the movies', *Religion and American* Culture, 10/2, 2000, pp.225–39.

Williams, Raymond, 'British film history: new perspectives', in Curran and Porter (eds): *British Cinema History*, pp.9–23.

Winock, Michel, 'Jeanne d'Arc et les juifs', *H-Histoire*, 3, 1979, pp.227–36.

Wojtas, Olga, 'A burning passion that's close to worship', *Times Higher Education Supplement*, 11 July 2003, pp.20–1.

Wood, M.G., *America in the Movies or, "Santa Maria, It Had Slipped My Mind"*, London: Secker and Warburg, 1975.

Wright, Alex, *Why Bother With Theology?*, London: Darton, Longman and Todd, 2002.

Wright, Melanie J., '"Don't touch my Holocaust": Responding to *Life is Beautiful*', *Journal of Holocaust Education*, 9/1, 2000, pp.19–32.

—— *Moses in America. The Cultural Uses of Biblical Narrative*. New York: Oxford University Press, 2002.

—— *Understanding Judaism*, Cambridge: Orchard Academic, 2003.

—— '*Cinema and the Romantic Legacy: Through a Glass Darkly*, by Paul Coates' [review], *Reviews in Religion and Theology*, 11/1, 2004, pp.113–16.

—— 'Lights! Camera! Antisemitism?: Jewish–Christian relations and the cinema', in Kessler and Wright (eds): *Themes and Issues*, pp.171–200.

—— 'Shot, burned, restored: *La Passion de Jeanne d'Arc*', in Christianson *et al.* (eds): *Cinéma Divinité*, pp.63–79.

—— 'Cinema and film', in Kessler and Wenborn (eds): *Jewish-Christian Relations*, pp.97–99.

Young, Robert J. C., *Postcolonialism: A Very Short Introduction*, Oxford: Oxford University Press, 2003.

de Zengotita, Thomas, *Mediated: How the Media Shape Your World*, London: Bloomsbury, 2005.

Film Index

Film Index

Film Index

Name and Subject Index

Name and Subject Index

Name and Subject Index